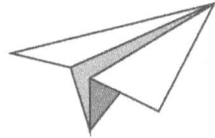

Followship

MARCUS YOARS

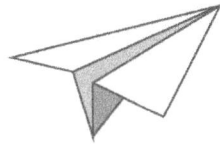

Follow ship

~~ENDURING~~ *Enjoying*
JESUS' LEADERSHIP,
EVEN IN THE UNKNOWN

TINDEN
MEDIA

FOLLOWSHIP by Marcus Yoars
Published by Tinden Media
2020 Washington Ave.
Sanford, FL 32771
tindenmedia.com

Unless otherwise noted, all Scripture quotations are taken from the Holy Bible, New International Version®, NIV®. Copyright © 1973, 1978, 1984, 2011 by Biblica, Inc.™ Used by permission of Zondervan. All rights reserved worldwide. www.zondervan.com. The "NIV" and "New International Version" are trademarks registered in the United States Patent and Trademark Office by Biblica, Inc.™

Scripture quotations marked ESV are taken from the Holy Bible, English Standard Version. Copyright © 2001 by Crossway Bibles, a division of Good News Publishers. Used by permission.

Scripture quotations marked MEV are taken from the Modern English Version. Copyright © 2014 by Military Bible Association. Used by permission. All rights reserved.

Scripture quotations marked NKJV are taken from the New King James Version®. Copyright © 1982 by Thomas Nelson. Used by permission. All rights reserved.

Scripture quotations marked NLT are from the Holy Bible, New Living Translation, copyright © 1996, 2004, 2007. Used by permission of Tyndale House Publishers, Inc., Wheaton, IL 60189. All rights reserved.

International Standard Book Number: 979-8-9902337-0-6
E-book ISBN: 979-8-9902337-1-3
Library of Congress Control Number: 2024904430

While the author has made every effort to provide accurate Internet addresses at the time of publication, neither the publisher nor the author assumes any responsibility for errors or for changes that occur after publication.

To Amber, my perfect gift from the Lord:
I never imagined I would get to share life with such a loving wife,
supportive best friend, and beautiful woman of God. You have believed in me
far more than I deserve, and I'm so thankful for the ways you have helped
make this book possible. I love being on this followship journey with you.

To my boys, Brayden and Xander:
What an honor it is for me to be your dad! I am so proud of you both for
who you are and for how you continue to grow in your love for the Lord.
May He always be your everything.

CONTENTS

FOREWORD

"FOLLOW ME!"

Jesus' invitation, offered to Galilean fishermen nearly two thousand years ago, still hangs in the air, beckoning people in every generation.

The call to follow Jesus is the call to discover and experience destiny. It is the call that satisfies the deepest ache in the human soul and leads us into the life we were created to live. In his brilliant book, *Followship,* Marcus Yoars guides us into that call.

Followship is a remarkable work that outlines both the cost and the crucible, and the glory and the reward of following Jesus. It is true that following Jesus will awaken our purpose and introduce us to true life, but it will also cost us. Everything.

What is gained along the way is certainly worth the price, but it is still no small task to respond to God's summons. Jesus' calling challenges us, changes us, and moves us into new and unexpected areas. Fortunately, Marcus and his wife, Amber, are among those who have lived this message and can now serve as guides to others. On multiple occasions, they have responded to a calling from God that led them far beyond their comfort zones or their personal hopes and dreams. In each of these experiences God has taught, transformed, and used them in rare and wonderful ways.

As I write this, they teach and lead in a powerful ministry in Hemsedal, Norway, where a generation of leaders is emerging around them with deep faith and passion to change their world. I have watched Marcus and Amber's ministry in the United States and in Norway, and more importantly, I have watched their lives. They are real-deal, authentic ministers who increasingly model the spirit and ethos of Jesus.

The term *followship* is gaining traction in leadership circles today as thinkers and teachers realize how essential good following is for good leadership. However, Marcus moves it beyond the idea of merely following well to also enjoying the supreme fellowship that we can experience when the one we are following is Jesus. Following Jesus is the sweetest fellowship the human heart can know.

Marcus is a clear and compelling writer. His wisdom, profound scriptural insight, and vulnerable sharing will no doubt heal and revive your soul.

I am so grateful for people like Marcus and Amber who say yes to God and then back up their affirmation with lives that follow wherever He leads. Those kinds of people set other people free. You and I have been called into this too, and the same fellowship and power awaits us in our stories. As Marcus writes, "Followship is indeed a beautiful dance."

Let's begin!

—Chris Jackson, DMin
Senior pastor, Hope City Church
Claremont, California

INTRODUCTION

WHEN MY SONS were little boys, they loved it when I would hold onto them and, one at a time, swing them around in a circle until we were too dizzy to continue. "Faster, Daddy! Faster!" they cried as I held their hands tightly while their little bodies circled through the air parallel to the ground. As we spun around, I would sometimes notice them closing their eyes. Part of that might have been their dizziness, but I know it often was because they wanted to relish the feeling of flying in the air. They knew Daddy wouldn't drop them, and that was enough for them to completely enjoy the ride.

It's easy to do that as a five-year-old. It's not so simple when the years add up and life sends you crashing to the ground too many times. An unexpected job loss. A financial crisis. A rebellious child. A broken relationship or the pain of no relationship at all. Maybe even your connection with God seems to be hanging by a thread. You thought He would lead you through life—that He would hold onto you and keep you safe—yet it sure feels like you've been dropped a time or two. So maybe *enjoying* the ride called life is hardly your goal these days; you just want to get *through* it without another bump or bruise.

If that's you, you're not alone. Life seems to be spinning wildly for many people I meet these days, particularly with so much uncertainty in the air. They stumble from one season of life to the next, dizzy from trying to meet expectations and fulfill ambitions, yet rarely enjoying a moment.

For others, life hasn't been so dizzying, only disappointing. At one point they were convinced God would lead them down the right path—to the right guy or girl, the right career, and the right calling. Now they've become accustomed to not knowing what God is doing. Maybe that's you.

God's leading is one of the most mysterious, frustrating, and wonderful things in life. He has a history of making promises that are eventually put to the test. He assures us that He will always be with us yet inevitably sends us into the desert—seemingly alone—to see if we trust Him. Again and again, the Lord leads in a way that challenges us to the core.

The fact that you picked up this book means you haven't given up. Whether life has been smooth sailing or a rough ride, you've tried to stay close to the Lord and are probably looking for help to grow even closer to Him.

Kudos to you! One of the wonderful things about God is how much He honors us for even the slightest move we make toward Him.

I don't know how close you feel to Jesus right now, but I do know He's invited you to follow Him—and to continue following Him no matter where He leads you. As trying as that can be, you and I both know it's the only way to experience true life. What we gain in going after Him extends far beyond our lifetimes, yet we can actually enjoy the fruit here and now.

That's exactly what this book is about. How do we enjoy the sometimes-harrowing process of following Jesus? How do we not just white-knuckle our way through the journey He takes us on but instead truly enjoy the ride with Him? Jesus' leadership is like no other. That may sound nice and exciting at first, but the reality is that His way of leading is so different it can be scary for us, especially if we don't have a strong connection with Him. My hope, then, is that through the message of this book, your relationship with Him will grow. I'm not looking to just inform you about Jesus' leadership; I want to help deepen your trust in Him so you can enjoy Him more.

When simply enjoying Him is first and foremost in our lives, then we can enjoy our journey with Him. Many believers expect it to be the other way around; we expect life with the Lord to be fun even though we barely know Him or only know about Him from a distance. But think about it: How long would you enjoy traveling with a stranger or even a distant relative? At some point, you'd either tire of the small talk and hope the trip ended soon, or you would get to know your traveling companion in a deeper way!

Jesus longs for us to take the latter option in our journey with Him. But He isn't just our tagalong buddy; He is our leader—our Master. He's both our Maker and our Lord. As we will soon discover, this makes all the difference, both in how we respond to Him and in the level to which we can trust Him. His call for us to follow Him entails much, and many are surprised by Jesus' commitment to the journey. He isn't passionate just about where we end up but how we get there and what happens along the way. Above all, He's passionate about those He leads.

The core of "followship"—I'll explain that word in the coming chapters—is our relationship with Jesus, the one we're following. Jesus' invitation to follow Him is simultaneously about the journey and about Him. When we know Him more, we understand His leadership more, and therefore we can understand more about the journey on which He's leading us—and eventually enjoy both it and Him.

I have organized this book into four parts to match those dimensions of following Him. Think of it as if you were being summoned by Jesus to follow Him, just as the first disciples were along the Galilean shoreline. Because followship involves an invitation to a journey with Jesus of enjoying His leadership, this is exactly how the four parts are arranged.

Part I: *An Invitation*

Jesus has called each of us to follow Him, but it's important to know what this call is about. What are we called to do? Who is calling us? Why does our response to this call matter?

Part II: *... to a Journey*

In the second part, we'll look at the journey to which He's called us. We'll briefly map out the story of the world (no small feat!) by getting a biblical overview of how the Lord has led humans—and particularly His chosen people, Israel—throughout history.

Part III: *... With Jesus*

The world's storyline culminates in the life of Jesus Christ, and in the third section we will spend more time examining why He is worth following and what His multifaceted leadership means to each person. Because it's crucial for us to know who is leading us, this is a key part of understanding the concept of followship.

Part IV: *... of Enjoying His Leadership*

In the last section of the book, we'll dive into the practical side of moving beyond simply enduring Jesus' leadership to actually enjoying it. What does life look like when we take joy in Him and in the way He leads us?

I am not an expert in this journey of followship, but I do have a story to tell and some things I've learned along the way. As I shared those insights with others over the years, they encouraged me to put them down on paper for a broader audience. The result is this book, which I wrote during a unique time when the entire world faces a new degree of uncertainty. People everywhere are desperate for direction, clarity, and certainty. I happen to believe we won't find those things anywhere other than in Jesus. If we're willing to follow Him, we can walk a path entirely different from the way the rest of the world goes. Venturing His way costs, and it's not easy by any means. But from what I—and countless others—have discovered so far, it's worth leaving behind everything for.

Sound inviting? Interesting? A little dangerous and radical? Maybe even enjoyable? Good. Then you're getting the idea. Now let's begin the journey of followship.

PART I

AN INVITATION

From the moment God thought of human existence, He has desired relationship and partnership with us. His longing continues today, expressed in the form of an invitation for each of us to know Him through followship. Yet joining that partnership entails His leading and our following, which isn't as easy as we might think.

CHAPTER 1

A CALL FOR ALL

I REMEMBER WHEN Jesus had the nerve to ask my wife and me for everything. *Everything.* And to make matters worse, this was not the first time.

Our family was enjoying a wonderful season living in Orlando, Florida. Our house was a forty-five-minute drive from both Disney World and Florida's white-sand beaches—perfect for raising our two young boys. We were part of a growing church community and trusted by its leadership to teach, counsel, and disciple others. My wife, Amber, was thriving as a leader of a large parachurch ministry to young mothers, and I had a dream job that had been the reason for our relocating to Orlando only five years before.

As the editor of a Christian magazine, I oversaw a team of journalists reporting on what the Holy Spirit was doing around the world, which meant I interacted daily with Christian ministries and leaders—including many well-known ones—from across the globe. I was only the third editor in the magazine's almost forty-year history and was humbled that God (and my employers) had trusted me with such a position so early in my life. I was in my mid-thirties, leading a team that reached almost a million people each month, and I regularly heard stories of how our work impacted others. Sure, my job was stressful and demanding, but it was fulfilling. Life was good—*really* good.

And that's when Jesus began tapping me on the shoulder.

Do you want to follow Me?

It was not an audible voice, but one of those "what was that?" thoughts that feels like a whisper from someone behind. I was in the bathroom, brushing my teeth before going to bed, which made it easy for me to shrug off the impression as tired imagination. But I had walked with the Lord long enough to pay attention to moments like this. Not only had the phrase seemingly out of left field felt weighty, but also the offer seemed to entail leaving something behind.

Years before, Amber and I had moved across the US, led by a sense of following God. Our transition to Florida had begun the same way, with the Lord making a clear path for us. But we'd only been there for five years and were seeing so much fruit. Was God really wanting us to move again, or was this about something else?

Do you want to follow Me?

The question lingered throughout the next day. Of course, I wanted to follow Jesus. Yet deep down I sensed this probably meant a major life change—if not a relocation, then a new job or something equally as big. I had no idea what, where, when, or how it would happen. With Jesus, those details were secondary. What mattered was my response and, more importantly, that He was the one calling me. But the truth was, this did not just involve me.

I shared what I sensed with Amber, and much to my relief, she also had felt a similar call from Jesus. Over the next few days, we talked and prayed about it. Though the cost was relatively high, the decision was easy: We would follow because it was Jesus leading. He had faithfully led us through every stage of our lives—both as singles and as a married couple—so we knew this meant He would direct us to something, somewhere, at some point.

Because of my role at work, Amber and I could not tell anyone—although I have no idea what we would have shared anyway. We knew almost nothing other than Jesus had asked us to follow Him and we had said yes. Over the next few months, we continued to seek Him for more guidance. Yet each time we pressed in for more details, His reply was the same.

Just wait. Come be with Me.

Those words brought heaven right into our home. We basked in a season of enjoying Him more and more, with no strings attached. We weren't seeking what He could do for us or what we could do for Him. We just wanted Him and nothing else. We stopped asking for details and simply loved His presence.

While His nearness was sweeter than ever, my work became more difficult than ever. As a leader in the company, I often shouldered both the responsibility and the blame amid the chaos of a shifting media industry. During these stressful times, I often closed my office door during my lunch break to escape into God's Word and enjoy a few minutes of stillness with Him. Some days my longing for this intimate time grew so strong it hurt. Though nothing had really changed outwardly in our life situation to that point, still everything was changing.

After more than a year of enjoying God's nearness, Amber and I pulled out a map of the United States and bluntly asked the Lord, "OK, so where do You want us to go?" We had done the same thing almost a decade earlier in one of our cross-country moves, so we expected Him to again highlight a city or state, or at least to open doors in the supernatural way He had done before.

But nothing happened. No out-of-the-blue job offers or random calls from across the nation. For the next several weeks, the Lord said nothing about the details, all while we continued to grow in knowing and loving Him.

A few months later, we pulled out a map of the world. I wish I could say we saw a specific country glowing like burning embers while a scroll from heaven descended into our hands to reveal our divine assignment, but I would be lying if I did. Basically, we were left with the same thought we'd had for almost two years to that point: *You've called us to follow You, Lord. So where are we going?*

BECAUSE IT'S JESUS

Jesus may have an odd way sometimes of calling people to follow Him, but even stranger is the often-illogical response from those who accept that call. In Matthew 4, Jesus beckoned a fearless foursome of fisherman to follow Him, promising that He would show them how to "fish for people" (v. 19). But think about it: Why would catching people interest some outdoorsmen who spent most of their time isolated on the sea? Yet all four young men heard Jesus' invitation and *immediately* left everything to follow Him.

Later, Matthew responded the same way when Jesus summoned him—while at his workplace—to come be His disciple. Why would a tax collector, insulated by riches and Roman protection, willingly leave such security to follow a stranger? Did he not realize his momentary decision would cost him his comfort, his career, his connections, and eventually his very life? Yet like the others, Matthew *immediately* left everything to go wherever Jesus went.

Two of John the Baptist's disciples *immediately* left their well-known mentor to follow Jesus when John called this Nazarene the "Lamb of God" (John 1:36). From all indications, both Philip and Nathanael had the same response when they saw Jesus for who He really was. And that, I believe, is the key. The call itself is not what moves people; it is the caller. We follow because it's *Jesus* calling. There is something about Him that lures the deepest parts of us to step into a place of risk and uncertainty, yes, but also a place of life and purpose that we have never known before. When we get a true glimpse of Jesus—as I believe Peter, Matthew, Nathanael, and the others did—we will do whatever it takes to be close to Him.

That was why my family and I could leave behind our comfortable, American-dream life and eventually move to the middle of nowhere in Norway. We left not because of what we would do or where we would go, but simply because Jesus was the one calling us. Let me explain.

More than two and a half years after saying yes to Jesus' invitation to follow Him, we finally got some directions. They were not explicit directions like you would get to visit an acquaintance's house, nor did they come in a single download from heaven. Instead, our directions were a bit murky and came through multiple means: through reawakened aspirations that began decades before; through opportunities suddenly opening and others suddenly closing; through prayer-birthed impressions and "could this be God?" moments; and through unmistakably divine connections.

After our season of simply enjoying the Lord's presence, we sensed Him leading us to start dreaming again and think outside US borders. My wife had been on a ministry trip to Norway in the early 1990s and faithfully prayed for the country ever since, so she immediately began thinking of the Scandic nation. I had never been there, knew almost nothing about it, and, more importantly, had no work connections there. This was good, as it meant I couldn't create any opportunities through my own networking and then wonder if it was Jesus' leading. If He wanted our family there, *He* needed to make a way for us.

He did exactly that, and after a long season of wondering and waiting, our family of four boarded an airplane to Norway on a hot, August afternoon. We had been invited to serve as staff at a ten-week Bible school in a small, mountain town, and although we were excited to go, there was much we didn't know. We didn't know the language, barely knew anyone in the country, and weren't sure what we would be doing. We believed God had called us to leave behind everything and follow Him, and yet it felt more like we were stepping off a cliff.

Those first months in Norway were an unforgettable time for our family as we poured ourselves out to serve every person, family, church, and organization we could. Amber and I taught classes, led worship and prayer gatherings, discipled students, counseled couples, coached organizations, and prayed with countless people. God had equipped us for the season, and we used every ministry tool He'd ever given us on our toolbelts.

That made it even more difficult when the Norwegian government continued to deny us a visa to stay in the country. Though Norway's laws allowed us to remain there while we appealed, they also made it difficult for us to stay as volunteers who merely wanted to serve the nation's people. After sending in our final appeal, we drove for four days to a city three hundred fifty kilometers north of the Arctic Circle because we had been invited to help a local church community there. It was possible that upon arriving, we would have to turn around and leave the country. At that point, we did not have a home to return to in the United States and had sold most of our belongings, so there was no plan B.

Those days tested us. As days turned into weeks, we had plenty of opportunity to question Jesus and His leadership. If He was leading, wasn't He supposed to make a way? This was not our problem in the first place; *He* was the one who had called *us*!

The hardest part was knowing how to pray. Was the Lord closing a door to move us to the next place He wanted us? Or were we to persevere in spiritual warfare, seeing this opposition as the enemy's attempt to prevent us from staying in Norway? We believed Jesus had led us step-by-step through the entire process of leaving everything behind, and we also believed He had directed us to Norway. But if that were the case, why would He lead us into what seemed like a dead end?

With help from a precious couple in the northern church, we eventually received a one-year visa to stay as volunteer workers—a "mini-miracle" since Norway's government makes it difficult for missionaries not employed by a Norwegian organization. We did all we could to serve the small communities of believers in the north, many of whom felt unseen and forgotten (it's easy to feel that way when you're almost two thousand kilometers away from most of your countrymen). Some of these believers desperately needed encouragement, and at times we were unknowingly seen as a sign from God that He saw them and cared for them. Talk about a humbling way to meet people!

A few months later, the organization we first worked with invited us to join their team and help with the ministry. We relocated and sensed the Lord's guidance throughout the process. Yet again, we faced another roadblock with our visa, and this time we had to leave the country after multiple rounds of disputing our case. It would have been easy to revert to the same questions as before: *Jesus, if You're leading us, why isn't the way clearer?*

But there was a difference in how we prayed. We didn't just wonder if He wanted us back in Norway; we *knew* He did. How could we be so certain? Because of the ways He'd led us in the months before. The more we walked with Him, the more we knew how He was leading and, more importantly, the easier it was to trust Him. There we were, facing yet another seemingly unpassable obstacle, and the only person we could trust was the one who could part the waters and make a way where there wasn't one before.

CAN WE TRUST JESUS' LEADERSHIP?

I don't want to over-simplify things. I cringe at pat answers and dislike it when people feel compelled to wrap up the tangled messiness of life with nice, shiny, happy ribbons. So please don't hear me say that when we trust Jesus, everything lines up—we always get the visa, the job, the girl, the opportunity, or whatever else it is we feel He's leading us to. Life with Jesus isn't so simple. I have plenty of examples—from my life and others'—with not-so-happy endings, and yet those accounts all share a common denominator when it comes to following Jesus. Are we still willing to trust Him when things go awry?

Ultimately, the Lord made a way for my family to return to Norway, and we hope to remain as long as He wants us there. But amid all the obstacles, our journey of following Him has never been about Norway or Thailand or wherever we've thought He wanted us to go. In fact, it's never been about teaching or ministering or whatever we've thought He wanted us to do. No, ultimately, the journey has always been—and will always be—about trust. Will we trust Jesus' leadership?

How about in your life? What's your story of following Jesus? Is it easy for you to trust His different way of leading? Can you trust Him whether you're facing opposition and uncertainty or a clear path filled with hope and assurance?

This book is about that very question. I have met countless people whose once-fervent faith in the Lord became a mere shadow because of disappointment, doubt, and mistrust in His leading. People like Maria, a forty-one-year-old woman who has spent half her life longing for a husband. Maria loves Jesus more than anything and has seen Him come through in countless other areas of her life. But while everyone tells her to just hang on and offers well-meaning Bible verses about the Lord giving her the desires of her heart, she finds it hard to not be disappointed—and even harder to not pin her deep frustration on His way of leading her life.

Or there is my friend Peter, who at age nineteen felt Jesus leading him to be a teacher but succumbed to expectations of becoming a doctor like his dad. Peter is now in his mid-thirties, settling into a thriving medical career, yet he still cannot shake a nagging sense that maybe he missed out on a more meaningful path in life.

I also remember Anne, who prayed for her mother to be healed from cancer and was convinced Jesus would bring about a miracle. She and her mom were the only believers in their family, which made things challenging, especially as her mother suffered through excruciating pain. Ever since her mom died, Anne has had the same burning question as her unbelieving family: Why would a God who leads His followers—and says He cares for us—let us go through so much pain?

We all wrestle with the deep issues of our broken world. I would argue that those who truly follow Jesus will undoubtedly wrestle even more. Many of us walk with a limp, brought about from times when following Him resulted in pain, suffering, or what seemed to be failure. While some are grateful for the limp and see it as evidence of a Jacob-like blessing, others end up bitter toward the one who has allowed—some would say *caused*—their hobbling.

One of my first limps in life came from when my dad suddenly died when I was twenty-three years old. We had a special relationship. I can hardly remember a day as I grew up when he did not tell me how proud he was of me—that's how loving he was. I also will never forget the days after he died, having to do the mundane things of life—going to the grocery store or the gas station—with a newfound sorrow while the rest of the world carried on as usual. Inside, I felt like screaming at everyone around me, "How can you just go on as if nothing has changed? Don't you realize *everything* is different now?!"

I faced an important decision in those moments, as if I were at a junction with two paths headed in opposite directions. On one, I could shake my fist at God; blame Him for my father's far-too-early heart attack; doubt His sovereignty, goodness, and faithfulness; and continue down the road on my own terms, under my own leading. *Lord, I've trusted You my entire life, and this is how You lead me? No, thank You. I think I can do better.* Choosing this pathway seemed logical and easy—*Isn't it OK to question God when you're grieving?*—especially because the pain was as close as my next breath during those days.

But I could also take another path. This other way was far more difficult because it involved trusting a God I couldn't physically see and surrendering to promises He had yet to fulfill. I would not be the one leading on the journey, and it was impossible to see far enough ahead to know how badly the road twisted and turned. Something inside me knew that if I went this route, I might not get my deepest questions answered or have things make sense. Ultimately, I knew I would lose control on this path.

I made my choice that day. Call me foolish, but I chose the harder way.

I am writing this book now because I want others to experience the joy I have as I continue down this more difficult path. It is a joy that comes from letting Jesus lead, of losing control over my life and trusting that He can and will guide me in an infinitely better way than I ever could. It is the joy of dying to myself each day and finding a new life in Christ. Simply put, it is the joy of following Him.

Of course, I still struggle sometimes. I still have days when I would prefer having more control over my life, when I question His leading, or when I want to go a safer way than how He is guiding me. The Bible and church history make it clear: Following Jesus is not easy. His way is not without pain, nor does it always make sense to us. But His leadership is perfect, regardless of whether that is easy for us to believe. As we will see throughout this book, Jesus' track record as a leader is flawless. There is truly no one like Him, no one more dependable or trustworthy.

A NATURAL PROBLEM

The fact that you are reading this book reveals at least two things about you. First, it indicates that you have a desire to follow Jesus, even if His way is difficult. Few would pick up a book about followship (a term I will explain in the next chapter) and enjoying Jesus' leadership if they did not already long to surrender more of their life to Him. So I commend you for wanting to grow in being a true follower of Jesus.

Second, it reveals that you have experienced some crossroads in life similar to the ones I have described from my life. You may not have sensed the Lord leading you to move to another place or faced the roller coaster of emotions after a loved one's death, but I am positive you have faced the same ultimate decision I did.

Whenever we come to any junction in life—whether a time of crisis or challenge or anything between—we all have a choice: to lead or to follow. Stated another way, either we have control over our lives, or someone—or some*thing*—else does. Either we are leading the way, or someone else is.

Our modern world tells us we are each in the driver's seat. You make your own destiny. Be what you want to be. Have it your way. The world is your oyster. Life is what you make of it.

When we truly follow Jesus, we give up this worldview. (Don't worry—the world's idea of control is flawed anyway.) Inherent to the idea of following Jesus is that He leads, not us, and that He gets to control our lives.

But there is a problem, and it is a big one. In fact, it is so massive you can trace it back to the beginning of human history (which we will soon do), and it is so important that it lies at the core of every person's dealings with God.

The dilemma is simply this: We do not like to follow. We want to lead. We believe we should have control over our lives and that we can lead best.

Unfortunately, this disposition to lead rather than follow is in our blood. It is human nature—theologians call it our fallen, sinful nature—and every person on earth inherits it the moment he or she is born. This innate nature within us is ultimately why we reject Jesus' leadership over our lives. It is why the apostle Paul often wrote of an ongoing wrestling match between our flesh and spirit, or our old self and new self. We do not want someone else calling the shots in our lives, even if it is our Creator; we want to be in control.

I realize I am making some dramatic statements here—some would argue they are too simplistic or absolute—so let me back up a bit.

FOLLOW THE LEADER

Did you ever play the game Follow the Leader as a child? The rules are so simple they can be stated in one sentence: One person is appointed the leader, and whatever he does or says to do, the others must follow.

There are different twists to the game, of course. When I was growing up, we called one version Simon Says, and if someone followed an order from the leader that was not preceded with the words "Simon says," he was disqualified. The game goes by different names, depending on what country you are in—in France the leader is called Jack, in Israel it's Herzl, and in China and Brazil it's the more generic "teacher" and "master" respectively.[1] But whatever terms you use, the goal of the game is the same: to be the leader.

I have never met a child who did not want to be the leader in Follow the Leader, Simon Says, or any other similar game. No one wants to follow all the time; at some point, we all prefer to lead. That fascinating instinct is why these games work regardless of where in the world children play them. Even when we grow older that nature continues, which is why no matter what culture you are from, leading is seen as better than following.

Why do we prefer leading over following? Because when you lead, you are in command. You have control. Leading inherently means you have power, authority, and influence. It means you shape and set the course not only for your own life but also for a group of people, an organization, a community, or even an entire region or nation.

Now, you may have no desire to lead a city or county, much less a home Bible study. But I am almost certain you would still prefer having control over your own life rather than being forced to follow someone else's directives for it. Even those who shun leadership positions would still choose to have *some* degree of influence and control over decision-making in their lives rather than none.

Following puts us in a vulnerable position. We no longer have the final say-so, and therefore it is always possible that something unforeseen could happen: The leader can take a longer route that we think is unwise or a waste of time. Or the leader can even assign us a task we would rather not do. Leading, then, is safer. There is less risk going your own way than having to follow someone else's. In that regard, we all most definitely prefer to lead rather than follow!

Jesus challenges our human nature, however, and His challenge comes in the form of a simple, two-word invitation: *Follow Me.* At first glance, His offer seems soft, generous, and harmless enough. After all, who wouldn't want to follow the Creator of life itself? He made everything; therefore, He knows the perfect way for each of us.

Although that is true, countless Christians mistake Jesus' perfect way for a path that is safe, easy, obstacle-free, and full of nothing but blessings in the form of health, security, and prosperity. But as one author warns, "To everyone wanting a safe, untroubled, comfortable life free from danger, stay away from Jesus. The danger in our lives will always increase in proportion to the depth of our relationship with Christ."[2]

Jesus was unapologetically blunt in describing what following Him meant. "If any of you wants to be my follower, you must give up your own way, take up your cross daily, and follow me," He told the masses who followed Him like a celebrity (Luke 9:23, NLT). Whereas most would use such star power to increase their following and influence, Jesus did the opposite, offering progressively difficult hurdles: "Whoever does not take up their cross and follow me is not worthy of me" (Matt. 10:38).

To the rich man who wanted what Jesus offered, He went straight for the jugular: "If you want to be perfect, go, sell your possessions and give to the poor, and you will have treasure in heaven. Then come, follow me" (Matt. 19:21).

To the man who wanted to say goodbye to his family before following Jesus, the Lord replied: "No one who puts a hand to the plow and looks back is fit for service in the kingdom of God" (Luke 9:62).

And later: "If anyone comes to me and does not hate father and mother, wife and children, brothers and sisters—yes, even their own life—such a person cannot be my disciple. And whoever does not carry their cross and follow me cannot be my disciple" (Luke 14:26–27).

Jesus' extreme statements have been problematic ever since He uttered them. He made it clear that nothing was too sacred to be included in what the "cross" entailed—not family, wealth, or security. Taking up our cross means going the way of our own death. Just as Jesus died for us to gain life, we must die to ourselves to gain life in Him.

Can you see a major problem developing? Following Jesus exposes an inherent dilemma for us—a crossroads. We want to lead so that we can protect ourselves. Jesus says the only way to follow Him is to die to self. Worse still, this death is not partial. He does not want only sections of our lives. He doesn't want just the areas we are most proud of, nor does He only want the messed-up parts. He wants *everything*. And only when we follow Him on this way of death and full surrender, only then can we call Him Lord. As Hudson Taylor, the famous nineteenth-century missionary to China, said, "Christ is either Lord of all or He is not Lord at all."[3] Similarly, the great preacher Charles Spurgeon offered this twist: "If Christ is not all to you He is nothing to you. He will never go into partnership as a part Savior of men. If He be something He must be everything, and if He be not everything He is nothing to you."[4]

Jesus has not altered the terms of following Him since calling His first disciples. The cost is the same. Countless Christians have grown accustomed to calling Jesus Lord on Sundays but ruling the rest of the week. Others have twisted the Way, as it was originally called by the early believers, to include greasy grace and a pain-free life of prosperity. But I have seen firsthand that amid the growing movements preaching false gospels and distorted teachings, Jesus is still preparing a church made up of disciples whose lives belong fully to Him, just as we find in the early church.

Jesus does not change. He is "the same yesterday and today and forever" (Heb. 13:8). His way of leading has not changed, and neither has His call for all. While the world—and even those calling themselves Christians—may alter its standards based on what is popular or brings the most personal convenience, Jesus is still tapping people on the shoulder and asking the same question: *Do you want to follow Me?*

CHAPTER 2

FOLLOWING ON JESUS' TERMS

WHEN I WAS a teenager, my family took a fall vacation in the picturesque Blue Ridge Mountains of North Carolina. Though not majestic in height or grandeur, the mountains are nonetheless stunning in October as the changing leaves showcase every imaginable shade of red, orange, yellow, and green. I was enjoying the colors up close one day on an afternoon hike with my two older sisters and their husbands, particularly noticing how the trees on our path created a dense canopy above us that seemed to shade us from the rest of the world. It was as if we were walking through a jungle in the mountains.

After a couple hours, my brother-in-law, Kendall, who spent most of his summers in these mountains, suggested that we begin making our way back to the car. Daylight was limited, he said, and we needed to be safe.

About an hour into our return, however, Kendall suddenly stopped, turned, and looked around. The puzzled expression on his face told the story: he did not recognize the path we were on. He was the only one in the group who had been in this area before, and none of us had been paying attention—we had just trusted that he knew the way. We hiked a bit longer, and every now and then, Kendall would again stop and try to get his bearings. That did not happen, however, and within minutes the sun was setting, further darkening our path. Even our attempts to find a clearing among the trees and get some perspective on the mountainside failed. We were officially lost.

As evening set, a sense of panic rose in the group. None of us had brought any gear other than some water bottles, and since this was years before cell phones were common, we didn't have any lights on hand. We were *completely* dependent upon Kendall; wherever he went, we followed. And based on his body language and few words, he was clearly concerned as well. As we continued in silence, trying to retrace our route to the top, I know I was not the only one praying that somehow Kendall would come across something familiar.

Around eight o'clock, almost two hours after the sun set, we finally saw some lights in the distance, found our way to a road, and made our way home. But that sense of having to completely rely on someone else's ability to lead has stuck with me. I did not like feeling so helpless; I wanted to do *something* other than just follow Kendall.

18

Have you experienced this unsettling feeling? Have you ever had to "blindly" follow someone through a tough situation—or even season—in life, knowing their leading determined the outcome for you? It isn't easy to trust someone else with your wellbeing in a circumstance, much less your entire life. Yet that does not diminish the truth that who—or what—we are led by is directly related to where we end up in life. Stated another way, your direction in life is dictated by who—or what—leads you.

As we unpacked in the first chapter, in life we are always either leading or being led (which is simply another aspect of following). Obviously, this means leadership is an important thing, not only in our personal lives but throughout humanity. Whoever leads—whether it is us or someone else—affects where we end up. This is why good leadership is critical everywhere we turn: at home, in school, at our workplace, in the church, and in our town, city, state, or country.

But have you ever stopped to notice *how much* we emphasize leadership today? In many cultures, we tell our children as soon as they can understand, "Be a leader, not a follower!" Today virtually every level of education, from primary schools to universities, offers a leadership training program. The most elite schools boast of developing the world's next generation of leaders. I have seen classroom posters, company banners, and T-shirts touting the famous Margaret Thatcher line: Don't follow the crowd; let the crowd follow you (a fitting sentiment from the Iron Lady). Meanwhile, Fortune 500 companies pour millions of dollars into MBA and leadership studies programs to produce leaders who will change not only their industries but the entire world.

Why is there such an emphasis on leadership? The common belief is that "everything rises and falls on leadership," as leadership expert John Maxwell says.[1] Strong leaders, not "weak" followers, win wars, championships, and challenges while helping organizations and even nations overcome obstacles. We value good leadership because it helps advance people from point A to B. And wherever humans gather with a purpose—from massive companies such as Google to an isolated tribe in Papua New Guinea—good or bad leadership is the difference between success and failure.

THE OTHER SIDE OF EVERYTHING

But what if leadership is not actually *everything*? What if the success of a company, school, or country is not merely based on whether a leader is good or bad but also on those who are being led? Amid all the hype surrounding leadership, what if it's only one side of the coin?

This is where followship comes in. In recent years academics have increasingly used the word *followship* (or sometimes *followership*) to describe an important dynamic in business. As they study successful organizations, they have found that equally important to those who lead are the ones who follow. A leader might have great vision for the future, but unless she has people willing to follow that vision, nothing will be accomplished. Likewise, even the most charismatic leader will be forgotten if people do not actually follow him. Simply put, leaders need followers.

Followship in the business world is a straightforward concept; it is the ability to receive direction and perform the tasks assigned to you. Followship is how well you "fall in line" and do your part when working under a leader on a project. Its fruit is most apparent when you deliver on what you have been given to do, regardless of what kind of leadership you serve. Ultimately, the idea of followship in the business realm underscores a core principle: how followers follow is equally as important as how leaders lead.

In a world obsessed with leaders, pioneers, influencers, and trendsetters, I find this growing movement refreshing. It helps to balance what I believe is a global overemphasis on "reaching the top"—something Jesus Himself certainly disrupted when He described servant leadership. Followship flies in the face of the "leadership is *everything*" mantra and argues that although leadership is certainly important, so is followship. So while everything within my human nature instinctively prefers to lead in terms of having more control over my own life, Jesus' call to me remains the same: deny myself, take up my cross, and follow Him (Matt. 16:24).

The term *followship* fits even better, then, in the Christian context because it perfectly describes the core calling for every disciple of Jesus Christ. If one of life's key questions is whether we will lead or follow, then every would-be disciple of Jesus is forced to rephrase the question this way: *Will I follow Jesus or will I lead my own life?* If we call ourselves Jesus' disciples, then we must follow Him. Conversely, we cannot be disciples and go our own way. We cannot lead our own lives and call ourselves Jesus-followers—that is a contradiction.

Followship as it relates to Jesus (which is how I'll use that word from here on) can be defined as following Jesus in fellowship with Him. The term entails two ongoing actions: following Jesus and fellowshipping with Jesus. Often those two intersect, overlap, and even meld into one. Yet they are distinct, and I believe you cannot have one without the other. Let's begin our exploration of followship by focusing on the first and most obvious part: following Jesus.

FOLLOWING AS A DISCIPLE, NOT A FAN

Jesus' invitation to follow Him means something profoundly different from the type of following we are accustomed to today. In the current social media era, people equate following someone with knowing about that person, not necessarily with knowing him or her personally. Social media allows average Janes and Joes like you and me to get up close with celebrities we have never met, and even some we'd never want to meet—all with the click of a "follow" button. When we follow them online as fans, we get instant access to "know" them through a stream of Photoshopped Instagram images depicting their perfect lives and misspelled tweets revealing just how real they are.

But no matter how many posts or photos we scan through, we don't *really* know these people. Our twenty-first-century version of following someone is more about marketing and messaging than about developing authentic relationship.

If we could go back two thousand years to Jesus' time, we would find a vastly different approach to following someone. Back then, to follow someone meant you were a disciple of that person, and this involved far more than the click of a button or the occasional interaction. At that time, Jewish culture revolved around the Torah. Most children were educated through reading, writing, and memorizing the Torah from ages five through twelve or thirteen. After their bar mitzvah, almost all boys entered their family's trade. A handful of the brightest (typically those from wealthy families) had the opportunity to essentially apply to continue their education and follow a rabbi, or teacher, of their choice.[2] This would not be a long-distance following but an up close, intense commitment to become like that rabbi. As one scholar writes:

> A disciple was expected to leave his family and job to join the rabbi in his austere lifestyle. Disciples would live with the rabbi twenty-four hours a day, walking from town to town, teaching, working, eating, and studying. They would discuss the Scriptures and apply them to their lives. The disciples were also supposed to be the rabbi's servants, submitting to his authority while they served his needs. Indeed, the word "rabbi" means "my master" and was a term of great respect.[3]

A rabbi was responsible for teaching his disciples God's laws (part of the Torah) according to his own interpretation of those laws. Unlike our modern,

Greek-inspired approach to teaching, however, the rabbinic method of instruction was less focused on head knowledge and more on disciples understanding the rabbi's way of life and, from this, developing discernment on their own. This is why disciples would often mimic their rabbi's way of eating, thinking, speaking, praying, organizing, studying—and it all stemmed from how he interpreted and followed God's commands. As the rabbi went through everyday life, real-life situations gave him and his students opportunities to discuss deeper principles. After continually being around the rabbi for a few years, the disciples would naturally develop the same characteristics, methods, and ways of thinking as their teacher. In fact, you could spot a disciple from a distance and tell whom he followed simply by the way he dressed or walked. A disciple's mannerisms were a telltale indicator of who was "master" over his life.[4]

Are you catching the parallels to our life as followers of Jesus? As His disciples, we are not called to be casual followers like the massive crowds who followed Him in the same way we follow celebrities today. We are not to be distant fans; instead, we have a personal invitation to be up-close disciples, just like the twelve disciples Jesus handpicked. He has shown us God's way of life (He *is* the way!), and now we are to walk in it. We are to look, sound, think, act, and live like our Rabbi. In fact, we want to follow and mimic our Teacher so closely that people mistake us for Him. This is the kind of following to which Jesus calls us!

BREAKING BARRIERS ... FOR US

Jesus not only was raised in this rabbinic culture, but He was a rabbi Himself. Although some during Jesus' time questioned the extent of His formal training (John 7:15), He was still recognized as a rabbi by everyone from commoners (Mark 9:17) to the most highly educated Pharisees (Luke 19:39; John 3:2) and Torah teachers (Matt. 22:35–36). Considering how fervent Israel's religious leaders were in ensuring their ranks were not "defiled" by unworthy teachers of the Law, it is remarkable how universally respected Jesus was for His knowledge of Scripture and for His holy lifestyle, both of which surpassed those leaders. I love how Matthew 7:28–29 describes it: "The crowds were amazed at [Jesus'] teaching, because he taught as one who had authority, and not as their teachers of the law."

Jesus was just one rabbi among many at a time when Israel was filled with multiple religious sects, all adhering to their own interpretation of God's laws.

But what many people today do not realize is just how much Rabbi Jesus stood out by breaking the rabbinic mold of His time.

As stated earlier, normally a highly educated teenager would seek out a rabbi, who would then decide whether he wanted to take on the youth as a disciple. No respected rabbi would willingly lower himself to recruit a disciple, much less a group of disciples. And yet Jesus humbled Himself to incredible depths by seeking out His twelve disciples and inviting *them* to follow *Him*.

Jesus could have declared Himself to the masses and performed enough miracles *before* obtaining His disciples so that hundreds of adolescents would clamor to be in His inner circle. If He had only marketed Himself better—maybe some "Disciples wanted" signs in town or a few CareerBuilder and LinkedIn posts—He could've had Israel's best and brightest vying for His attention. But instead of having His disciples pursue Him, here was the ultimate rabbi, God Himself, walking around and asking young men to follow *Him*.

Stooping to such a low level could have been a career-killing move if Jesus cared about that. (He didn't.) At the very least it would have been embarrassing for Jesus, providing fodder for other rabbis and religious leaders to poke fun at Him. ("Look—this guy had to go around begging people to follow Him! What a joke!") And yet Scripture gives no indication of shame when Jesus uttered the words, "Follow Me." Why would there be when He knew the history-changing mission He was calling these young men to?

Equally as detrimental for Jesus' reputation as a rabbi was whom He selected. The more respected you were as a rabbi, the more educated and elite your disciple selections would be. Israel's most prestigious rabbis picked only from the cream of the crop. Yet Jesus went straight to the lowest and those who typically would have had no chance at being invited. Not only was He seeking His own disciples rather than having them petition Him, but many of those He asked came from undesirable backgrounds—circumstances that could be scandalous for Jesus' reputation. A tax collector hated by all Jews. A group of uneducated fishermen, two of whom were known for having tempers. A political zealot whose past would likely get you in trouble with Roman authorities. Even the towns where some of the disciples came from made them easy targets for ridicule. For sure, none of the twelve Jesus chose would have been on a who's who list at the time, and yet these were the men Jesus handpicked. It's not as if the Son of God didn't have time to think about this before coming to earth!

Such is the unmeasurable, unfathomable extent Jesus goes to invite us to be His disciples and follow Him. He leaves the ninety-nine to find the one who is lost. He goes after the sick, sinful, and scorned even when it costs Him His reputation. "I have come to call not those who think they are righteous, but those who know they are sinners," He said in Mark 2:17 (NLT).

Jesus takes upon Himself scandalous people from every walk of life and invites us into a real, up close, intimate relationship with Him. Like the man in His parable who threw a great banquet, Jesus has gone into the streets and alleys of every town and brought in "the poor, the crippled, the blind, and the lame" (Luke 14:21, NLT). That's us! And yet such is the way of His kingdom, where "whoever is the least among you is the greatest" (Luke 9:48, NLT).

STRANGERS DISGUISED AS FOLLOWERS

Before we continue, let me offer a reminder when it comes to following Jesus. We could spend the rest of this book focusing on Jesus' humility and grace shown in how He called the Twelve then and how He calls us still today. But we also must not forget the conditions involved in that calling. Jesus has never been interested in developing part-time disciples, much less half-hearted followers. His call to follow Him comes on His terms, and those terms are clear: either we fully surrender to Him by daily dying to ourselves, or we are not His disciples. As Jesus said, "Whoever does not carry their cross and follow me cannot be my disciple" (Luke 14:27). Therefore, there is no such thing as a disciple of Jesus who still controls his own life.

Tragically, the Christian community is full of people who claim to follow Jesus but still sit in the driver's seat of their lives. Many are convinced they are following Him because they attend a church worship service each week, pray every now and then, read the Bible sometimes, and mostly try to be "good Christians" (which simply means they don't swear, lie, cheat, sleep around, and possibly a few more things). Based on what Jesus said, doing or not doing those things does not necessarily mean we are following Him. In fact, Jesus reserved His harshest words for Israel's most religious people—those who thought their pious lifestyle meant they were following God more closely than anyone else and therefore knew Him the best.

Jesus responded to this attitude with a sobering warning: even performing the most supernatural "spiritual" acts—prophesying, casting out demons, doing miracles in His name—does not mean we are following Him. (See Matthew 7:22–23.)

Imagine if a stranger walked into your church gathering and, praying in Jesus' name, brought sight to a blind person, removed someone's tumor, delivered dozens of people from demonic attacks, and even healed a couple people from cancer. I am certain your congregation would assume that person was sent by God and therefore close to Him. And yet Jesus said it is possible for Him to *not even know*—to have no relationship with—this healer. How haunting when we consider the ramifications of this!

First Samuel 16:7 says God "does not look at the things people look at. People look at the outward appearance, but the LORD looks at the heart." Following Jesus, then, starts with a heart surrendered to Him. It is an inside-out journey. If it is possible to follow Jesus with our actions yet never know Him, then it is crucial that our hearts are purely set on knowing Him first, not just doing things for Him or appearing super-spiritual on the outside. The more we get to truly know Him, the more of our lives we want to give Him.

Unfortunately, many people stop there and forget that what we do matters as well. It is a both-and situation, not an either-or. A heart yielded to Jesus will eventually, by grace, produce fruit that carries His attributes. Such godly fruit can be seen in our actions, attitudes, motives, and even our thoughts, but this can only be produced if we "remain in Him," as Jesus said in John 15:4. We cannot remain in Jesus without there being true fellowship between us. And if we are truly in fellowship with Him, then we will produce fruit.

The key to following Jesus, then, is being in real fellowship with Him rather than having a religious connection to Him—which is what we'll examine next.

CHAPTER 3

THE ULTIMATE FELLOWSHIP

MOST PEOPLE MISTAKE the word *followship* for *fellowship*, which is a fitting error given what followship entails. Jesus' call to follow Him is not an emotionless command but an invitation to deep, intimate relationship with Him. Simply put, He invites us into a union that is like no other. Through it, we literally fellowship with God.

But what does this fellowship look like? What does that word even mean? If you grew up in Christian circles, the meaning of fellowship sadly may have been watered down for you. I was raised in a denomination where fellowship basically meant potluck lunches after a worship service. Today in many church services, fellowship has been reduced to a segue between the musical worship and the sermon—the time when we're instructed to "fellowship with your neighbor and tell them God loves them," or something equally as awkward and, dare I say, artificial. On the other hand, fellowship can also describe the closeness some believers develop in a small-group community, where they can be more honest and open in sharing their lives than with their own families.

Our understanding of fellowship depends upon our personal experience. Yet we see in the Bible that God describes fellowship as being both vertical and horizontal. It involves both our individual relationship with Him (the vertical) and our relationships with others (the horizontal). Jesus alluded to this when He said the greatest commandment was to "love the Lord your God with all your heart and with all your soul and with all your mind," quoting from the Law given to Moses. But Jesus didn't stop there: "*And the second is like it*: 'Love your neighbor as yourself'" (Matt. 22:37–39, emphasis added).

Jesus overtly linked the vertical (loving God) with the horizontal (loving people) in a way that redefined true fellowship. Enjoying God and enjoying people were now intertwined.

We see this new way put in action in the first few chapters of the Book of Acts, where the early believers had such an intense, God-produced love for one another that they shared all they had within their community and experienced tremendous joy and favor. Where did this love stem from? It was based on "remaining" in the source of this life and love: Jesus. "If you remain in me and I in you, you will bear much fruit," He promised (John 15:5).

We cannot experience the ultimate fellowship we were made to have with God without loving others, and we cannot experience the depths of true fellowship with others without loving God. In this book we will talk about both aspects, but I admit up front that we will focus more on our fellowship with God because of what I see as a growing crisis in the church today: forsaking our "first love," which Jesus warned the believers in Ephesus not to do (Rev. 2:4, NKJV).

Our first love is always to be the Lord. Nothing changes that. He is our source of true life. Jesus used the analogy of a vine and branches: He is the vine, and we, His people, are the branches. "No branch can bear fruit by itself; it must remain in the vine," He said. "Neither can you bear fruit unless you remain in me" (John 15:4). Without that life-giving, nourishing attachment, we die. "If you do not remain in me, you are like a branch that is thrown away and withers," Jesus continued. "Such branches are picked up, thrown into the fire and burned" (v. 6).

It's wonderful when followers of Jesus fellowship together. That should be a key part of every believer's life. But as much as we may give life to one another, the only way we are able to give this is because of the life we have received directly from Jesus. When we remain in Him, we become channels of His life—living branches through which He can fill others with the same life that is in us.

This means it's crucial that each of us is truly connected—in fellowship—with Him first. Unfortunately, I meet many Christians who love to receive the blessings from the vine but are barely attached to it themselves. They may fill their time with church gatherings, conferences, and ministry activities, and they may even have some of their deepest needs met because of the godly love they experience through others. Yet they neglect to nurture a personal relationship with the one who is life and love itself. Phrased another way, they love hanging out with spiritual brothers and sisters yet barely know their Father because they don't spend time with Him.

I once counseled someone over the course of several months, during which we saw significant signs of transformation. This young man forgave those who had deeply hurt him in the past, experienced a newfound sense of hope after feeling depressed for many years, and was better equipped to overcome the anxious thoughts he frequently battled. Yet the more I got to know this man, the more I saw how heavily he depended on others to help him connect with God. Although we all need help in our journeys of faith, I noticed that he never talked about anything he had discovered on his own in the Bible, never prayed out loud with others, and never shared anything of what the Holy Spirit was teaching him on his own. When I mentioned this, he admitted that even though he had been around Christians for years, he had grown tired of "not getting anything" when he tried to spend time alone with the Lord. Because of this, he was content to simply engage with God through others.

From that point on, I tried to help him develop a personal, intimate fellowship with the Lord. Unfortunately, we lost contact after he moved to another city, and I later heard that he stopped connecting with other believers. I hope he found his own way to commune with the Lord despite not being in fellowship with others. But sadly, my hunch is that he did not.

There is no such thing as riding the coattails of other believers. We are fooling ourselves if we think their fellowship with God is our own. The truth is, it is too easy to hang around a church community and appear close to God while neglecting our own one-on-one time with Him. No one and nothing can replace our own fellowship with the Lord.

At times I have been so busy ministering to others that I neglected being alone with God. During some of those times, I convinced myself that I was still spending time with Jesus as He used me in serving others—and there is some truth to this. God delights in our fellowship with others and our service to them, particularly when He is placed at the center of both. Yet there is nothing like our own, personal time with the Lord, when we can talk with Him, discover more of Him, and simply be in His presence. When I neglect this and put other things ahead of Him—even good things like ministering for Him—I risk venturing down the same path of those who have done miracles in His name but whom He says He never knew. (See Matthew 7:21–23.)

I am convinced that one of our primary goals in life is to "know [Christ] and the power of His resurrection, and the fellowship of His sufferings" (Phil. 3:10, NKJV). Everything else we do stems from this fellowship, just as every fruit produced on the branch of a vine stems from that branch remaining in the vine.

TO ENJOY HIM

The more we abide in Jesus, the more we will enjoy Him. After all, He *wants* us to enjoy Him! I believe the Holy Spirit was speaking through King David when he wrote, "Taste and see that the LORD is good. Oh, the joys of those who take refuge in him!" (Ps. 34:8, NLT). Or when Habakkuk prayed, "I will rejoice in the LORD, I will be joyful in God my Savior" (Hab. 3:18). Or when Paul encouraged believers to "rejoice in the LORD always. I will say it again: Rejoice!" (Phil. 4:4). To rejoice in something is to take joy in it, and simply put, to take joy in something is to enjoy it. Throughout Scripture, from Genesis to Revelation, we find evidence that true joy is found in God alone, and we are challenged—even commanded—to enjoy Him.

Too often I meet believers who don't enjoy their fellowship with God but instead see it as a duty. Like eating vegetables, walking with the Lord has become something they are told is good for them but that they do not actually enjoy. I have counseled enough people to know there are many reasons for this. Life can get complicated, especially if our life history is full of layers of wounding, disappointment, and tragedy.

I discipled a young man years ago who had become almost incapable of feeling joy. No matter what good thing happened in his life, he would eventually see the glass as half-empty. His was not simply a bad case of pessimism; it was as if he couldn't even understand the purpose of joy, much less feel it. Together we discovered that, as is often the case, he had been deeply hurt as a child and had made an inner vow to protect himself from ever feeling such pain again. In doing so, he had agreed with the enemy's agenda to steal from his life and thus had built walls around his heart that kept him from experiencing the joy of the Lord. I praise God that He broke down those walls when this young man repented and invited Jesus to be Master over this area of his life.

Countless others have not experienced such freedom, however. Some mistake joy for the worldly, fleeting feeling of happiness. They expect giddiness and goosebumps, whereas God's joy is typically found more in stillness and suffering. Though it is wonderful to feel excitement in our fellowship with Jesus, the reality is that joy goes deeper than emotion. Enjoying fellowship with the Lord starts with an awareness that we are with *Him*, the supreme God. We get to be in a relationship with the Master of all creation—and He actually wants us! He cares about us and even loves us!

Bible teacher John Piper says: "What could be more liberating, more thrilling, more amazing than that the God who made the universe would come to you, a hopeless sinner, and point you to the death of his Son where sins are paid for, and then say to you, 'Your first and greatest obligation is *that you enjoy supremely what is supremely enjoyable*? Namely, me and my Son in the power of my Spirit.'"[1]

That God is the one who invites us into fellowship with Him should be reason enough to for us to "enjoy supremely what is supremely enjoyable": Him. What a privilege that the Lord enjoys us so much He longs to have the most intimate of relationships with us! That invitation is extended purely because of His grace. We do not deserve it, yet we can enjoy it forever because of His love for us, expressed through Jesus' sacrifice on the cross.

But what often keeps people bound like that young man is a belief that they can do absolutely nothing to enjoy God—that they simply must wait on Him to deliver them from their depression, apathy, or hopelessness. It's no wonder, then, why following Jesus becomes a joyless obligation for them. The Bible offers a different perspective when it comes to joy, however. Most often, especially in the New Testament, the word *joy* is mentioned in the context of an imperative statement or command. Simply put, there's an action attached to it. And almost always, that action is directly linked not only to God but also to a person. God offers joy, and we are to *take it* ("Take delight in the Lord" [Ps. 37:4]). He offers it *in* Jesus, and we are to abide *in* Jesus. Thus, Paul commands us to "rejoice in the Lord always" (Phil. 4:4), and he says, "We can rejoice in our wonderful new relationship with God because our Lord Jesus Christ has made us friends of God" (Rom. 5:11, NLT).

You cannot force someone to enjoy something. I could not force the young man I counseled to enjoy his fellowship with God. But because he wanted to grow in that relationship, I urged him to take action, as the Bible often encourages believers to do, by *taking joy* in God's desire for fellowship with him. It helped this young man immensely to realize he wasn't just waiting for an emotion to sweep over him, but instead that he could step into a relational position that the Lord had already defined. Jesus enjoyed him; therefore, he could enjoy Jesus no matter how he felt—and this became the turning point of their relationship. A true revelation of the Lord's love for this young man freed him to grow in sincere fellowship with Jesus rather than just maintain a distant connection out of duty. He began to *want* to know Christ more, and from this desire he began to know and experience Him more—which included having the fruit of real joy.

PHASES OF FOLLOWSHIP

This book is about enjoying Jesus and, more specifically, enjoying His leadership. As we follow Jesus in fellowship with Him, which is the most basic way to define followship, we should naturally mature toward a true enjoyment of Him. I hope you can already see how intertwined following and fellowshipping are in our lives with Jesus. It is possible to follow Jesus from a distance for many reasons: out of a sense of obligation, because of intellectual curiosity, because we come from a Christian family, and so on. But we will never begin to enjoy Him without developing a close relationship. Stated another way, it is impossible to follow Jesus closely without truly fellowshipping with Him. Think about it: Thousands of people in Jesus' time followed Him around, but only a select few enjoyed intimate fellowship with Him. The masses knew *about* Jesus, but those few knew Jesus personally, and out of that knowing came an enjoyment so great they were willing to give up everything for Him.

In the next chapter we will begin to look at what made Jesus so impacting that His followers would even die for Him. What we find in their stories, as relayed in both the New Testament and first-century historical documents, are traits of a leader so compelling they were willing to follow Him anywhere and do anything for Him. Indeed, Jesus' leadership is so profound it radically changes the life of every person who relinquishes control to Him. His track record is still flawless; He has never led a single person astray, nor has He ever made a wrong decision.

If Jesus is such a perfect leader, why would anyone not want to follow Him? We will continually ask that question throughout this book as I provide you with a new lens through which to read the overall story of the Bible. There are many lenses with which we can read God's Word to gain greater insight and revelation. For example, an end-time lens helps us find the thread of prophesies, statements, and descriptions regarding the last days that runs throughout the entire Bible. The lens we will apply in this book—we can call it the followship lens—examines Scripture through the filter of our universal, age-old problem with God, which we identified at the beginning of this book: Humans inherently want to lead rather than follow. This is especially true when it comes to responding to Jesus' call to follow Him as disciples. As we see how the entire scope of the Bible—past, present, and future—relates to this theme, we find Jesus in the middle of it all, serving as both the centerpiece of history's greatest conflict and its glorious resolution.

I believe that by viewing Scripture through the followship lens, we can develop an even greater awe for Jesus and the way He leads. Ultimately, I hope this book causes you to worship Him more and, at times, to stop reading because you simply want to *be* with Him.

If that happens, then I have successfully conveyed what followship is all about. The closer we get to Jesus by following Him, the more we enjoy Him through fellowship. The way of followship is life's most priceless journey because its endpoint is Christ Himself. Yet along the way, every disciple of Jesus encounters a few distinct phases as we grow in Him. Before we end this chapter, I think it is worthwhile to map out this common experience of following Jesus and, in particular, examine each phase.

I hesitate to describe these as *phases* because we commonly connect that word with steps or sequences like in a to-do list, and the thought of presenting anything in our spiritual lives as a three-step, quick-fix solution makes me cringe. The "Five Easy Steps to Inner Healing" approach may work on magazine covers, but I have not found it to be helpful in life with Jesus. However, the word *phase*, which means "a stage in a process of change or development," precisely captures what makes up the parts of the followship journey.[2] As we are in the process of change—namely, growing closer to Jesus and becoming more like Him—we can see some distinct stages that we pass through along the way of followship.

Let's identify these four phases of followship, each of which can be best examined in the form of a question.

1. Will we *surrender* to Jesus' leadership?

The starting block for every disciple of Jesus is the obstacle of surrender, of giving up "lordship" over our own lives and relinquishing ourselves to Him as Master. As we have already seen, following Jesus comes on His terms, and His terms of surrender are no less than everything. He asks for it all—our careers, families, rights, time, thoughts, dreams, personalities, possessions, health, emotions, expectations, and much more. This involves what we do, what we think, who we are—*everything*.

Given the scope of such a demand, I would argue that surrender is not a one-time decision but an ongoing journey as the Spirit of Jesus reveals more and more of the things we hold onto, often without realizing it. The good news is that the Lord is more gracious, gentle, patient, and loving than anyone else. So although He demands everything, He walks with us through a lifetime of surrendering. Still, the overarching questions remain: Will we accept that Jesus is the rightful leader over all things? And will we surrender to His authority?

2. Will we *submit* to Jesus' leadership?

In war, it's one thing to surrender to the enemy; it is an entirely different matter to actually submit to them. Submission involves us yielding our will to another's. We may have surrendered our "stuff" to Jesus, but the next challenge is whether we will willingly bow to Him and serve Him. When you yield to someone while driving a car, you give way to that driver and allow her to go before you. In an infinitely deeper way, Jesus asks us to yield to His leadership in our lives. Will we give way to Him in all things? Will we willingly and continually do His will rather than our own?

3. Will we *trust* Jesus' leadership?

It is technically possible to surrender and submit to a person without trusting him. But to follow that person with a willing, eager heart takes trust. We usually establish this kind of trust through our senses; we trust people because we've seen them do something or because we've heard stories of their accomplishments. We often say trust is earned and not given; it takes time. Yet Jesus challenges this notion to the core, asking us to trust Him in things we cannot see simply because He is the one leading.

Most people get stuck in this phase of followship with the Lord. After more than thirty years of ministry, I have observed that most believers can decide in their heads to give up things for Jesus, and they typically have the desire and will to see that through and serve Him. Yet when push comes to shove, their hearts are what hold them back in the journey because they find it hard to trust a leader who often remains completely unseen to them.

Do we trust that Jesus really has what's best for us—*always*? We often think we know how things should go in our lives. Will we trust that as the supreme leader, Jesus actually knows best and that His way is perfect?

4. Will we *enjoy* Jesus' leadership?

This is the phase I hope you can experience most in life. The culmination of knowing Jesus is to enjoy Him. As the Westminster Shorter Catechism of the seventeenth century famously states, "Man's chief end is to glorify God, and to enjoy him forever."[3]

Indeed, there is nothing better than enjoying the Lord simply for who He is. When we can surrender everything to Him, submit to His ways, and trust both Him and His leadership, then we can truly enjoy the only perfect leader this world has ever known. Again, I believe this is the ongoing, lifelong journey called followship. But I can assure you, it *is* possible to enjoy Jesus every step of the way and in every phase of the journey.

Notice that these four phases and the questions they raise are not just for us as individuals. These stages are the same ones all humanity must go through. One day, the issues of surrender, submission, trust, and enjoyment will be the pivotal issues for every nation of the world. All humanity will have to answer questions regarding Jesus' authority. As we will explore later, Scripture speaks of an end-time conflict, and it is clear one of the core issues will be Jesus' leadership. Will humanity give up the right to lead ourselves? Will Jesus be honored as the rightful leader of all creation? Will we trust His way of leading? Will we eventually enjoy it? These are the crucial yet culminating questions of history. And once again, they all revolve around Jesus.

This is actually why I have used and will continue to use the phrase *Jesus' leadership* instead of the more generic *God's leadership*. For some it may make no difference, while for others the description is more awkward than anything else. We typically speak more of God's leadership than we do Jesus'. I am being intentional in referring specifically to Jesus and His leadership.

Obviously, I would not be a Christian or follower of Jesus if I did not believe He is God. I believe Jesus when He said, "I and the Father are one" (John 10:30), and, "I am in the Father and the Father is in me" (John 14:11). Jesus' position in the Trinity as the Son of God is not up for debate here. Jesus is God, as virtually every New Testament writer testifies.

Why, then, do I keep referring to Jesus' leadership rather than God's? First, because it is Jesus who asks us to follow Him. Just as Jesus called the Twelve during His time of earthly ministry, He beckons each of us today with the same invitation: "Follow Me." We are Jesus' disciples, and we live to serve Him.

The better and more specific answer, however, lies in the end-time scene that we will examine in greater detail later in this book. For now, it's important to understand that Jesus was hated by His people (the Jewish nation) during His first coming on earth, and He will be hated by His people (all humanity) upon His second coming as well. In Psalm 2, which is full of allusions to Jesus, David prophesied that in the last days global leaders and entire nations will rage and plot "against the LORD and against his anointed"—a clear reference to the Messiah (v. 2). Jesus said the world "hates me because I testify that its works are evil" (John 7:7)—and in today's "don't judge me" era, His words are as offensive and hated as ever. As Scripture says, end-time believers who claim that Jesus is the only way will be mocked, persecuted, and killed everywhere.

The focus of all this hatred will be Jesus. Why will the nations be so angry, as Psalm 2 asks? Because they don't want His leadership.

Let's turn our attention, then, to what makes Jesus' leadership so unique and why it causes such a stir.

CHAPTER 4

JESUS, THE PERFECT LEADER

WHILE TEACHING IN Norway a few years ago, I asked a group of young professionals—teachers, lawyers, social workers, doctors, engineers—a seemingly simple question: What makes for a great leader? In other words, what are the characteristics of a great leader? They had enough workplace experience to have observed good and bad leaders, so the answers came quickly: humble, trustworthy, safe, inclusive, a good listener, compassionate, daring, bold.

Their responses didn't surprise me, as I have lived in Norway long enough to understand the unique perspective Norwegians—and Scandinavians in general—have on leadership. Their approach is called "flat leadership," and it's a style that highly values group dialogue, communal decision-making, and ensuring each person's opinions are considered. A Scandic leader is separated from the pack only in terms of responsibility, not status—which is why it's incomprehensible for a leader to "pull rank" over others. As one business school explains, "Scandinavian leaders don't get respect from their employees just by being the boss."[1]

In Nordic nations, a good leader earns respect by creating space for each person in the group, fielding any challenges or disagreements with humility, and putting the group's desires and vision ahead of his own. Social democracies generally think in terms of "we" more than "me," and leaders are gauged more by how they narrow the gap between themselves and colleagues rather than what they achieve individually. Many Scandinavians subscribe to Chinese philosopher Lao Tzu's leadership proverb, "A leader is best when people barely know he exists."[2]

Is that how you would define good leadership? Does "flat leadership" sound like strong leadership to you? Before you answer that question, let me present another angle.

My hometown of Hong Kong (I was raised there as a missionary kid) has long been known as the city where East meets West. Although local culture has been far more influenced by the Western world than mainland China in recent generations (it was a British colony for more than one hundred fifty years), the Eastern element is still ever-present—especially when it comes to leadership. I remember a few occasions when my dad returned from organizational meetings frustrated at his Chinese coworkers who, in the name of honoring their leader, refused to tell the truth about the leader's detrimental decisions and bring any hint of shame upon that person.

In Asia, as in much of the Middle East and South America, the belief is that leaders inherently deserve respect because of their position. Leadership in these regions is typically patriarchal, meaning most organizations are led by a father figure through whom everything runs and to whom everyone submits with respect (whether deserved or not). This is why in countries such as Russia, Egypt, and Mexico, bosses typically have large, lavish offices, where they sit behind massive desks in throne-like chairs higher than everyone else's while multiple assistants follow their orders. The more decisive and dominant that person is in guiding the organization, the stronger his perceived leadership.

My Norwegian friends may shudder to think of working under such authoritarian leaders, while my Chinese friends may feel it's an honor to submit to such strong leadership. Who is right? Which leadership style is better? The truth is, how we define great leadership depends on our culture. We categorize a leader as "strong" according to our own cultural standards. So what a Dane describes as a great leader will often sound like a weak leader to someone from Malaysia. And what a Guatemalan considers brilliant leadership will likely offend an Australian.* This doesn't mean one is right and the other wrong; it simply means we define leadership by different standards according to where we live.

This also means if I were to ask people from every nation the same question I asked those Norwegian students—What makes for a great leader?—I would get an impossibly broad list of adjectives covering everything from decisive to diplomatic to divinely inspired. As much as we honor history's "greatest" leaders—Julius Caesar, Napoleon Bonaparte, Mahatma Gandhi, Alexander the Great, Nelson Mandela, Winston Churchill, Abraham Lincoln, Martin Luther King Jr.—none of those men could be described with all those adjectives at once.

And yet Jesus can be.

He is the only person in history who can meet the leadership expectations of *every* culture. Take a moment to wrap your head around that truth. Jesus is the

---

* If cultural differences in leadership interest you, I recommend checking out Geert Hofstede's studies on "power distance" and his Power Distance Index, which measures how much a society embraces the gap between leaders and subordinates.

humblest, most "we"-thinking leader ever and yet still the most authoritative. He is more uncompromising than the world's most renowned dictators, yet His compassion for people in every sphere of society is unmatched. He shows mercy to those whom even the most gracious judge would not pardon, and simultaneously He will challenge those whom the world considers beyond reproach. His leadership is complex, profound, and beautiful. It is perfect.

AUTHORITY AND SUBMISSION

Jesus stands out among all of history's other leaders for countless reasons. He is, after all, the only human who is also God in the flesh, with the "government … on his shoulders" (Isa. 9:6). Yet one of Jesus' most remarkable traits as a leader is how He leads in a dualistic way that the world cannot comprehend: with full authority and full submission.

By earthly standards, authority and submission seem contradictory, or at least polar opposites. The more authority I have, the less I need to submit to anyone or anything. Authority leads to power, and in our world, power is the ability to influence others—in plain English, to tell them what to do. As strongman-turned-politician Arnold Schwarzenegger once said, "Ninety-five percent of the people in the world need to be told what to do and how to behave."[3] So according to this thinking, a powerful person is not one who submits to others; instead, his power is revealed based on how others submit to his authority.

Jesus, as usual, turns worldly leadership on its head by ruling with both authority and submission. How does a person rule with submission? We find the answer in Paul's glorious description of Jesus in Philippians 2:

> Though he was God, he did not think of equality with God as something to cling to. Instead, he gave up his divine privileges; he took the humble position of a slave and was born as a human being. When he appeared in human form, he humbled himself in obedience to God and died a criminal's death on a cross.
>
> Therefore, God elevated him to the place of highest honor and gave him the name above all other names, that at the name of Jesus every knee should bow, in heaven and on earth and under the earth, and every tongue declare that Jesus Christ is Lord, to the glory of God the Father.
>
> —VV. 6–11, NLT

Jesus was divine before coming to earth, yet His humble obedience to the Father's plan resulted in His current position of having authority over everything "in heaven and on earth and under the earth." He is now in heaven, seated at the right hand of the Father and exalted "to the place of highest honor." And though His glory hasn't been fully revealed, we know one day, when He has established His eternal kingdom in a new heaven and new earth, *every* person will recognize Him as Lord.

So even if the world we live in hasn't seen or experienced the full extent of Jesus' power, is there any question whatsoever about His authority? Absolutely not! Jesus has *all* authority. Even in a still-broken world contaminated by sin where the forces of darkness have yet to be expelled, He is still in charge.

Why, then, has He not revealed that authority to everyone? Why has He waited so long to unleash His power against all that corrupts this world? Answering that requires looking at how Jesus has handled His authority and power in the past.

I'VE GOT THE POWER!

Imagine you came to a party at my house and I introduced you to two of my friends. I then announced to the group that there would be a twist to the evening: We would be heading out into the wild and would need to follow the orders of one of these two friends, but it was up to you to pick who would command us.

One of the guys looked old and serious, acted a bit reserved, and was not that talkative, while the other was young, charismatic, likable, and clearly the life of the party. Which one would you naturally pick to lead us? What if I told you the first friend was actually a retired Army general who had led hundreds of thousands of soldiers, and that my other friend stocked inventory at a local grocery store? Would that change your pick?

It's amazing how quickly we will follow someone with authority.

Jesus had every right to tout His authority as soon as He arrived on earth. It was His prerogative to demand the world's attention and notify every human that God Himself was now walking the planet. He didn't just have power; He had *all* power! As the Son of God, He didn't have just a little bit of authority; He had *all* authority over every other form of authority on the planet! Yet God the Son allowed Himself to be "made lower than the angels for a little while" by taking on human form (Heb. 2:9), and as a man named Jesus, He allowed Himself to be underneath the authority of those on earth.

Rather than immediately showing everyone how great and powerful He was, Jesus took the humble route of growing up a craftsman's son in a tiny farming village. If you or I were Master of the Universe, I'm certain we would've picked another path more suited for divinity. Nevertheless, Jesus remained perfectly obedient to the Father's plan, which was the way of submission.

Jesus did not only obey His heavenly Father, however. He also spent His entire childhood—and probably more—following directions from His earthly father, Joseph. Though the Gospels' accounts are silent on most of Jesus' upbringing, we know Joseph was a craftsman who raised Jesus as his son.[†] As the eldest son in a Jewish family, Jesus would have been expected to take over His father's business. That means He probably spent much of his youth and possibly even young adulthood working as Joseph's apprentice, learning everything He could from His father about how to build things. Yet can you imagine what it was like for Joseph to teach Jesus, knowing his earthly son/apprentice was ultimately his supreme Master?

Once again, Jesus' humility and self-restraint are astounding. He never abuses His authority, nor does He force His power upon anyone without submitting to His heavenly Father's wishes. In His own words:

> The Son can do nothing by himself; he can do only what he sees his Father doing.
>
> —JOHN 5:19

> For I have come down from heaven not to do my will but to do the will of him who sent me.
>
> —JOHN 6:38

> I do nothing on my own but speak just what the Father has taught me.
>
> —JOHN 8:28

> I love the Father and do exactly what my Father has commanded me.
>
> —JOHN 14:31

[†] Whether Joseph and Jesus were carpenters is uncertain, given a centuries-old translation issue with the Greek word *tekton*, which is more accurately translated as "craftsman" or "builder" and leads some scholars to think Jesus worked more with stones because Nazareth was near a major stone quarry. For more information, see Robby Galatty's book, *The Forgotten Jesus.*

What humility, obedience, and submission! Throughout His life on earth Jesus modeled this way as a different kind of leadership, one built upon submission in which the master becomes the servant. Jesus submitted to Joseph as a youngster, even when He did not have to. At times, He submitted His plans to meet others' requests (such as performing a miracle at His mother's appeal or healing the Canaanite woman's daughter). And He always perfectly submitted to His heavenly Father's will.

Jesus was willing to submit in a way no one else ever has. Remember, just because He had taken on human form doesn't mean He was any less divine. He had every right and, as God, had all power to say at any moment, "No, I do not want to do this." I wonder how many times during Jesus' life on earth He was tempted to go that way. Obviously, His prayer in the Garden of Gethsemane gives us a snapshot of Jesus' thoughts at the pinnacle of pressure. Praying with such intensity that His sweat was like drops of blood, Jesus said, "Father, if you are willing, take this cup from me; yet not my will, but yours be done" (Luke 22:42). Matthew's account records a second prayer in which Jesus' submission to the Father seems to have grown stronger even as His anguish increased. He doesn't even mention His own will: "My Father, if it is not possible for this cup to be taken away unless I drink it, may your will be done" (Matt. 26:42).

This type of submission is not only remarkable and unworldly but also unsettling. For the leader of the world to be submissive like this turns our natural value system upside down. It dismantles the foundations of our humanistic ideals (especially regarding power and authority), and if we are honest with ourselves, it offends us to the core. After all, it's one thing to yield to God, but what kind of all-powerful leader caters to the will of no-name, unruly outcasts (lepers, beggars, Gentiles, the "unclean")? How strong of a leader are you when you refuse to do *anything* without first consulting another authority in heaven? Based on our earthly understanding of what a leader should be like, Jesus' leadership seems weak and even absurd. Why would we ever want to follow Him in the way He followed His Father?

LEADING THROUGH … SUBMISSION?

My wife and I teach a marriage course based on Paul's instructions to husbands and wives in Ephesians 5. It's a passage that gives believers fits if misunderstood and one that unbelievers use to mock Christianity, all because of one word: *submit.* Indeed, as soon as I start reading verse 22 aloud in our class, "Wives, submit yourselves to your own husbands," I feel the tension rising in the room. Is there any wonder why? Generations of globally accepted sexism and misogyny—especially in the church—prompted a feminist revolution that has transformed many cultures. As a result, the word *submission* now brings to mind apron-clad housewives having dinner ready as soon as their dominating husbands return home from work to remind them that the man is the "head of the household."

Jesus had another way to define submission—both for women (His valuing of them was revolutionary) and men—that did not involve holding power over someone. Instead, Jesus' way was about going "lower" than others, even when you were rightfully above them. He modeled the radical concept of leading through humility and service.

How did Jesus model this so perfectly? How did submission come so naturally to Him? I believe it came out of His identity within the Godhead. And I believe that by seeing how the term *submission* works within the context of the Trinity, we can rediscover its original intent and meaning. Let me explain.

Whereas today we associate submission with domination, Jesus modeled submission as a posture of going low not just to serve but also to lift up someone else. His definition of submission was about deferring to others and even preferring their "exaltation" over your own. Within the Trinity, this is what is constantly happening. Each member lifts up the others. Jesus loves to bring glory to the Father, the Holy Spirit loves to exalt Jesus, and the Father loves to honor His Son by His Spirit.

The early church fathers used the word *perichoresis* to describe this unique relationship within the Trinity. Each person of the Godhead is intimately part of the other (the theological term is interpenetration) yet still unique. Perichoresis, then, describes this divine relationship of indwelling with union yet uniqueness. Within the very Triune nature of God is not the exaltation of "self" but instead a desire to bring glory to another. As author-pastor Tim Keller described, "The life of the Trinity is characterized not by self-centeredness but by mutually self-giving love."[4]

Jesus perfectly submitted to the Father's will, even to the point of giving up His life and dying in the worst possible way. That submissive act—along with Jesus' entire life of submission and obedience—brought glory to the Father, yet the Father in turn glorified the Son. Through perfect submission, Jesus received all authority, as we read earlier in Philippians 2:9: "Therefore God exalted him to the highest place and gave him the name that is above every name." And yet at the end of this beautiful description, what is the ultimate purpose of every person recognizing Jesus' lordship over all? It is "to the glory of God the Father" (v. 11). Even as the ultimate leader and the rightful Master over everything, Jesus *still* seeks to glorify the Father. Meanwhile, the Holy Spirit submits to both the Son and the Father while forever seeking to glorify Jesus. What an incredible relationship!

If diving into the Trinity confuses you, don't worry—trying to explain the Triune God has baffled the church for generations. My desire is not for you to get lost in theological pondering over the Trinity, but simply to sense the power of submission through this beautiful picture of the Godhead. God, the Triune being, is the ultimate leader. If within Him exists constant submission—ongoing service to one another—then how much more do we need this aspect ingrained in our thinking of leadership. If we are offended by Jesus' submission as a leader and see it as "weak," then maybe our definition of leadership has been defined more by this world's standards than by God's.

Jesus served to perfection. He is the definition of servant leadership, and He showed us how perfect leadership involves both authority *and* submission. He led that way while on earth, He continues to lead that way in heaven now, and He will one day return to this world and display this perfect leadership as its rightful ruler.

A RAGING WORLD

Let's be honest, though. Does it look like Jesus is leading the world right now? Even if Jesus leads with perfect submission, does it seem like He is still in control? Hatred dominates the headlines in the form of racism, sexism, anti-Semitism, homophobia, and xenophobia. The world's economies are in chaos. Leaders flaunt their godless agendas while the masses applaud. Violence, poverty, famine, corruption, disease—these are the conditions of everyday life. As believers, we cry out for Jesus to do something, yet people mock us for believing in an ancient God who seems to no longer respond. And so, as evil continues to escalate, we're left hanging onto this thing called faith, believing—*hoping*—that the Lord sees all and one day will bring about justice.

Do you realize the Bible paints the exact same picture of the era immediately preceding Christ's return—what we call the end times? I briefly mentioned in the last chapter that Psalm 2 gives us a snapshot of the world raging at Jesus. King David wrote these prophetic words more than three thousand years ago, yet they could easily describe what is emerging today:

Why do the nations conspire and the peoples plot in vain? The kings of the earth rise up and the rulers band together against the Lord and against his anointed, saying, "Let us break their chains and throw off their shackles."

—PSALM 2:1–3

The "nations" of this passage—leaders of all types and people from everywhere—oppose God because they feel He is restricting them. More specifically, they "conspire" against Yahweh, the God of Israel and "his anointed," which is Jesus the Messiah. (Our word *messiah* comes from the original Hebrew word *mashiach,* meaning "anointed one.")[5]

The people's common hatred for the Lord galvanizes their attempts to "break their chains and throw off their shackles" (Ps. 2:3). What chains and shackles do these raging rebels want to be rid of? The ways of God. The people no longer trust God's definitions of what is right and wrong but instead feel they are confining, restrictive, and outdated. In true humanistic fashion, the nations believe humanity is so advanced that they should be the ones defining truth and morality, not God. Their rebellion is like a looping video throughout human history: We want to lead rather than follow. Ultimately, the people of Psalm 2 want to be God—to act like Him, lead like Him, rule like Him.

If you don't think this applies to today, let me remind you that within the last sixty years we have witnessed a global moral revolution unlike any other, particularly in nations with Christian roots. Societies once established on biblical truths and values have now become the leading proponents of defying those very morals. Increasingly, both governmental authorities ("the kings") and cultural leaders ("the rulers")—celebrities, CEOs, sports stars, academics—believe they are doing people a favor by removing the Bible's "old-fashioned" morals from society. In recent years, nation after nation has established legislation directly opposing God's Word on such foundational social issues as marriage and divorce, immigration, sexuality and gender, poverty, parenting, identity, and life in general (from when it begins to when it ends). This tidal wave of godless legislation continues to impact other nations and, in turn, shape beliefs, morals, and lifestyles.

WHEN JUSTICE SEEMS LATE

The world is raging and will only increase in its hatred of Jesus, His ways, and His leadership. Of course, not *all* nations, peoples, and leaders will shake their fists at God, nor will everyone plot against His anointed. The Book of Revelation reveals a remnant of end-time believers who refuse to yield to the onslaught of humanism and who remain true to the Lord, even at the cost of death. Today an estimated one hundred thousand people around the world die each year for their faith in Jesus, while millions of others are persecuted.[6] Yet their collective cry is the same as that of those in the last days:

> When he [the angel] opened the fifth seal, I saw under the altar the souls of those who had been slain because of the word of God and the testimony they had maintained. They called out in a loud voice, *"How long, Sovereign Lord, holy and true, until you judge the inhabitants of the earth and avenge our blood?"* Then each of them was given a white robe, and they were told to wait a little longer, until the full number of their fellow servants, their brothers and sisters, were killed just as they had been.
>
> —REVELATION 6:9–11, EMPHASIS ADDED

How long, Sovereign Lord? How long? Faithful followers of God have asked that question throughout history. In Psalm 94 the psalmist describes the Lord as "a God who avenges" and the "Judge of the earth" who pays "back to the proud what they deserve." Yet only two verses later, he asks, "How long, LORD … how long will the wicked be jubilant?" (94:1–3). Asaph sang with a more loaded tone: "How long will the enemy mock you, God? Will the foe revile your name forever? Why do you hold back your hand, your right hand?" (Ps. 74:10–11). The prophet Habakkuk brought even a tinge of accusation into his questioning: "Your eyes are too pure to look on evil; you cannot tolerate wrongdoing. Why then do you tolerate the treacherous? Why are you silent while the wicked swallow up those more righteous than themselves?" (Hab. 1:13).

The question of God's justice remains as relevant for us today and can make it difficult to trust the Lord in the journey of followship, much less enjoy Him through it. Every recent generation has seen protestors marching through city streets around the world, standing up against injustices such as racial profiling, police brutality, governmental oppression, and the denial of human rights. Their voices may temporarily change situations, but at the end of the day, history proves we will still be left with evil in the world, which will always lead to more injustice. How, then, as believers do we reconcile a just God with the injustice we see around us every day? If Jesus is perfect in His leadership, why does He allow evil to rule the world instead of putting His foot down and saying, "Enough is enough!"

How long, Lord?

God knows His followers will continue asking this question until the day He brings full justice. I believe this is *exactly* why Jesus gave us the parable of the persistent widow in Luke 18:1–8. If you have never read the parable, here's a summary (though I encourage you to study the passage on your own): A widow repeatedly approached a crooked judge to grant her justice against "her adversary." We're not sure who this adversary is, what charges they brought against her, or why she was continually having to appeal to this judge. What we do know is this judge "neither feared God nor cared what people thought" (v. 2). Stated another way, he did not care for truth nor what was right. The very person who was supposed to represent justice and function as its extension was himself unjust.

I have been at the mercy of a judge only once in my life, to appeal a speeding ticket as a young man. Even then, I approached the judge's bench to explain my case with trepidation, knowing this man had the power to affect my future. (The penalty of losing my appeal was worse than if I had not appealed in the first place, so that should explain my nervousness.) Can you imagine, then, what the widow must have felt going to a judge she—and the whole town—knew was unjust? And to think this was the only person who could make things right for the widow!

Despite this, the widow continued to appeal time after time, only to be met with deaf ears and complete apathy. It seemed her adversary would triumph. Still, she did not give up and continued to voice her appeal. Eventually, the meager widow wore down the powerful judge, and he consented not because of any sense of justice within him, but simply out of a selfish motive to no longer have to listen to her annoying appeals.

Jesus created such juxtaposition between the evil judge of His parable and His righteous heavenly Father that His concluding questions are almost rhetorical: "Will not God bring about justice for his chosen ones, who cry out to him day and night? Will he keep putting them off? I tell you, he will see that they get justice, and quickly" (Luke 18:7–8).

God is nothing like the evil judge. He cares more about us than we will ever know, and He hears when we cry out to Him for justice. But do we believe what Jesus said? Do we believe God actually is just? Do we believe His "chosen ones" really will get justice? And quickly?

I have found that last part to be where many believers struggle. We question if God's "quickly" is anywhere close to ours. As ludicrous as it sounds, we often question the Creator of time's sense of timing. And we tend to conclude that if things don't happen the way we think they should—in our lifetime, in a way we can prove and experience with our senses—then God is unjust. From there, our view spirals downward, because if God is not just, then how can He be trusted to be fair? And if He isn't fair, then how do we know He won't keep "putting [us] off"? And if it's possible that He might ignore our cries for justice, then what is the point of crying out to Him day and night?

Can I let you in on something? God is just, whether we think He is or not. It's who He is. He is the very definition of justice. As is the case with each of God's attributes—love, mercy, peace, joy, and so on—we find the origin of those attributes in His very being. But simply because God is just does not necessarily mean He is always fair. And for that, we should be thanking Him, not giving up on Him. Let me explain.

There is not a person on this planet who has not sinned. Psalm 51:5 makes it clear that we are born into sin ("Surely I was sinful at birth, sinful from the time my mother conceived me"), while Romans 3:23 says that "all have sinned and fall short of the glory of God." We don't measure up to God's standard of holiness. Whether we've sinned once or a billion times makes no difference in regard to our standing with a perfect God. Just as a single stain makes an entire carpet stained, a single sin makes the whole person sinful.

That's a problem, because justice says there must be a payment for sin, and that payment, according to Romans 6:23, is death—not just physical death, but spiritual death. It's eternity without God—an eternity of darkness, turmoil, loneliness, unrest, and all the things God is not. So our sin put us on a track destined for hell.‡ Our only hope of rescue from this death sentence was someone who could make the payment of death, someone who despite being born into a fallen human race would never sin.

Enter Jesus.

---

‡ If at this point you're arguing that it isn't fair for God to condemn us for something we're born into, then try living the rest of your life without ever sinning. You'll quickly discover that it's in our nature to sin. Why would God make us this way? He didn't; He made us perfectly in His image with free will to choose or reject Him. Unfortunately, just as the first humans discovered, our free will takes us down the wrong path every time and proves we must be rescued from ourselves. For more on this dilemma—and God's solution—read Romans 6–8.

The perfect, sinless man ended up dying in our place, and this is why God is not fair. It's not fair that Jesus died for us. It isn't fair that He was mocked, tortured, and crucified. It's not fair that we did not get what we deserved. But thank God He isn't fair, and that His lack of fairness doesn't affect His justness. He is still completely just in everything He does.[5] And that leads us back to Jesus' parable of the persistent widow.

FINDING FAITH

Jesus promised in Luke 18 that God will "bring about justice for his chosen ones, who cry out to him day and night" (v. 7). But notice the way Jesus finished His teaching with a cliff-hanger: "However, when the Son of Man comes, will he find faith on the earth?" (v. 8).

I used to find Jesus' question puzzling, as if He had suddenly changed topics and forgotten to wrap up His parable with a nice bow on top. (As if He ever did that!) The truth is, Jesus once again used a piercing question to not only challenge His listeners' image of God but also ingeniously connect the parable to the issue of His end-time leadership.

What does it take to believe that God is just, despite what our world, our eyes, and even our experience tells us? It takes faith!

What does it take to cry out to an invisible God who doesn't seem to answer the way we think He should? It takes faith!

What does it take to believe this invisible, slow-to-avenge God will bring about justice quickly for His chosen ones, even when it seems our adversary is the one triumphing? It most definitely takes faith!

And what does it take to believe this God will one day return to right all wrongs and, in complete justice, destroy the nations that conspire against Him, rise up to break off the "shackles" of God's Word, and even persecute those who are crying out to Him for justice? It takes the ultimate faith!

We are still waiting for Jesus' return—the return of a perfect leader who will reign with complete authority, power, submission, and yes, justice. Such waiting takes faith since we have yet to see Him return. We know from the Book of Hebrews that "faith is confidence in what we hope for and assurance about what we do not see," and that "without faith it is impossible to please God" (11:1, 6). Faith, then, inherently involves both belief (head knowledge)

---

[5] For a deeper look at the questions surrounding God's justice and His fairness, I recommend Jennifer Rothschild's cleverly titled book, *God Is Just Not Fair*.

and trust (heart knowledge). It's the latter that makes it easier to persevere and never give up, just like the persistent widow. We don't have faith only because we intellectually believe Jesus will return in justice; we have faith because our hearts trust *Him*. It's Jesus who has said He will return; therefore, we know He will.

I will admit that at times it's hard to believe Jesus is in control over this world, especially when evil, chaos, and injustice seem to rule our day. Our faith can be tested when the world mocks us for believing in a just God whose sense of justice seems to be failing and whose timing seems off. We may even face persecution for our faith, but the question Jesus posed two thousand years ago remains the same today: *"When the Son of Man comes, will he find faith on the earth?"*

Will Jesus find a people who have trusted Him, remained loyal to His Word, and expected His return? Will He find a people who have continually called out to Him, day and night? Will He find a people who long for His perfect leadership?

A GLIMPSE OF THE END

Eventually, all history will culminate in one man named Jesus. He is already the centerpiece of human history, yet when He returns, humanity will witness a climax like never before. I'll elaborate more on this return in a later chapter, but for now, let me give you a glimpse of how things will end.

The human journey begins and ends under the leadership of Jesus, and in Revelation 5 we find Him at the center of everything, just as He should be. The apostle John, who wrote the Book of Revelation, was caught up in a vision of God's throne room, where in the previous chapter he described an incomprehensible yet glorious snapshot of worship in heaven: lightning, thunder, rainbows, a sea of glass, twenty-four thrones with twenty-four elders wearing crowns, seven blazing lamps, four mysterious creatures that never stop declaring God's holiness.

It's a mesmerizing scene. But as chapter 5 begins, the focus shifts to a single scroll. We don't know what the scroll is or what it says, only that there is writing on it. (We find out a bit more later in Revelation.) But we know there is a problem: No one can open the scroll. It is sealed with seven seals. In verse 2, an angel inquires, "Who is worthy to break the seals and open the scroll?" Yet no one—not a single person in heaven or on earth—is worthy to open it. This is so unsettling that John begins to weep bitterly—until an elder taps him on the shoulder, says a few words, and gets John to wipe away his tears so he can see what happens next.

Jesus stands up.

With all heaven and earth fixated on Him, Jesus rises, walks over to the scroll, and takes it out of His Father's hand. I can just imagine the silence of the entire universe at that moment, with everyone mesmerized by this God-man who is called the Lamb. He can open it! He is the *only* one who can open the scroll. Not only is He able to, but He is worthy enough to. And this eternal truth sends the heavens into a massive, historic frenzy of worship.

The four living creatures, who until that point have not stopped declaring God's holiness, and the twenty-four elders suddenly throw themselves to the ground and launch into a song never heard before:

> You are worthy to take the scroll and to open its seals, because
> you were slain, and with your blood you purchased for God
> persons from every tribe and language and people and nation.
> You have made them to be a kingdom and priests to serve our
> God, and they will reign on the earth.
>
> —REVELATION 5:9–10

Their singing is followed by a booming chorus from millions of angels who encircle the throne:

> Worthy is the Lamb, who was slain, to receive power and wealth
> and wisdom and strength and honor and glory and praise!
>
> —REVELATION 5:12

Then, as if the universe cannot contain itself, every creature—in heaven, on earth, in the air, and in the sea—shouts the loudest, most glorious sound of worship the earth has ever heard:

> To him who sits on the throne and to the Lamb be praise and
> honor and glory and power, for ever and ever!
>
> —REVELATION 5:13

No movie can capture the sights and sounds of this scene, nor can a book or painting depict what it will be like when everything in creation worships Jesus. He is the culmination of it all, the centerpiece of existence. He is the only one worthy of such adoration. He is the longing of every nation and every person. And He is our perfect leader.

Why, then, would *anyone* not want to follow a leader so glorious and worthy? The answer requires us looking back in history to see how this conflict all started, which is what we will do in the next part.

PART II

... TO A JOURNEY

Each of us is part of a bigger story—and a bigger struggle—that began before the world was created. As we commit to following Jesus, it's crucial that we not only understand the ongoing dilemma we face but that we place it in the right context. History really can help us avoid making the same mistakes as those before us!

CHAPTER 5

THE ORIGINAL PLAN

"IN THE BEGINNING God created the heavens and the earth" (Gen. 1:1).

The first sentence of the Bible fittingly establishes God's supreme leadership. He existed before everything else; prior to anything, He was. Therefore, as the originator of all life, whatever came next would be under Him.

When God made Adam, however, something extraordinary happened: The Creator separated him from the pack. He specifically made mankind to be over the rest of what He had created, just like He was. This likeness to Him was not a mistake, nor was it merely a matter of similar appearance. When God announced, "Let us make mankind in our image," He immediately followed His statement with an explanation of the function for that likeness: "so that they may rule over ..." (Gen. 1:26).

Different Bible translations use a variety of words there—to rule over, to reign, to have authority, to have dominion, to have power over, and so on—but they all boil down to a single concept: We were meant to *lead* creation on earth. Just as God leads, we were created to lead. In fact, God stated our function twice in a matter of three verses (Gen. 1:26–28). He wanted us to know our purpose.

God also wanted us to know who we are. Three times in two of those same verses the Lord highlighted our likeness—our replicated similarity—to Him, each time using the word *image*. God made us "in His own image." The original Hebrew word, *tselem*, connotes a representation or shadow that points to someone or something else.[1] Just as photographs are visual representations of an actual scene captured by a camera lens somewhere else, we were created to be living photographs—images—of God in heaven. We were to be a representation of Him on earth, divine image-bearers who *re*-presented Him just as He was.

Part of that re-presenting, then, involved His way of leadership. We were to lead all the earth just as God would. Simply put, we were made to lead like Him. We were not God, but we were like Him. In fact, He made us so similar to Him that one of His purposes for us was to extend His leadership on earth in the same way He would.

What is God's way of leading? As we discovered in the last chapter, Jesus gave us a perfect picture of this when He walked on earth, and He continues to provide this leadership now in heaven. The Lord leads with supreme authority and submission. He wields all power over everything, but instead of glorifying Himself, Jesus delights in continuously lowering Himself to serve the Father. In this regard, He leads *with* the other divine persons of the Trinity in perfect partnership—and that is key.

Do you remember the term *perichoresis* mentioned in the previous chapter—the intimate connection between the Father, Son, and Holy Spirit? Each is unique as a person, yet each is profoundly interconnected to the other as one being. Within that indwelling, they continuously elevate one another, glorify one another, and delight in the exaltation of one another. This is how they exist together as one, and it's also how they lead. The triune God leads out of who He is, and therefore everything is done out of the joy of fellowship.

When God created mankind, I believe He longed for the same type of fellowship with us. (The Bible unveils this theme throughout its pages but especially when Jesus prayed in John 17:21 "that all of them may be one, Father, just as you are in me and I am in you. May they also be in us.") I believe God opened up the most divine, intimate relationship and invited us in. Though we must be careful to not overextrapolate this idea—after all, we aren't God, nor were we invited to become God—still, God's invitation to partner with Him reveals His longing for fellowship. As theologian Sam Storms writes, "God created us so that the joy he has in himself might be ours. God doesn't simply think about himself or talk to himself. He enjoys himself! He celebrates with infinite and eternal intensity the beauty of who he is as Father, Son, and Holy Spirit. And we've been created to join the party!"[2]

If, then, we were made to lead like God, we were to lead both *over* and *with*: *over* planet Earth, which was our given dominion, and *with* God, whom we were to represent in continual, joyful partnership. Humanity's leadership upon the earth was to be in perfect sync with our Creator. We were to lead in fellowship with Him. Ultimately, then, you could say *we were made to lead and to be led.*

I cannot stress this point enough, because not only is it the foundational principle for everything in this book, but it's also crucial to understand as we spend this chapter and the next few walking through the biblical timeline of followship. Humans were made *to lead* because, unlike any other creature on earth, we were made in God's likeness, and we were made *to be led* in perfect partnership under God's supreme authority. God wanted us to lead like Him, over His earth, and with Him.

This was the original plan.

A QUICK FALL

One bite. That's all it took for the perfect life to be ruined. Paradise was indeed lost when Adam and Eve succumbed to temptation, disobeyed God, and ate from the tree of the knowledge of good and evil. Though they had an entire territory of trees to eat from—who knows how large the Garden of Eden was—they still wanted to taste fruit from the only tree from which God had said they *couldn't* eat. Here we have history's first instance of humanity facing the timeless issue: to lead or to follow. Whether they knew it or not, Adam and Eve's desire to make their own rules—to lead their own way and not follow God's—would leave a lasting imprint on every person.

The first humans didn't have to wait long to see the effects of their decision either. Immediately strange things began to happen. They felt emotions they had never experienced: guilt, shame, anger, frustration, resentment, fear. Sin's curse crept in like swelling storm clouds, and when they were overcome by the internal darkness, they tried to avoid it by blaming their faulty leadership on someone else. Adam blamed Eve (and in a not-so-subtle way, God), desperately attempting to gain whatever higher ground he could to avoid his own fall. "The woman *you* put here with me," he told the Lord, "*she* gave me some fruit from the tree" (Gen. 3:12, emphasis added). In Adam's statement we find the initial evidence of mankind elevating himself over another to justify his own desire to lead *above* rather than *below*—to lead in a God-less way rather than a God-like way. This was not natural to how God created him, but it was now a new nature by his own choice.

Adam wasn't alone in his infection. Eve caught it too and quickly blamed someone else: "The serpent deceived me, and I ate" (Gen. 3:13).

I wonder if either human recognized then how tragic this new type of "leading" was. Both wanted to lead, yet neither was willing to lower themselves and submit to their Creator's authority.

Adam and Eve's original sin doomed humanity in every way. It also distorted the divine leadership structure God originally planned. Man and woman were supposed to rule *with* each other, together with God—not *over* each other. Yet because we wanted to rule over God by choosing our way rather than His, and because it's impossible for anyone to rule over God, He granted us the next possible thing. "He will rule over you," the Lord said to Eve while pointing to Adam (Gen. 3:16).

Some Bible translations replace the phrase *rule over* with words like *dominate* or *have dominion over*, which helps us connect this outcome to God's original plan, but it also makes it more tragic. Prior to this, neither human dominated the other. Our dominion was to be over the earth, not one another. Though Adam was first to be created, he was to lead like God, which meant whatever "leading" he did of Eve involved willingly serving her, exalting her, and enjoying their fellowship.* She was his God-given helper (Gen. 2:18, 20), and he was her servant leader. Human fellowship was to be like the divine fellowship of perichoresis. We were to lead with perfect authority and submission.

Through sin, however, humanity was introduced to the concept of domination rather than dominion. Dominion is a holy order of God's governance, and He willingly shares it with all who will enjoy fellowship with Him. Domination, on the other hand, is the order of hell. This is why authority and rank matter so much to the devil and his demons. They are obsessed with self-exaltation and gaining power over someone or something.

The fall of mankind meant we no longer ruled in Godlike partnership but instead through domination. As a result of sin, God declared that one gender would rule over the other. This new order not only initiated a battle of the sexes, but more significantly, it redefined leadership. From this point on in history, people's way of leading would forever be defined in terms of domination. In addition, submission—part of God's holy way of leading—would also be defined in terms of being "over" or "under" others rather than with them. Instead of being an expression of fellowship, submission became a mark of domination. Can you see how truly tragic this was? Sin ushered into the world a whole new order, a new way of leading, a new kingdom, and indeed, a new "king."

THE PROBLEM OF FREE WILL

By the very next generation of humans, the new model of leadership—of ruling *over* someone else—was distorted even more. Adam and Eve had a pair of sons, and years later these brothers brought offerings to the Lord. Cain, the older brother, who was a gardener, "brought some of the fruits of the soil," while the

---

* This is why Paul instructs husbands to "love your wives, just as Christ loved the church" (Eph. 5:25). Jesus reminded us of God's original plan for the marriage relationship, which reflects the relationship within the Trinity. Husbands, we are to stoop so low to serve our wives that we're willing to die for them, just as Christ died for His bride, the church. Talk about loving someone to death! This is the opposite of male chauvinism; it's God's original pattern of leadership—His heavenly way—being restored to a redeemed earth!

younger, sheep-herding brother, Abel, offered "fat portions from some of the firstborn of his flock" (Gen. 4:3–4). You know how the story goes: Cain was jealous because God favored Abel's offering, and the older brother eventually murdered his younger brother.

Murder is the ultimate expression of domination over someone. We don't usually think of killing in terms of leadership, but in the crudest way, murder is the ultimate negative leadership over others: You "lead" them to death by killing them! Within the first two human generations, then, we went from seeing God's perfect leadership, to God creating humans in His image so they could lead like and with Him, to the man sinning and ruling over the woman, to humans now leading others in a negative way, with the ultimate consequence of bad leadership: death. How could things go so bad so fast?

To answer that, we need to pause on our timeline journey and take a deeper look at the problem. It's pointless to read the Bible's story with the "followship lens" if we haven't established some foundational truths about the story itself. For starters, it's important that we clarify a few things related to God, humans, sin, evil, and everything between. That's no small task!

God's original design, as we've already seen, was for us to lead and be led. We were made to lead because we were created in God's likeness, and we were made to be led in partnership with God under His sovereignty. Because of God's perfect character, He didn't force us to be led but gave us free will to enjoy relationship with Him. We can choose to enjoy the perichoresis kind of relationship He invited us into, or we can willingly step out of the fellowship at any point. This is the essence of love, because love cannot be forced; it is a choice. The first humans' decision to love God, then, was a choice to follow His way and submit to His leadership. They then enjoyed not only everything found in God but the spoils of His kingdom as well: life, blessing, abundance, even the authority He'd given them to lead on the earth with Him. By remaining in relationship, they enjoyed everything good.

Before Adam and Eve took their fatal bite from the forbidden fruit, this goodness was all they had ever known. The Lord desired for Adam and Eve to never experience life without Him. He prohibited them from eating from the tree of the knowledge of good and evil because He didn't want them to know evil, which was the absence of Him, and for such evil to exist eternally. Paradise meant the absolute best for humanity, and that perfection was enjoying the fullness of God Himself. But notice that the Lord still gave Adam and Eve a choice. They had free will. He would not force them to *not* eat from the tree, but for their own well-being He led them away from it by forbidding it.

When my sons were young I forbade them from touching the stovetop whenever it was hot. My leadership came out of pure love; I didn't want them to experience the pain of a burned hand. But I also gave my boys a choice. I didn't lock up our oven in another room so they couldn't get to it. I gave them free will to touch it or not, even though I knew there was the possibility they would choose to lead themselves (doing what they wanted rather than obeying me) and experience the negative consequences of that decision.

That's a weak comparison to the situation in the Garden of Eden, but the point remains. As Adam and Eve stood before the forbidden tree, they faced the same decision they had each day. There were ultimately only two choices, just as there continue to be for us today: Will I be led by God or will I choose to lead? Phrased in a way we've used throughout this book so far, the question was simply: Will I follow God's leadership, or will I follow someone or something else (including my own leading)?

When we fell—and it's "we" because any of us would have made the same choice as the first humans (Rom. 5:12)—we chose to lead ourselves. In short, we sinned. The Bible defines sin as rebellion against God (Deut. 9:7; Josh. 1:18) and as "lawlessness" (1 John 3:4). So sin is simply when we turn against God and rebel against His ways.

When Adam and Eve made this choice to oppose God and eat from the forbidden tree, they faced consequences infinitely greater than a burned hand from a hot stove. Can you imagine what thoughts ran through their minds as they suddenly became aware of their nakedness, scrambled to cover themselves, and then embarked on the worst game of hide-and-seek in history? Life would never be the same. In an instant they lost their freedom and became slaves to a new master called sin. Every human after them would be born with the same desire to, by their own free will, oppose God, and that path would lead them to an eternity devoid of God if they couldn't be saved.

But the bad news got worse. Adam and Eve's fallen nature would now be reflected throughout the earth, as the first human sin brought the entire planet under the rule of another force: evil. Many people see evil as a created substance, but God didn't create evil. Evil is simply the absence of good, just as darkness is the absence of light. As one study states, evil is "the sad corruption of what was intended for good."[3] It's borne out of relationship gone awry. When we choose to go against God and break relationship with Him, the result is evil. So despite what you might have heard, God didn't create evil and store it in a single forbidden tree in the garden; He created something that possessed a knowledge of what life would be like if we decided to lead—that is, chose to be our own "God" and rule ourselves—rather than follow Him. Evil would have never entered Paradise had the first humans not willingly chose to rebel against God and lead themselves.

They did just that, obviously, and the rest is (human) history. But according to Scripture, they were not the only ones to make this fateful choice.

BEAUTY TO ASHES

When God pronounced a curse in Eden, He responded not only to Adam and Eve but also to the serpent, whom Scripture later explains is "the devil, or Satan, who leads the whole world astray" (Rev. 12:9). The word *satan* means "the adversary" or "one who stands against" and is more of a job description.[4] Over time, however, we've adapted it as a proper name for the same spiritual being Jesus called "the evil one" (Matt. 13:38–39) and whom John described as the deceiver (Rev. 20:2–3, 8, 10).

Indeed, Satan's nature is to oppose God and deceive others into doing the same. Many Bible scholars believe Genesis 3 simultaneously tells the rebellion story of both humanity and the devil. (Otherwise, why would God curse an already fallen Satan?) Other scholars believe Lucifer's fall happened prior to Eden, which is the current majority view within the church and is based on two key passages that seem to give us a backstory to this original rebel.[†]

Despite pop-culture depictions, Satan is far from being an equal and opposite force to God, nor is he a grotesque creature with horns, wings, and a pitchfork. In Ezekiel 28, we discover that God created Satan as "the seal of perfection … perfect in beauty" and adorned him with some of the most valuable elements and stones (vv. 12–13). A passage in Isaiah 14 describes him as a "shining star" (v. 12, NLT). If the Bible describes you as *perfectly* beautiful with star-like radiance, then I think it's safe to say you were nothing less than stunning, considering all of God's creation that still leaves us speechless today!

[†] Ezekiel 28:2–19 and Isaiah 14:4–17 are clearly addressed to the human kings of Tyre and Babylon, respectively. Though the passages never directly mention Satan, they also include supernatural, figurative descriptions that seem to tell a deeper narrative than just the tales of two prideful kings of earthly kingdoms—for example, "You were in Eden … anointed as a guardian cherub … on the holy mount of God" (Ezek. 28:13–14); "How you have fallen from heaven" (Isa. 14:12).

Ezekiel 28 also tells us the devil was "full of wisdom" (v. 12); God *anointed* and *ordained* him as a guardian cherub (v. 14). The cherubim, along with the seraphim, seem to be among the highest-ranking heavenly beings whose purpose is to worship the Most High and magnify His holiness. Ezekiel's description of the devil as being "on the holy mount of God" (28:14) indicates this former cherub had a position near the Lord's presence, which elevates his status even more.

How could something so beautiful, wise, anointed, ordained, and close to God willingly give up perfection? Ezekiel 28:15, 17 tells us:

> You were blameless in your ways from the day you were created till wickedness was found in you. ... Your heart became proud on account of your beauty, and you corrupted your wisdom because of your splendor. So I threw you to the earth; I made a spectacle of you before kings.

The devil was so stunningly beautiful that it went to his head—technically, his heart—and this developed into pride. At its core, pride is thinking more of ourselves than we should. It's exalting ourselves to such an extent that we begin to act as if we were God, defining the worth of things. Lucifer's beauty eventually caused something in him to relish in his own valuation rather than being content with the worth God gave him. God's love and enjoyment of him were not enough; he wanted more.

C.S. Lewis described pride as spiritual cancer: "It eats up the very possibility of love, or contentment, or even common sense."[5] Indeed, Lucifer's pride spread to such a cancerous degree that he lost sight of reality and was willing to throw away perfection to seek his own gain. Ezekiel 28:2 says, "In the pride of your heart you say, 'I am a god; I sit on the throne of a god.'" The prophet Isaiah expanded on this part of the devil's story:

> For you said to yourself, "I will ascend to heaven and set my throne above God's stars. I will preside on the mountain of the gods far away in the north. I will climb to the highest heavens and be like the Most High."
>
> —ISAIAH 14:13–14, NLT

Satan wanted God's position of authority. He was not content with God being the supreme leader; he wanted that position. Whether he desired to be over all creation or merely master of himself makes no difference (though most believe it was the former). Here we have the very origin of sin, and it's no coincidence that the core issue is God's leadership. Just as Adam and Eve introduced sin into the earth by trying to elevate themselves with one bite, heaven found a mismatch the moment Lucifer aimed to raise his throne higher than God's—or at least above everything else in creation. Remember, the very essence of God's leadership is the delight He takes in sharing His authority. Though He is all-sufficient and lacks nothing, He takes pleasure in others experiencing His glory. As perichoresis shows, He lowers Himself in profound humility so others will be exalted in Him.

The devil apparently missed that memo and allowed pride to consume him. Instead of being content with the glory God gave him, he wanted to exalt himself. It cost him eternity, but not simply because of a one-time "mistake"; his heart continues to be so consumed with evil that he is beyond saving. Because of this, both Ezekiel and Isaiah mention how the Lord responded to Satan's supreme pride:

> I threw you to the earth ... and I reduced you to ashes on the ground in the sight of all who were watching.
> —EZEKIEL 28:17–18

> You will be brought down to the place of the dead, down to its lowest depths.
> —ISAIAH 14:15, NLT

Earlier in Isaiah's passage, the Lord describes the devil's new domain as "the realm of the dead ... [where] maggots are spread out beneath you and worms cover you" (vv. 9, 11). Isn't it interesting to see the connection between this and the Lord's curse upon the serpent in Genesis 3:14 ("You will crawl on your belly and you will eat dust all the days of your life")? The one who wanted to be like the Most High was instead forced to be the lowest of all. While Christ's way of humility willingly chooses submission and has led to Him being exalted, Satan's way of pride chooses self-exaltation and has forced him into a position of eating dirt.

To this day Satan has not changed. He still desires to be exalted, and his pride keeps him lowered. He still wants the glory God receives as creation's rightful leader for himself. Sin—opposing God—continues to drive the core of his existence, and he is eaten up by pride. His ongoing mission, as Jesus revealed, is to "steal and kill and destroy" (John 10:10). It's fueled by an unquenchable hatred and jealousy for people. Why? Because while Satan wanted to be *like* the Most High, guess who was created in God's likeness, with the innate opportunity to lead *like* Him? Us!

I believe the devil has never been able to let that one slide, and it's why throughout the Bible we find his rage so often directed at humanity. He knows that if he's already lost his battle against God, then the next best thing he can do to satisfy his fury is to steal, kill, and destroy whatever he can within humanity.

CHANGING LEADERS AND KINGDOMS

Satan went right to work on taking from humanity as soon as he was driven out of Eden. We see that blatantly in the influence he had on Adam and Eve's children, leading Cain to murder—which is why Jesus said the devil "was a murderer from the beginning" (John 8:44). But before that, Satan took something even more significant—he took the authority God gave humans to rule the earth.

Whether the devil technically stole this authority or had it handed over to him makes no difference; the loss and the fault was ours. When we chose to lead ourselves and no longer be led by God, we gave up our position of leadership on earth. What God had given us—the authority to rule over earth like Him—was relinquished to Satan through sin. This is why the New Testament calls him the "god of this world" (2 Cor. 4:4, NLT) and why Jesus referred to him as the "ruler of this world" (John 12:31, NLT). When the adversary tempted Jesus in the wilderness, he showed Jesus all the kingdoms of the world and said, "I will give you all their authority and splendor; it has been given to me, and I can give it to anyone I want to" (Luke 4:6). For once, the devil wasn't lying! He could only say this because humanity's fall gave him the authority to lead this world. As the apostle John wrote, "The whole world lies in the power of the evil one" (1 John 5:19, ESV).‡

---

‡ One of the amazing facets of the gospel is that Jesus reclaimed this authority and has given it to us once again! As followers of Jesus, commissioned by Him to pronounce *His* kingdom on earth, we now have *His* authority to go into the darkness and evil that permeate this world and, with *His* power—through *His* Holy Spirit—enforce *His* will "on earth as it is in heaven" (Matt. 6:10). Do you see how this is all about Him? Jesus has "all authority in heaven and on earth" (Matt. 28:18), and His kingdom is established in this world, no matter how bad things seem or whether we choose to be part of enforcing His will.

When the devil gained authority over this world, it changed the entire landscape—spiritually and literally. God's kingdom is one of light, goodness, righteousness, peace, love, generosity, holiness—the characteristics go on and on, just as He does. After all, kingdoms tend to reflect the nature of their king, don't they? When the devil "moved in" as the earth's new ruler, his nature also ushered in a kingdom fit for its king. The world began to experience a leading in directions it had never gone before; evil, darkness, wickedness, violence, pride, and selfishness now ran rampant throughout the land. The fruit of God's kingdom had been life, blessing, and abundance; now this kingdom of darkness bore death, suffering, pain, and destruction.

Make no mistake: These changes not only affected the earth physically but overwhelmed its inhabitants as well. As citizens of a kingdom (whether light or dark), we inherit the "fruit" of whoever reigns in that kingdom. To repeat the leadership principle I shared in chapter 2, our direction in life is dictated by who leads us—whoever we choose to follow. Paul put this principle in extreme terms when he said, "Don't you know that when you offer yourselves to someone as obedient slaves, you are slaves of the one you obey—whether you are slaves to sin, which leads to death, or to obedience, which leads to righteousness?" (Rom. 6:16). Adam and Eve's decision resulted in the ultimate condition of slavery. With the powers of darkness now in charge, humanity was mastered by a new way (sin) that was driven by a new force (evil) and produced new results (deterioration, destruction, and ultimately death).

It's fascinating to see that God warned humanity of sin's viral dangers soon after the fall. Before Cain killed Abel, the Lord urged Cain to return to His perfect way of leading: "If you do not do what is right, sin is crouching at your door; it desires to have you, but you must rule over it" (Gen. 4:7).

Obviously, Cain didn't rule over sin but instead allowed it to master him. And in so doing, sin continued to expand its power in this rapidly growing kingdom of darkness.[§] By the time of Noah, "The LORD saw how great the wickedness of the human race had become on the earth, and that every inclination of the thoughts of the human heart was only evil all the time. The LORD regretted that he had made human beings on the earth, and his heart was deeply troubled" (Gen. 6:5–6).

[§] The parallel fall of spiritual beings—the "sons of God," as described in Genesis 6:1–4— accelerated this rapid descent into evil.

I doubt we can fully grasp these verses. To say a perfect God *regretted* something is amazing within itself, but even more so when we consider that He regretted making the crown jewel of His creation. He had formed humans in His image, empowered them with authority to rule over the earth like Him, and given them free will to choose His perfect leadership. Now, within just a handful of generations, not only had they rejected His leadership, but they ruined all of creation with their wickedness. The word Scripture uses is *corrupt*: "Now the earth was *corrupt* in God's sight and was full of violence. God saw how *corrupt* the earth had become, for all the people on earth had *corrupted* their ways" (Gen. 6:11–12, emphasis added).

If we summarize the first few chapters in Genesis, then, we find a world corrupted by people who led their own lives, refusing to submit to any leadership other than their own. Sin and all its evil consequences had ruined the planet. Godlessness reigned as the world was full of people simply living for themselves.

That sounds a bit like today, doesn't it?

PLANET EARTH 2.0

God decided to do a reboot. He would start over with the human race through one man, Noah, and his family. Why Noah? Two verses tell the whole story: "Noah was a righteous man, the only blameless person living on earth at the time, and he walked in close fellowship with God. … And Noah did all that the LORD commanded him" (Gen. 6:9; 7:5, NLT). Those verses bookend an almost hundred-year journey of faith in which the Lord asked Noah to do the unthinkable: build a massive boat that would protect Noah and his family from God's righteous judgment on the earth. The reign of evil upon the earth had contaminated it so much that God needed to start over for humanity to have a chance at redemption. It would take a complete reboot of the planet for us to once again walk in partnership with the Lord and His perfect leadership.

If you attended Sunday school as a child, you undoubtedly know the story of Noah—albeit probably a G-rated, felt-board version full of animals, rainbows, and smiling humans. The real version is anything but feel-good, given the rampant evil ruling the world at that time and the total annihilation required. This was truly as bad as it gets, and we know this from God's response.

Yet even now as you mentally revisit this epic account, I hope you catch the incredible parallels between Noah's story and our salvation through one man, Jesus. I realize I'm drastically fast-forwarding our timeline journey here, but it's crucial for us along the way to not miss how Jesus fulfills every aspect of God's perfect way for humanity, as shown in the Old Testament. Noah's family members weren't "righteous" or "blameless" (Scripture says Noah was "the only blameless person living on earth" then), yet they were spared destruction because of Noah's obedience to God. Likewise, we couldn't save ourselves, but simply because of Christ's perfect obedience to the Father we can now be adopted into His family, counted righteous, and protected by His blood. In the same way they were sheltered from God's just wrath, we can now be protected from His righteous judgment of our sin. Hallelujah!

Again, why Noah? Because Noah followed God's leadership. He not only walked faithfully with the Lord, as some translations say, but he also enjoyed close fellowship with the Lord like no one else on the planet. Do you remember the phases of followship discussed at the end of chapter 2? Noah is a prime example of someone who most definitely walked through each phase.

- He *surrendered* to the Lord's leadership even when things didn't look good and evil ruled the world. He did not hesitate to give God everything in his life—from his resources to his reputation and from his family to his future.

- Noah *submitted* to the Lord's leadership in what we can imagine was an incredibly difficult environment. The Lord gave him a task that seemed not only crazy but absolutely foolish: build an ark. And he wasn't to build just any ark, but a three-story vessel so large its size wouldn't be surpassed until the 1800s![6] Oh yeah, and Noah was supposed to run a zoo at the same time, collecting pairs of every kind of creature on earth. (Later that became seven pairs for some of the animals!) Uh-huh. And where would Noah keep all this? Who knows! Yet twice Scripture points out that Noah obeyed the Lord in everything.

- Noah *trusted* the Lord's leadership. How do we know this? After he built the ark, he was to wait for a promised flood. We don't know what the weather was like at that time, but given the time lapse—it probably took Noah decades to complete the ark—it's more than likely there were times when Noah was a laughingstock among his people. Yet we have no indication that his faith ever wavered. Hebrews 11:7 even points out that Noah "obeyed God, who warned him about things that had never happened before" (NLT). Noah had the kind of relationship with the Lord where He told him secrets. That requires serious trust on both sides!

- Noah *enjoyed* the Lord's leadership, not only before God called him to such a crazy assignment (as indicated in Genesis 6:9) but also afterward. As soon as he and his family were able to leave the ark after the flood, Noah worshipped God. And by all indications, their close relationship continued.

Noah changed the world and all human history because of his obedience to God's leadership. When God gave him a seemingly absurd task, Noah followed through. Did he ever struggle? We don't know. I wish the Bible gave us more details into Noah's journey, but it doesn't. From what it does reveal, however, we can conclude that Noah had a close relationship with the Lord. I'd venture to say that anyone willing to put up with as much as Noah did, remaining righteous in a wicked world, surely had to *enjoy* the Lord. You don't faithfully continue following someone for hundreds of years unless you enjoy that person; otherwise you would give up at some point out of frustration, doubt, cynicism, bitterness, or a host of other reasons. Yet we know from Scripture that Noah did everything God asked Him to do and was credited for his faithfulness.

Would you be that obedient? God probably hasn't asked you to spend a hundred years building a boat for an impending global catastrophe. But what has He asked you to do? Have you done it? If He asked you to do something out of your comfort zone, would you still follow Him? Or would you question His leading and come up with reasons you shouldn't do it?

God's way of leading is perfect, but that doesn't mean it always makes sense to us. In fact, let's be honest: Too often His ways seem downright strange compared to how we would do things! How else can we explain a God who has a history of leading people through such things as hardship, trials, ridicule, and pain? Noah surely suffered while he was obediently building an ark. There was a high cost to his obedience. But despite what Noah had to endure, I'm positive he would also say the price was worth it because the Lord is worth it—that's the kind of relationship he had with Him. Can you say the same thing? Is what you've had to go through worth it because of Him?

Noah's obedience came out of his fellowship with God. He walked with the Lord in the way originally intended for all humans. Adam and Eve may have fallen, relinquished their authority on earth, and ushered in a world full of sin, but Noah represented a renewed hope for all mankind. With God starting over again with a new humanity, surely Noah's descendants would take after him and walk in righteousness with the Lord. Surely this would be a return to Eden.

CHAPTER 6

AFTER THE REBOOT

MY FIRST DOG was a science project. That sounds strange, but technically she was. I got her in the seventh grade as part of a semester-long experiment for Mr. Rohr's science class. I had begged my parents for a dog for years and, as a twelve-year-old, finally got clever enough to add a new twist. My science-fair project was about determining how much a dog's running speed changes with its growth (an earth-shattering discovery, I know), but to complete the project, obviously I needed a dog.

It worked. One night my parents drove me to the closest animal shelter an hour before it closed, where we noticed the only dog not barking at us when we walked down the hall full of kennels and immediately fell in love with her floppy black ears and oversized puppy paws. Poochi, as my mom named her (you can see what kind of "arm-twisting" went on there!), was a dream dog and would be for years to come. She was all mutt—part German shepherd, part Akita, part who-knows-what—and all fun.

I took my responsibility of caring for Poochi seriously, and from the first week began training her. Though house-training her was of course top priority, I had visions of her sitting, lying, and rolling around on command and endlessly fetching sticks like all dogs are supposed to do. Instead, during those first few weeks, she mostly wanted to mark her territory outside, where she would also sniff poop and occasionally eat grass. This would cause her to vomit, which she would then eat (yuck!). I tried to keep her from doing this for her own good, even scolding her at times.

Within months Poochi was house-trained and could do most of my envisioned tricks. I even got an A on my science project. But for her entire life, no matter how many times I tried to get her to avoid those other less-than-refined actions of poop sniffing, grass eating, and vomit licking, she just couldn't help herself; it was in her nature. I discovered firsthand why Solomon wrote, "As a dog returns to its vomit, so fools repeat their folly" (Prov. 26:11).

When God rebooted the human race through Noah, I imagine He hoped Noah's descendants would not return to the sinful ways of the wicked generations before them. The Lord desired that people follow His perfect way instead. Even though sin was still a possibility—humans still had free will, after all—surely the eight people who boarded the ark could produce a different kind of future for humanity.

Sadly, just as a dog can't avoid its own nature, humans couldn't seem to avoid their sinful nature. As soon as they settled on dry land, God made a covenant with them and gave them relatively simple instructions. In fact, these instructions were almost verbatim what He'd given the first humans. To Adam He said, "Be fruitful and multiply. Fill the earth and govern it. Reign over the fish in the sea, the birds in the sky, and all the animals that scurry along the ground" (Gen. 1:28, NLT). To Noah and his sons He said, "Be fruitful and increase in number and fill the earth" (Gen. 9:1).

Did you notice something missing between God's instructions to Adam and those given to Noah and his sons? That's right: There's no mention of governing the earth. Humans couldn't be commanded to reign over the earth and its creatures because they no longer had authority over it. They had relinquished that authority to Satan. What's fascinating is that despite this, God still caused a "fear and dread" of humans to fall on all creatures of the earth (Gen. 9:2). He was actually using domination—forced power over someone that can result in fear—to still give humans a form of dominion, even though they had messed up His original plan. As always, the Lord was redeeming something bad to bring about something good.

God gave Noah and his sons instructions, then repeated them only moments later, just in case some of the family had missed it the first time: "As for you, be fruitful and increase in number; multiply on the earth and increase upon it" (Gen. 9:7).

Why was the Lord so concerned about them growing the population and filling the earth? Because He was still serious about His original plan of sharing His glory throughout the earth.

Humans' fallen nature would not prevent God from desiring the type of fellowship with them that would bring heaven to earth, just as it had been in Eden. Neither would sin keep the Lord from wanting to lead humanity. His desire was still for people to reflect His leadership on earth in partnership with Him. God's original plan was not destroyed when Adam and Eve sinned; things just got more complicated when they (and future generations) chose to reject God's perfect leadership. The Lord gave humans free will, but He also has always made a way for redemption even when we've rejected Him. (And this theme runs throughout the biblical narrative, as we will see.)

THE RABBLE AT BABEL

Noah's sons did what they were told, and eventually "from them came the people who were scattered over the whole earth" (Gen. 9:19). Before that scattering occurred, however, we get the famous story of the tower of Babel, which not only tells us how those people groups were dispersed but also sheds light on whether humanity continued to desire the Lord's leadership.

Remember, God had given Noah's family a simple task: Multiply. Expand. Spread out. He wanted His leadership to be reflected throughout the whole earth. What happened instead? People did the exact opposite, as Genesis 11:1 indicates: "Now the whole world had one language and a common speech."

How do we know from this one verse that they didn't obey the Lord's command? Think about what happens over generations when people spread out over a continent. Among the first things to emerge are different ways of doing and saying things. We call that culture! As more cultures emerge, so do more languages—and vice versa.

I live in a country (Norway) where you can barely travel thirty kilometers down the road without people speaking a different dialect. Some dialects are so different that even other Norwegians don't understand them! The Philippines has two official languages, Filipino and English, yet its people speak more than one hundred and eighty languages (not just dialects) among the seven thousand-plus islands that make up the nation.[1] If you think that's confusing, imagine life in Papua New Guinea, where citizens speak more than eight hundred fifty different languages![2]

Whenever and wherever people congregate in separate groups, language is affected—and usually, new ones get birthed. So when the Bible says the whole world had a single language, we can say within reason that most people must have been gathered together in one place. Had they obeyed God's command to spread out, there would have been more languages.

Yet Babel reveals other ways humans were once again rebelling against the Lord's leadership. While Genesis 11:4 explains their attempt to build an Eden-like city with a tower, verse 3 curiously mentions the construction materials: Those at Babel "used brick instead of stone, and tar for mortar." Why did the biblical writer point out this seemingly random detail? To indicate just how fractured the relationship already was between God and His people. According to the ancient Jewish historian Josephus, the reason for using brick and mortar was to construct a waterproof tower—sealed with bricks and mortar in such a way that water could not penetrate, it would be "too high for the waters to be able to reach" if God "should have a mind to drown the world again."[3]

Wait, hadn't the Lord repeatedly promised Noah that He would never destroy the earth again with a flood (Gen. 9:11, 15)? Yet the people feared that God would do just that and were doing whatever they could in their own strength to ensure their survival. They didn't trust Him! Think about it: This is not even two generations removed from Noah, the model for followship, and already humanity doesn't trust God's leading or His character.

To make matters worse, verse 4 reveals the pride that now infected human hearts and motivated their building: "Then they said, 'Come, let us build ourselves a city, with a tower that reaches to the heavens, so that we may make a name for ourselves; otherwise we will be scattered over the face of the whole earth.'" Not only were humans blatantly opposed to God's instructions to spread throughout the earth, but they also wanted to "make a name for" themselves. Simply put, they wanted to elevate their own status and fame by building something everyone would marvel at—an indication of pride's growing grip on them.

Bible scholars almost universally agree that the tower of Babel was actually a ziggurat, which was the centerpiece of all Mesopotamian temples. In ancient times, these structures were believed to be sacred mountains, where the gods could dwell and where heaven supposedly met earth. People used ziggurats to summon the gods and, essentially, to barter with them.[4] In Babel, the ziggurat was either an attempt to elevate mankind to the heavens or to bring God down to earth—or both. Whichever the case, here we have people trying to restore their connection with God on their own terms—namely, by summoning and commanding Him like a pet.

God would have none of it.

Let's remember, the Lord had established heaven on earth in the paradise of Eden so humans could partner with Him. But humans, by their own choice, didn't want the kind of partnership the Lord offered. God's original relationship with Adam and Eve was a perichoresis-like fellowship, where human submission resulted in being "lifted" into God's glory. Noah had enjoyed the Lord's leadership by trusting and serving Him, and through his obedience God "elevated" him above the deadly waters, saving him out of wickedness and making him the starting point of humanity's reboot. Now, however, those left on earth wanted the exact opposite. They wanted to act like God, make their own decisions, and have full control. They wanted to lead, not follow. And they wanted to elevate themselves, both literally and figuratively.

It's not coincidental that their actions reek of similarities to Satan's fall, as the events of Babel give us yet another significant rebellion.

This time, God didn't respond by casting out any rebellious beings from heaven but instead by halting the world's most united construction project. His response wasn't because He felt threatened that "if as one people speaking the same language they have begun to do this, then nothing they plan to do will be impossible for them" (Gen. 11:6). God was not worried that a tower might get too close to heaven, as some have thought. No, the Lord knew that humanity's united defiance and arrogance would simply repeat the pre-flood story and quickly fill the earth with evil, and He had other plans—plans to redeem.

Indeed, if we read this story with the followship lens, Babel offers a tragic account revealing our ongoing rebellion against following the Lord's leadership. Yet if we see with a lens highlighting God's redemptive story, we get a different perspective. The Lord confused the people's language to scatter them for His greater purposes (Gen. 11:7–9). He loves diversity within His kingdom and longs to fill the earth with His glory. He wants different ethnicities, cultures, languages, and expressions—it's partly why in heaven we find representatives "from every nation, tribe, people and language" worshipping the Lord (Rev. 7:9).

Despite humans defying God at Babel, He still accomplished His mission. His desire for partnership had not changed; He still wanted all people to enjoy His presence and leadership, and He knew what was best for them. Even though they didn't want this perfection, God still had a plan to make a way for them. He would start over again, this time without flooding the earth. Once again, however, the Lord had to find someone from within all the evil on earth who would follow Him.

Enter Abraham.

GOD WILL MAKE A WAY

The Bible doesn't give us the same kind of introduction to Abraham as it does with Noah. There is no indication that he was the lone righteous man amid a sea of human wickedness. But what we do see is a man, flawed though he was, willing to not only follow the Lord's leadership but also enjoy it.

As always, the relationship started with God. Immediately after the account of Babel in Genesis 11, the very next chapter begins with God making a covenant promise to Abraham. This time, instead of a man trying to make a name for himself, it's the Lord who promises the man, "I will make your name great" (Gen. 12:2). Not only that, but Abraham would become a blessed nation through whom all other nations will be blessed. God's divine plan still involved the nations of the world, even though they essentially disowned Him. He wanted to bless all people because that is who He is. Even if they wouldn't receive His blessings directly, He would make a way through His own people and His own nation.

This nation, however, would be unlike any other. Mesopotamian history indicates that most people on earth at that time had become polytheistic, believing in multiple gods and worshipping various idols. To believe in only one god was seen as foolish. How much more to call that lone god *the* God above all others! Yet that's exactly what the Lord required of Abraham, and by all indications, he obeyed. As soon as Yahweh gave His first instruction—"Go from your country, your people and your father's household to the land I will show you" (Gen. 12:1)—Abraham went. No specific directions, no specific country, no destination to plug into his GPS or Google Maps—just, "Go."

God tends to give vague directions. Near the end of my college education I faced a major crossroads in my life. I had only months left before graduating and didn't know what I would do after finishing or where I would go. I had applied for a few jobs in nearby cities but was open to go anywhere; I just needed some guidance from the Lord.

Although I'd prayed for months about my future, I hadn't sensed anything. One afternoon while taking a power nap before heading off to work, I was suddenly awakened by what seemed like an almost audible voice: "Go, and I will lead you." I jumped up and glanced around—not a normal reaction considering I'm almost always groggy after sleeping. After looking throughout my apartment and confirming that, yes, I was alone, those simple words began to sink in. I knew it was God. But as logic began to sink in further, my first thought was equally as clear as the voice: *I'll go ... but where?!*

I wonder if Abraham had the same immediate question. In the months that followed my wake-up call, I never received any further specific directions from the Lord, but I did experience a strange peace as some job opportunities fell through and others opened up. I took one risky step at a time in faith, not knowing what would follow. But the more steps I took, the easier it became to trust the Lord was somehow guiding me—and this trust grew my love for Him.

I've since discovered that is God's way. He most often directs us not with specific, point-by-point directions but with general guidance. While we want more details and information, He wants more time and trust. He's after real relationship, after all, and anyone who has experienced true intimacy with another person knows that is only developed by being with each other and journeying through experiences together.

The fact that Abraham left everything behind with such vague instructions reveals a deep trust he had already developed in the Lord. Of course, Abraham's journey of faith wasn't without the occasional stumble. More than once his trust wavered to the point that he took matters into his own hands. Yet Abraham's humanness can actually encourage us. He was far from perfect, despite being listed among Hebrew 11's faith hall of fame. Indeed, the Bible is filled with men and women who, like Abraham, faced the same question: *Will I follow God's way and yield to His leadership, even when it seems ridiculous?* The Lord often tests our commitment to Him by calling us into the seemingly impossible.

I can't imagine a more gut-wrenching test than what Abraham faced when the Lord asked him to sacrifice his son. Isaac was already the culmination of Abraham's faith journey to that point, the proof of both Abraham's faithfulness to the Lord and Yahweh's faithfulness to him. This beloved son was the seed of promise that took almost three decades to come to fruition. And now it seemed that God wanted to kill the promise.

Other than Jesus, there may not be a more powerful example of followship in the Bible than how Abraham responded to this heavy request. What God asked Abraham to do seems, well, ungodly. It seems unfair, unreasonable, unloving, even abusive—like a father who finally gives his little daughter the toy she's begged for all year, only to tell her she must throw it in the garbage. Because God's command to Abraham feels so brutal, I've often tried to dampen its sting by reminding myself of the historical context. Child sacrifice wasn't uncommon at that time in history. Sadly, parents often thought they would appease the gods by sacrificing a child. Some cultures even viewed this as an honor killing. From a religious perspective, then, people at that time wouldn't have recoiled as we do today at the thought of human sacrifice being part of worshipping a god. Yet beneath all these historical facts lies a sobering truth: Abraham would still have to plunge a knife into the heart of the son who mattered most to him.

Somehow, Abraham trusted God enough as his leader to accept whatever outcome the Lord decided. Hebrews 11:19 says Abraham "reasoned that God could even raise the dead," which indicates he believed he wouldn't lose Isaac. We also get signs of this hope in Genesis 22 when Abraham assures his servant that Isaac and he will *both* return from the sacrifice (v. 5). And when Isaac asks where the sacrificial lamb is, his father tells him straightforwardly, "God himself will provide the lamb for the burnt offering, my son" (v. 8).

Despite Abraham's strong faith, I can't imagine what thoughts ran through his mind as he ascended Mount Moriah, knowing he would have to bind Isaac's hands without explanation and then, with tears in both of their eyes, hold his son down as he prepared to kill the sacrifice. Abraham still had to go through with God's painful plan that seemingly involved death, just as Jesus would have to do two thousand years later. And like the Messiah, Abraham still had to make the same profound statement Jesus made: "Not my will, but yours be done" (Luke 22:42).

What if the Lord asked you to "kill" what is most precious to you? What if He asked you to put to death something He's promised? Maybe it's a talent He's given you, even one you've used faithfully for Him. (Surely He wouldn't ask for that, would He?!) Maybe it's the dream of being married or someday having children. Maybe your Isaac is future comfort or security. Or what about happiness? That's a big one. Are you willing to follow the Lord to places or seasons of life that don't necessarily bring you happiness, comfort, pleasure, or all the other things we prefer in life?

These are deep questions, and I know some people strongly object to asking them. They believe God already provided the ultimate sacrifice when He allowed His only Son to be killed, and because of Jesus He no longer asks us to suffer in the same way. Besides, they argue, what kind of a trustworthy father would God be if He gave us something and then asked us to kill it?

I don't believe God delights in crushing our dreams. And yes, Scripture clearly proves that we can't add a single thing to Jesus' costly accomplishment on the cross, where He "took up our pain and bore our suffering" (Isa. 53:4). But if God no longer tests us—either by causing or allowing trials, depending on what you believe—how do we account for the numerous New Testament verses that speak of enduring trials that test our faith (e.g., Jas. 1:2–4, 12; 1 Pet. 4:12–19)? What do we do with passages that link this suffering to the Lord's discipline, which He administers to those He loves (Heb. 12:5–11)? And what about Hebrew 11's reminder that every single person listed there never saw the ultimate fulfillment of what God promised? I have met countless believers in the persecuted church who've had their personal dreams crushed and yet came out the other end with gold in the form of loving, knowing, and trusting God more. They could relate to Job's cry, "Though He slay me, yet will I trust Him" (Job 13:15, NKJV). Is that not the acme of followship?

Abraham's test was as severe and difficult as they come. I strongly doubt God would ask any of us today to physically sacrifice our children, but I do know that when we make Him Master over our lives, He asks for *everything*. When God required Abraham's "everything" in the form of giving up Isaac, He wanted to see if this was someone He could trust with more than just a normal assignment. This would be the man through whom He would change the world.

Why was God's test so extreme with Abraham? Because the Lord's redemptive plan for the entire planet was extreme as well, and it would be founded upon Abraham's followship. Through him, God was making a way. And one day that way would lead back to the exact same mountain, where God Himself would show His love by sacrificing His only Son—only then, the knife would not be stayed.

THE MOSES MODEL

As we continue examining Genesis using the followship lens, we find that each of Abraham's successors ultimately faced the same question from God: *Will you trust My leadership?* All were flawed individuals, from Isaac to Jacob to Joseph. Some typically took matters into their own hands, while others learned how to depend on this unseen God. Yet ultimately, the key factor for their success or failure in life boiled down to trusting the Lord's leadership.

As the Book of Exodus begins, the spotlight turns to a new man through whom God would continue His redemptive plan: Moses. Perhaps no one in the Old Testament had as unique a relationship with the Lord as Moses. He was the only person on earth with whom the Most High spoke so directly and intimately. The Lord shared secrets with Moses. He vented around him as you would only with a close friend. God even showed Moses part of His glory (at least from behind), which no person had seen before and still lived. As with many other individuals highlighted in the first few books of the Bible, Moses had plenty of highs and lows in his life. Still, he was a beautiful example of leading in partnership with God.

I could spend the rest of this book on Moses alone, given his pivotal role in Israel's history and his personal journey of enjoying God's leadership. Yet what I want to highlight most is the shift in God's leadership structure that came through this man. With Noah, God rebooted the earth. With Abraham,

God selected a man to be the channel for reestablishing His kingdom on earth through a specific nation of people. With Moses, God shifted to actually operating in partnership *with and through* one man's leadership. God would still lead His people, but He would choose to lead through a single representative. In the same way Adam re-presented God on earth, Moses would re-present God to His own people.

This wasn't exactly how God wanted it, and Exodus 19–20 reveals the sad reason. Up to that point in the Exodus storyline, God had delivered His people from four hundred years of slavery in Egypt, given them much of Egypt's wealth, and miraculously provided for them in the desert. He supernaturally guided them as a pillar of cloud during the day and a pillar of fire at night. (What a sight to see!) Even though Moses continued to be His spokesperson, at Mount Sinai the Lord wanted to gather all of Israel and speak with them up close. In essence, He wanted to lead them more directly. They were, as He lovingly reminded them, His "treasured possession" (Exod. 19:5).

To get even remotely close to Yahweh, however, the people had to be cleansed, so they spent two days consecrating themselves. On the third day, the Lord arrived in spectacular fashion, with thunder, lightning, and ear-piercing trumpet blasts from heaven. "Mount Sinai was covered with smoke, because the Lord descended on it in fire. The smoke billowed up from it like smoke from a furnace, and the whole mountain trembled violently" (Exod. 19:18). In front of everyone, the Lord called Moses to the top of the mountain for a private meeting and reminded him of the lethal dangers should any Israelite get too close to Him. But there He also gave Moses the keys to a life of blessing for the Israelites: the Ten Commandments, which were essentially a summary of the Law that would come later. True to God's character, He was simultaneously expressing His holiness, generosity, power, justice, kindness, and a million other things. He was, after all, Israel's perfect leader.

But sadly, this was too much for the Israelites. God may have been the perfect leader for them, but He was just too frightening. The powerful display of God's holy presence caused them to tremble with fear (Exod. 20:18). They begged Moses, "Speak to us yourself and we will listen. But do not have God speak to us or we will die" (Exod. 20:19). Even when Moses reminded them they had nothing to fear—that God was simply testing them so they would walk as holy people and not sin—they still recoiled from the Lord. And in one of the saddest verses of the Old Testament, Exodus 20:21 says: "The people remained at a distance, while Moses approached the thick darkness where God was."

Only one man in Israel trusted God enough to get close to Him.

As a result, Moses became an intercessor, a go-between. He stood between God and His people—a critical function that would become even more important in the days ahead as this "kingdom of priests" (Exod. 19:6) would, in reality, have only a few priests who could meet with God.

STUCK IN A CYCLE

Despite a new model, Moses' generation wasn't content with God's leadership, even when it came through a fellow human. God wanted His people to enjoy the land He'd promised, yet a journey that should have taken weeks took forty years, not because of physical distance but because of the posture of their hearts. The Israelites grumbled, complained, and fell into idol worship. The Lord, therefore, had to do yet another reboot, only this time within the nation of Israel.

God was determined His new nation (complete with actual territory now) would be full of inhabitants wholly committed to His leadership. Remember, it's through this nation that He planned to re-present His leadership—His dominion, government, and way of life—on earth. The Lord wanted to bless all the earth through Israel. Therefore, He needed a new people dedicated to following and partnering with Him.

That came in Joshua's generation. The successor to Moses, Joshua led a new generation into the land of Canaan, which God had promised them. During Joshua's term as Israel's intercessor-leader, all was finally well. God's people had the land, they loved God's leadership (even if it was indirect), and they kept their hearts pure. They were blessed to be a blessing. Life was good.

But as you might predict at this point, the good life didn't last long. The beginning of the Book of Judges depicts how quickly things went south for Israel:

> The people served the LORD throughout the lifetime of Joshua and of the elders who outlived him and who had seen all the great things the LORD had done for Israel. … After that whole generation had been gathered to their ancestors, another generation grew up who knew neither the LORD nor what he had done for Israel.
>
> —JUDGES 2:7, 10

What a tragedy! Within one generation of God's people seeing the fulfillment of His promises, they abandoned Him. (If this sounds like a broken record by now, get used to it—there's more to come.) How could things change so quickly? Part of the blame must go to Joshua's generation since their children grew up knowing "neither the Lord nor what he had done for Israel." What pathetic spiritual leadership on the home front! That verse alone proves how vital it is for parents to lead their children in the ways of God, reminding them of what He has done and showing them who He is.

There was more to Israel's story than just bad parenting, however. Clearly, this new generation did not want the Lord's leadership. Once life was comfortable in Canaan for long enough, they would turn to worship other gods. It didn't take them long to notice the nations and cultures around them and, more significantly, the gods they served. Sadly, this would become a pattern for future generations.

What did God do with such a short-sighted people? He showed extreme mercy and executed another reboot of sorts. This time, He began to lead through a different means: judges.

For the next three hundred-plus years, God appointed what we call judges to serve as His representatives to lead His people. In fact, another word for judge is simply *leader*. Their roles went far beyond what we today see as courtroom figures adorned in black robes and presiding with gavels. Israel's judges were God's appointed overseers to the nation when His people needed salvation or course correction—or both.

From Deborah to Gideon to Samson and others, these judges served God's people as governmental leaders unifying a nation that was geographically split into separate tribe-states. Militarily, the judges brought all the tribes together to defend the confederation of Israel, and some of these judges were tremendous warriors. Others also functioned as national judges in the sense we think of today and presided over legal hearings according to the Torah.

Though God appointed these leaders to serve various functions, most importantly, they were to remind the Jewish people of God's leadership. He was their God, their ruler. Not only that, but He would lead them supernaturally—making them unlike any other nation—just as He'd always done. Despite such supernatural leadership and countless reminders of God's perfect guidance, Israel became trapped in a vicious cycle that went like this.

1. Israel experiences a season of peace and prosperity until ...

2. The people fall into sin and idolatry and abandon God's ways.

3. God judges Israel by giving them over to the influence of a foreign nation, which leads to enslavement.

4. Eventually, the people cry out to God and ask Him to deliver them.

5. God raises up a judge to rescue His people.

6. Israel experiences a season of peace and prosperity until …

(Repeat cycle.)

This continued for more than *three centuries.* That's a long time to continually refuse to learn from your own history! Yet sadly it reveals a powerful pattern we see deeply entrenched not only in Israel's history but in all humanity: We do not want God's righteous leadership. Even when we experience the good life, as Israel did when it submitted to God's ways, we eventually turn and want to lead ourselves. And when we suffer the disastrous results of leading ourselves and God rescues us, even then we inevitably forget the polar-opposite outcomes between His leadership and ours—and we once again begin to long for our own way.

By the end of the Book of Judges, we see this in full operation, and the results are utter chaos throughout the land. The book ends on a haunting note: "In those days Israel had no king; everyone did as they saw fit" (Judg. 21:25).

Toward the end of the three hundred-plus years of God leading through judges, He began to appoint men and women leaders to serve in other capacities as well. Eli, for example, was not only a judge but also a priest. His successor, Samuel, grew up as a priest in the tabernacle, yet God also called him as a prophet to the nation. In essence, he wore three hats as a priest, prophet, and judge.

Does that sound like a foreshadowing of anyone? Later we will look at how every aspect of God's perfect leadership was expressed in the person of Jesus. But for now, it's fascinating to see how even during Israel's centuries-long cycle of obedience and rebellion, the Lord still had a redemptive plan at work. He was moving closer and closer to the type of leadership He ultimately wanted: someone who would re-present Him perfectly and live in fellowship with Him the way Adam was originally meant to lead on the earth.

CHAPTER 7

THE FORGOTTEN KING

FOR MORE THAN three hundred years God sent one judge after another to remind His people that they were infinitely better off when they followed His leading. If they would submit to His leadership, they would be lifted out of captivity and foreign invasion, and instead receive divine blessings. They were, after all, a nation set apart by God Himself to show all the earth what life could be like under perfect leadership.

Yet from Israel's first judge (Othniel) to its last (Samuel), God's people displayed an astounding tendency to forget or ignore their past mistakes. Sure, they would eventually repent and return to the Lord each time after turning to other gods, but over time their cycle of rebellion took a toll. By the time Samuel grew old, even those he appointed to lead the nation (his own sons) were corrupt. And this is the context for a pivotal chapter in the Bible regarding God's leadership: 1 Samuel 8.

During each of Israel's rebellious periods, the people lusted after what surrounding nations had—from their women to their possessions to their gods. This envy reached a new low, however, when Israel's most respected local leaders, the elders, came together in solidarity with a demand for Samuel: "Now appoint a king to lead us, such as all the nations have" (1 Sam. 8:5).

When you think about this, it was an idiotic request. Israel was the only nation on earth whose king was divine. Other nations may have worshipped gods like Baal, Dagon, or Ashtoreth, but none of those gods offered perfect leadership (or anything, for that matter). Yahweh had rescued the Israelites from four hundred years of slavery, even parting a sea so they could escape the Egyptian army. He supernaturally provided food and resources for His people in the wilderness. And once the Israelites entered the Promised Land, their true King repeatedly proved His power.

Despite their small numbers and size, the Israelites continued to wipe out opposing forces as long as they followed the Lord. In fact, most often God would do all the fighting for them, in logic-defying ways. At Jericho they blew trumpets, took some walks around the fortified city, and watched God flatten Jericho's walls, which were possibly as large as two meters thick and eight meters high.[1] (See Joshua 6:1–21.) At Gibeon the Lord confused Israel's enemies, killed many with large hailstones, and even made the sun and moon stand still for almost a full day. (See Joshua 10:1–14.) And if there was any doubt who really fought Israel's battles, it was settled when the Lord used a Gideon-led army of only three hundred men to defeat tens of thousands of Midianites. (See Judges 7:1–25.)

This tiny nation was known worldwide because its God actually fought for and defended His people and land. Even when the Israelites suffered from historical amnesia, other nations didn't! They most certainly remembered being defeated by supernatural means, such as the numerous times Yahweh caused their own soldiers to kill one another. Israel was divinely blessed, and this was clear to everyone. So why in the world would they want a mere human king when they already had the perfect, divine King of kings?

That may be a rhetorical question, but it's important for us to recognize something else at work here—something we can trace back to Eden and even back to the heavenly realm before the devil fell. Whether it's among humans or supernatural beings, something rises up to oppose God's leadership. No matter what He does, no matter how good and faithful He is to us, we still tend to refuse His leadership and not follow Him. We want something else, and usually it's for us to rule. In the Israelites' case, they wanted an earthly king to rule them rather than a divine one. They forgot the blessings of life under their true King and instead offered a pathetic, illogical reason for wanting an earthly one: "We want a king because … um, well, everyone else has a king."

ISRAEL'S IDENTITY CRISIS

God's people wanted what everyone else had. They wanted to be like the nations around them. But there was a fundamental problem with this: Israel was meant to be *different*! Their foundational purpose—the very reason for their existence, if you will—was to be unlike any other nation or people. God had set apart the Israelites to show the rest of the world what partnership with Him looks like and how His kingdom operates. They were a walking, living billboard proving to the rest of the world the Most High was above all other gods. "If you walk with Me," He told His chosen people, "in the fellowship I originally wanted—which includes obedience—you will be blessed. From that blessing you will in turn bless all the other nations of the world, because that's ultimately why I made you and have sustained you. I promise, you will make them jealous if you just partner with Me, and you'll live life the way it was supposed to be lived."

Somehow Israel managed to continually forget this arrangement. They forgot how to be a blessing to others. They forgot their own identity. Most critically, they forgot their relationship with the one who had made them His "portion" and His "allotted inheritance" out of all other nations (Deut. 32:9).

When you think about it purely from a leadership standpoint, the Israelites' desire for a human king made no sense whatsoever. Ever since they left Egypt more than four hundred years earlier, God had been gracious enough to steer them back to His perfect leadership time and time again. He had repeatedly shown mercy and forgiven them for worshipping other gods. He had even changed how He led them to better suit their liking; instead of leading them directly, He guided them through human vessels—intercessor leaders, warrior leaders, judicial leaders, priestly leaders, prophetic leaders, and even leaders who blended those categories.

Still, Israel wanted a king like everyone else had. So when the nation's elders demanded that Samuel appoint a king, the Lord, in His divine wisdom, relented. "It is not you they have rejected," He told Samuel, "but they have rejected me as their king" (1 Sam. 8:7).

What a heart-breaking statement. From the moment Adam fell, God longed to restore humanity to its original state of perfect partnership with Him. He wanted Eden again: God dwelling with mankind, spirit with flesh, the divine with the mortal. Unfortunately, only God could establish this the right way because each time humans tried to lead the process their sinful nature got in the way.

God's redemptive plan had already gone through Noah, Abraham, Isaac, Jacob, and Moses. He had established His own people, liberated them from slavery, and led them supernaturally. When they partnered with Him, He offered them blessing, protection, provision, goodness, and countless other things Adam and Eve received in humanity's original, intended state. God's people existed because of Him, and yet now they didn't want His leadership.

Isn't that the essence of the human condition? We exist—we take each breath—because of God. He allows us to be, and yet we don't want Him to lead us.

I want you to notice in 1 Samuel 8 how God's character still shone through at this moment of utter heartbreak and disappointment. Even when He was being rejected and could have fumed against Israel's idiocy, instead He comforted Samuel and assured him the people weren't rejecting him. "As they have done from the day I brought them up out of Egypt until this day, forsaking me and serving other gods, so they are doing to you," the Lord explained to Samuel (1 Sam. 8:8). The prophet was disheartened and frustrated at his own people, though his emotions were nothing compared to what the Lord felt. Yet amid His own pain and rejection, God still comforted His appointed mediator.

The Lord then gave the Israelites an opportunity to back out of this terrible, horrible, no good, very bad decision. He "warn[ed] them solemnly" (1 Sam. 8:9) and painted a detailed picture of what life would eventually be like under this requested king:

> He will take your sons and make them serve with his chariots and horses, and they will run in front of his chariots. Some he will assign to be commanders of thousands and commanders of fifties, and others to plow his ground and reap his harvest, and still others to make weapons of war and equipment for his chariots. He will take your daughters to be perfumers and cooks and bakers. He will take the best of your fields and vineyards and olive groves and give them to his attendants. He will take a tenth of your grain and of your vintage and give it to his officials and attendants. Your male and female servants and the best of your cattle and donkeys he will take for his own use. He will take a tenth of your flocks, and you yourselves will become his slaves.
>
> —1 SAMUEL 8:11–17

In short, this king will be a tyrant. He will take what is most precious to you for his own selfish gain. Although he is one of your own, he will oppress you and put you in shackles, just as the kings of other nations have done. And then the Lord offered maybe His most sobering warning: "When that day comes, you will cry out for relief from the king you have chosen, but the LORD will not answer you in that day" (1 Sam. 8:18).

I once knew a guy who loved the wrong woman. This girl wasn't just wrong for him; she was bad news for virtually everyone who knew her. Even her family called her manipulative, demanding, overbearing, and just plain mean. At times she would publicly humiliate this guy so badly that others had to intervene to stop the verbal abuse. And yet always, despite what others said, he would go back to her. "She just makes me feel something that no one else does," he told his bewildered friends when announcing their engagement. A few years later, to no one's surprise but his own, they were divorced.

Like this unfortunate man, Israel had been warned in advance. God didn't exaggerate the situation but simply gave them the truth: *Life will be really bad if you get what you want.* But also like that infatuated guy, Israel apparently had such blinders on that they couldn't shake the notion of being ruled by an earthly king, no matter how horrible life would be under him. So they ignored Samuel; the Bible says they "refused to listen" to him. "'No!' they said. 'We want a king over us. Then we will be like all the other nations, with a king to lead us and to go out before us and fight our battles'" (1 Sam. 8:19–20).

Not only were the Israelites foolishly defiant, but now they were being irrational. God had already gone into battles and fought for them—numerous times! Each time He did, they remained undefeated. No earthly king could claim such a perfect record, yet the people convinced themselves they would be better off with someone else to lead them.

Isn't it amazing how easily our pride blinds us to the truth? Satan's pride blinded him from the perfection of heaven. Adam and Eve's pride distorted the perfection of heaven on earth. The pride of mankind at Babel kept them from seeing God's intended plan to restore heaven on earth and bless *all* peoples. Still today the pride in our hearts rises up to convince us we would lead better than God. We begin to think, *I should be leading, not following.* And the more we allow that lie to take root, the more warped our perception of reality becomes—until we end up facing the consequences of being partnered to the wrong person (or force), who puts us in bondage.

Once again, God let the Israelites have what they wanted. They did not want His leadership, so the King of kings stepped aside and gave up His seat to a mere man. Let's see how that went.

THE HIGHER YOU RISE, THE HARDER YOU FALL

As we begin examining how Israel's human kings fared, it's important to keep in mind God's warning to His people that we just read in 1 Samuel 8:11–17. The truth is, this prophecy wasn't fulfilled with just one of Israel's kings; it was fulfilled in king after king after king, as we will see.

Israel's first king, Saul, had all the outward traits to enamor people—he was strikingly handsome and tall. Inwardly, however, he struggled with timidity, insecurity, and self-esteem. (See 1 Samuel 9:21; 10:21–22.) The Lord wanted His people to have the best replacement leader possible, so He "changed Saul's heart," empowered him with the Holy Spirit, and "changed [him] into a different person" (1 Sam. 10:6, 9–10). This dramatic transformation was immediately evident, as one of Saul's first acts after being presented to Israel as its king was to rescue seven thousand men besieged by a neighboring enemy.

(See 1 Samuel 10:27; 11:1–11, NLT.) After the successful mission, people advised Saul to kill off some vocal dissidents, yet he extended mercy and rightly gave credit to the Lord for the victory: "No one will be put to death today, for this day the LORD has rescued Israel" (1 Sam. 11:13). Finally, Israel seemed to have the mighty king they wanted, and more importantly, he was leading like the Lord! Saul was submitted to a higher authority, the Lord, and refused to exalt himself. Maybe this would work out after all!

As Israel celebrated the new hope they had in Saul, a now-aging Samuel offered another sobering caution as part of his final address to all the tribes. He reminded Israel—and Saul—who the nation's real king was and said if they were faithful to the Lord, He would continue to be faithful to them. "But if you do not obey the LORD," the prophet warned, "and if you rebel against his commands, his hand will be against you, as it was against your ancestors" (1 Sam. 12:15).

It took Saul only one battle to neglect this warning. At Gilgal, Saul and his troops faced a Philistine army with "soldiers as numerous as the sand on the seashore" (1 Sam. 13:5). Saul had been told to wait seven days for Samuel to come and, presumably, ask for the Lord's favor in battle. But during that time, many of Saul's men were so terrified they retreated into hiding. When the seventh day came and Samuel still hadn't arrived, Saul took matters into his own hands and presumed the role of a priest by administering the burnt offerings to the Lord. As those at Babel had done a thousand years earlier, he was trying to summon God on human terms and control Him like a puppet. Just as Saul did this, Samuel arrived—and with a scathing rebuke and prophecy: Saul's disobedience would cost him the throne.

Scripture doesn't say how Saul responded to such bad news, but it does reveal how his growing pride led him into greater delusion. Although the Lord gave Israel supernatural victories against the Philistines and other enemies, Saul increasingly made these battles all about him—to the extent that he erected a monument at Carmel honoring not Yahweh but himself (1 Sam. 15:12). His descent into egotism came to a head when he disobeyed the Lord's blatant directions to eradicate the Amalekites along with all their animals and possessions. Instead of following through, Saul and his men kept the Amalekite king alive, then picked through the spoils to keep the best sheep and cattle.

To make matters worse, Saul lied to Samuel and, when exposed, still tried to save face by claiming he intended to use the plunder for worshipping God: "But I did obey the LORD. ... I completely destroyed the Amalekites and brought back Agag their king. The soldiers took sheep and cattle from the plunder, the best of what was devoted to God, in order to sacrifice them to the LORD your God at Gilgal" (1 Sam. 15:20–21).

How often do we try to cover up our sin with religious acts? Without real relationship, religion is ultimately humanity's attempt to work our way to God. It's Babel all over again, mankind trying to restore heaven on earth through our own ways rather than God's. When we succumb to a religious spirit, we often try to hide pride (exalting ourselves) behind a guise of worship (exalting God). Our heart's focus is no longer on God and His glory but instead on what we can do to get what we want from Him. While we engage in religious acts to get closer to the Lord, without real relationship, we will end up feeling distant from Him.

That was certainly the case with Saul, whose lame excuse revealed that a relational shift had already taken place. Notice again his response to Samuel: "The soldiers took ... the best of what was devoted to God, in order to sacrifice them to the LORD *your God* at Gilgal" (1 Sam. 15:21, emphasis added).

What happened? Since when did Yahweh become Samuel's God and not Saul's as well? This isn't a typo or a translation error; every version of the Bible captures the same shift in Saul's spiritual paradigm, to the point that he called the Lord Samuel's God instead of his own. Pride had created a chasm between Saul and his true King. In fact, Saul had elevated himself to such a degree in his own eyes that he wanted to act like God, determining right from wrong. He was unwilling to submit to the Lord's authority and leadership, even when confronted with his own sin.

Saul confessed after being both confronted and convicted. He appeared repentant when he grabbed Samuel's robe and pleaded with him to forgive him and allow him to worship God. But within a matter of minutes, Saul's true motive revealed itself: "I have sinned," he told Samuel. "But please honor me before the elders of my people and before Israel" (1 Sam. 15:30). There it is on full display. The glory of human exaltation had so seeped into Saul's heart that he was willing to forfeit true relationship with God for another fleeting chance to be adored by the masses. He loved his own stature more than God's. He feared people's opinions more than he feared the Lord.

At this point, it's far too easy to shake our heads in disgust at Saul without first looking into our own hearts. How often do I care more about what others think of me than what God thinks of me? If you're honest with yourself, are there times when your worship is more about appearances than what's actually in your heart? Are we willing to obey the Lord even when it kills our egos, or are we more concerned about our reputations?

I don't believe the Bible highlights Saul's life just so we can have a villain right before a hero (David) emerges. I believe it's a warning for each of us: The same pride that consumed Saul can just as easily consume us. Sadly, that pride runs in our bloodline, our fallen nature. Saul's downfall came quickly; ours can too if we aren't aware of how wonderful public adoration and self-exaltation can feel yet how subtly both can turn our hearts from God.

THE DIVERSITY OF DAVID

Though Saul's leadership continued, the pride in his heart not only destroyed his own life but also affected all Israel. Perhaps that's why God made sure the next king of His people would be "a man after his own heart" (1 Sam. 13:14). He longed for someone to accurately re-present His leadership on earth—first to His own nation and then to all nations.

The Lord found someone eager to do this in David, who is easily one of the most fascinating and celebrated figures of the Hebrew Bible. We all love David, partly because we can relate to him. Sure, few of us live the soap-opera life he did. (I'm all but certain you haven't ruled a nation, killed thousands, or plotted the death of a loyal commander to cover up your own infidelity with his wife.) Yet there's something in David's expressiveness and love for God—captured so vividly in the Psalms—that compel us to greater passion for the Lord.

We can relate when David sings, "As the deer pants for streams of water, so my soul pants for you, my God" (Ps. 42:1). We feel David's pain when he's down in the dumps because we've been there too: "I am worn out from sobbing. All night I flood my bed with weeping, drenching it with my tears" (Ps. 6:6, NLT). And we know what David is talking about when he writes of how the Lord "lifted me out of the slimy pit, out of the mud and mire; [and] … set my feet on a rock and gave me a firm place to stand" (Ps. 40:2).

David's ability to worship God through triumph and tragedy clearly inspires us to the same resilience. But regarding how much David's forty-year reign as king re-presented God's leadership to His people, the picture is anything but clear. As one biographer wrote, "For every Goliath in the story of David, there is a Bathsheba around the corner. For every soul to whom he showed compassion, there were a hundred he was personally responsible for slaughtering. … While David was no saint, neither was he a monster. He was a complex man, perhaps one of the most complicated and conflicted leaders of all time."[2]

David ushered Israel into a golden age of unprecedented prosperity, but he also brought constant war.[3] His family was so dysfunctional that one of his wives betrayed him and his own son led a national coup to dethrone him. David's weakness was women; in addition to the scandal surrounding Bathsheba, let's not forget he had at least eight wives and multiple concubines. Politically, his leadership skills were more comparable to the Mafia bosses of *Godfather* than God the Father (indeed, David ran a protection racket, operated a hired-mercenary business, and was renowned for executing people in grotesque fashion just to prove a point). David's double-crossing ways bely his worshipping-warrior heart, yet even on his deathbed he ordered hits on his enemies. And like Saul, David's pride cost the Israelite nation dearly. More than seventy thousand men died because David disobeyed God and conducted a census to prove how vast his kingdom had become. (See 2 Samuel 24.)

So to say David led like the Lord would be wrong. His heart may have been like the Lord's, but his actions often proved otherwise.

Despite this, God loved His anointed one—deeply. He was with David throughout his life, made his name great among the nations, gave him victories against all of Israel's enemies, and even promised him that his household and kingdom would last forever—a covenant fulfilled through Jesus.

RESTORING THE RIGHT LEADER

Why would God choose David? With other men such as Noah or Abraham, we could possibly point to their outstanding righteousness or faith, which the Bible emphasizes. But why would God choose such an obviously flawed leader to ultimately bring about the model of His perfect leadership (Jesus)?

First, God works through dirt. He created the first man from dirt and, ever since the fall corrupted the earth, has continually redeemed mankind from our "earthly" ways. Choosing David as the biological vessel through which God would bring His own Son was completely in line with His character. (In chapter 9, we'll look at Jesus' "flawed" lineage.) God redeems—that's what He does because that's who He is. Perhaps He chose David because no one else at the time would better prove that it's not about how sinful we are or how much good we've done, but it's ultimately about God's mercy and grace. He uses us not because we're worthy of being chosen but because He is who He says He is.

There's another reason I believe God chose David. Despite all his flaws, David was obsessed with glorifying God. He didn't just want to see how great God was—he wanted everyone else to see it too and have the same natural response of praise. As Israel's king, he successfully turned the desire of his people back to the Lord. The more David worshipped God, the more joy he found in who God is—in particular, how perfect His leadership is. And the more David experienced God's perfect leadership, the more he wanted others to experience this kind of leading.

This desire wasn't merely for Israel either. David wasn't satisfied with only his people experiencing God's leadership and glory; he wanted other peoples to know this as well because it was ultimately God's desire. I believe this was another reason God called David a "man after his own heart" (1 Sam. 13:14). David shared the same concern as God did for all humanity, as evident in his numerous psalms that involve "the nations." He grasped God's bigger picture: that Israel was blessed to be a blessing for all nations, so that God could restore His divine leadership, in all its glory, throughout the earth just as it is in heaven.

Because David was obsessed with glorifying God and seeing Him exalted among all peoples, it made sense that his lifelong desire was to see "heaven on earth" restored in the form of an earthly dwelling place for the Lord. "Here I am, living in a house of cedar, while the ark of God remains in a tent," David lamented (2 Sam. 7:2). (Throughout the Old Testament, the ark of God is directly linked to His presence.) David had experienced the Lord's presence countless times while worshipping in the tabernacle. But that was just a fancy tent; David knew God deserved more. He wanted to build a house—a temple—fit for the King of kings.

Though God informed David he wouldn't be the one building this temple—which must have been heart-breaking for David—that didn't deter the king from doing everything he could to help the process. (This reveals David's Christlike attitude of taking joy in submission as long as God is exalted.) David had already succeeded in establishing a massive system of day-and-night worship that included 4,000 musicians, 4,000 gatekeepers, and 288 singers (1 Chron. 23:5; 25:6–7). In addition, he amassed the materials needed for the temple's construction. Some Bible teachers believe David spent the modern-day equivalent of *twenty billion dollars* of his own wealth funding the tabernacle system and the new temple![4] David poured out his life, including his own possessions, to the Lord because he understood not only God's infinite worth but also that He was the source of every blessing in David's life.

David may have messed up in other areas of life, but when it comes to worshipping God, he is a model for us even today. Perhaps no moment of his life encapsulated his passion for God more than when the ark was being returned to Jerusalem. David was Israel's king, but that wouldn't stop him from leading the nation in glorifying God. He took off his royal robes, wore a linen ephod as a priest would, and danced passionately like a commoner. Even when David's own wife mocked him for leading the procession in a "vulgar" manner that wasn't kingly enough in her eyes, David's response indicates his wholehearted devotion to God: "It was before the LORD … I will celebrate before the LORD. I will become even more undignified than this, and I will be humiliated in my own eyes" (2 Sam. 6:21–22). As God's anointed king, David was willing to lead by submitting himself—regardless of the embarrassment or humiliation—so God was glorified.

A thousand years later, Jesus would take off His kingly robes, become our great High Priest, and live like a commoner. While David's actions may have been troublesome to his wife, Jesus' actions were offensive—even scandalous— to an entire human race and to His own Jewish people in particular. What kind of divine King leads His people by stooping so low? Would Yahweh really be so undignified as to make Himself "nothing by taking the very nature of a servant" and allow Himself to be "made in human likeness" (Phil. 2:7)? Jesus, God's anointed Son, chose to submit to His Father's plan, descend from heaven, and live in perfect obedience—even unto death—so His Father would be glorified. Though David was a typecast of such obedience, Jesus was the ultimate expression of a King willing to give up everything so another would be lifted up. David modeled an imperfect yet passionate form of leadership; in time, another King from his family line would model an absolutely perfect form of leadership.

SOLOMON'S SLIDE

Such perfect leadership wouldn't come through David's successor, however. After David's death his son Solomon inherited the throne of Israel. God again wanted someone to re-present His way of leading, so He blessed Solomon immensely. And once again the new king's reign showed incredible promise.

Solomon completed the temple in Jerusalem, making it the most glorious structure ever built for the Lord. With God in His house, heaven was now on earth, and Israel once again experienced blessing. Solomon submitted to the Lord, recognizing early on that he needed God's help. "I am only a little child and do not know how to carry out my duties," he prayed. "So give your servant a discerning heart to govern your people and to distinguish between right and wrong. For who is able to govern this great people of yours?" (1 Kings 3:7, 9).

The Lord in turn blessed Solomon more than he could have ever imagined. According to 1 Kings 10:23–24, he "was greater in riches and wisdom than all the other kings of the earth. The whole world sought audience with Solomon to hear the wisdom God had put in his heart." Yet for all of Solomon's wisdom and splendor, he apparently wasn't smart enough to detect the little things in his life that, over time, ate away at his dependence on the Lord. People turned to Solomon for his God-given wisdom, but privately he neglected to acknowledge its source. We know this because Solomon's personal life soon became a mess. More and more he took matters into his own hands—which, it should be noted, was the downfall of all three kings we have looked at so far. Each trusted more in his own decision-making and wisdom than the Lord's.

In Solomon's case, God had specifically told him and the Israelites not to intermarry with people from certain neighboring nations. This wasn't because God was racist but because He knew the patterns of His own people; as soon as they began taking foreign wives, they would take their gods as well. Israel had proven this tendency from the first time God blessed them with their own land, and it continued in a vicious cycle for hundreds of years. That they were now in a time of prosperity under Solomon didn't change things. In fact, God had warned Solomon specifically that if he and his people turned away from Him and began serving other gods, there would be severe consequences. Not only would the Lord allow their land to be taken from them, but the temple would be demolished.

You'd think such a sobering warning would put the fear of God in Solomon. But apparently pride went to his head, and he reasoned that God's warning to the Israelites somehow didn't apply to him. He blatantly disobeyed the Lord's commandments regarding a king's personal wealth. (Compare Deuteronomy 17:16–17 with 2 Chronicles 9:13, 25, 27.) In addition, he inherited his earthly father's weakness for women. One marriage to a foreign king's daughter led to another, which led to another, until eventually Solomon defied the Lord by taking an unfathomable "seven hundred wives of royal birth and three hundred concubines" (1 Kings 11:3; compare to Deuteronomy 17:17). The Bible explicitly blames his wives for leading him astray: "As Solomon grew old, his wives turned his heart after other gods, and his heart was not fully devoted to the LORD his God, as the heart of David his father had been. He followed [other gods]. ... So Solomon did evil in the eyes of the LORD; he did not follow the LORD completely, as David his father had done" (1 Kings 11:4–6).

Notice this was not an overnight plunge into evil. I doubt Solomon ever intended to fall away from the Lord. Instead, it was one unwise decision after another that led to his downfall. Each of those decisions ultimately involved the same choice: *Do I follow the Lord's leadership, the way He has instructed me to go, or do I follow my own leading, the way I think is best for me?* The Bible may credit Solomon's wives for influencing him enough to "follow" other gods, but that doesn't exonerate Solomon from his part in the matter. Remember, in life we're always either leading or following. At the end of the day, Solomon's pride caused him to value his own leading more than the Lord's, and unfortunately that placed him in direct opposition with what God wanted.

THE PROPHECY FULFILLED

Within only a few verses in 1 Kings 11 we're told that Solomon's heart went from divided in verse 4—"His heart was not fully devoted to the LORD his God"—to hardened in verse 9—"His heart had turned away from the LORD." Once again, this transformation didn't just affect Israel's king personally; it impacted the entire kingdom. God had promised there would be blessings if Solomon and all Israel followed Him obediently, but there would also be negative consequences if he and the Israelites went astray. The Lord was true to His conditional promise and, partly due to Solomon's choices, raised up adversaries as part of His divine plan for Israel.

Do you recall God's initial warning to His people when they first cried out for an earthly king to lead them instead of the Lord? Remember how He painted a bleak picture of a tyrant king who would take from the people the very things they held most dear (1 Sam. 8:11–17)? Saul fulfilled some of this prophecy when he took sons from families throughout Israel to build his army (1 Sam. 14:52; 24:2). Solomon was also part of its fulfillment when he created a national system of forced labor involving more than one hundred eighty thousand men to build the temple (1 Kings 5:13–16). But after Solomon's death the Lord's prophetic warning was fully realized.

Solomon's son, Rehoboam, inherited the throne, and like his father, he let pride affect his decision-making abilities. Instead of taking advice from his elders and easing the forced-labor system his father created, Rehoboam foolishly did the opposite to show how powerful he was as king. His political muscle-flexing backfired when the tribes used for forced labor rebelled, a response that would change the course of Jewish history. In 930 BC, the nation that was originally meant to display God's perfect leadership to the world instead divided into two kingdoms: The ten northern tribes became the kingdom of Israel while the two other tribes (Judah and Benjamin) became the kingdom of Judah in the south.

The geographical split of God's people represented a far deeper division that had already occurred between them and their true King. Under Solomon, the Jewish people again began worshipping other gods. When the northern kingdom of Israel split from Judah, idol worship grew rampant. And just as God had warned would happen if His people abandoned Him, Israel's kings became brutal despots, each one seemingly eviler than his predecessor. Jeroboam didn't just allow citizens to worship foreign gods; he made a mockery of Israel's worship, setting up two golden calves and heavily promoting (some would say *forcing*) idol worship (1 Kings 12:25–33). Omri apparently used manipulation and cruelty to expand the kingdom's territory.[5] And the Bible says Ahab was more wicked than all of Israel's previous kings (1 Kings 16:33). Now *that's* evil!

Though Judah occasionally had God-fearing kings who led the southern kingdom in seasons of repentance and restoration, inherently God's people there ended up turning away from Him as well. More than two centuries after splitting, the ten tribes of Israel were assimilated into the Assyrian empire and, within a few generations, were essentially lost. And in 586 BC, almost one hundred fifty years after Israel's destruction, the citizens of Judah were forced into exile as the Babylonian empire took over.

God's people—in both Israel and Judah—had altogether turned away from their true King, and the result was just as He promised: They would reap the full "benefits" of the earthly kings they wanted. What they clamored for—human leadership rather than the Lord's—became their ruin. Rather than experiencing freedom and blessing, they were enslaved and stripped of everything they had and were meant to be. Instead of showcasing to the world what followship is like when led by the one true God, they became an embarrassing testament of a God-forsaken people.

This was their fault, not His. And yet the Lord would not change His character. He still loved His people even as they continually rejected Him. He still wanted the best for them—and the best was Him. Yet He would not force Himself on those He loved; they had to choose Him and accept His way of leading. Israel needed to be rescued, just as humanity needed to be rescued—both from their situation and, more importantly, from themselves. Left to their own leading, they would always end up on a path of death, destruction, and evil.

They needed a Savior. They needed a Messiah.

And God, as always, had a way.

PART III

... WITH JESUS

Choosing to follow someone we can't physically see is not easy. In our invitation to follow Jesus, then, it helps to understand more of who He actually is, particularly as a leader. In this section of the book, we'll look at different facets of Jesus' perfect leadership and how each one can draw us closer to Him. Be forewarned: He is unlike any other leader.

CHAPTER 8

THE COMPLEX MESSIAH

"WHO HAS INFLICTED this on us? Who has set us apart from all the rest? Who has put us through such suffering? It's God who has made us the way we are, but it's also God who will lift us up again."[1] Anne Frank wrote those words in her famous diary some eighty years ago, and they continue to echo today. The mindset that "to be Jewish is to suffer" has been ingrained in the Jewish identity for generations, and understandably so. Israel's history is full of oppression, exile, and genocide. From Egypt to Babylon to the Holocaust, God's chosen people have endured suffering like no other and, by His divine purposes, still survived. But I don't believe the Lord wanted His people to go this way.

From the beginning, the Israelites were meant to be a people "blessed to be a blessing." (See Genesis 12:2–3.) As a kingdom of priests, they were to live by completely different standards from the world's, and in so doing, showcase the unending blessings of knowing God and following His leadership. Indeed, if Israel walked in followship with Him, He would make them the envy of all nations. Things wouldn't just go well; they would go supernaturally well! This covenant was conditional, however, and Yahweh made that clear from the start. He would always be faithful; He couldn't be anything else. But if Israel wasn't faithful to Him and the covenant they had made, He would give them over to their desires. The choice to follow Him was theirs.

We've covered enough ground so far in Israel's story of followship that you know how things went. Even when God gave them what they asked for to help them follow Him—earthly kings, prophets, and judges—they continued to abandon their true leader and revert to their own way. The Lord allowed the twelve tribes to split into two nations, both of which were ruled by successive evil kings (with some occasional godly ones). Amid all this heartache, He spoke to His people through prophets, calling them back and even reminding them of an ultimate leader He would send—a Messiah who would one day restore everything. (More on that shortly.) Yet when God's "stiff-necked" people refused to return to Him and walk in His ways—in particular, when they oppressed those in need instead of caring for them—He finally allowed judgment to come through the Assyrian and Babylonian empires, which ravaged the land and scattered the Jewish people into exile.

But something changed after the Babylonian exile, something that hadn't happened before. Rather than returning to idolatry, the remnant of Jews who traveled back to their homeland rebuilt a culture devoted to following God's way. Their adherence to the Law—Torah—became the centerpiece of Jewish life. The Torah's five books along with the prophecies (e.g., Isaiah, Malachi) and the "writings" (e.g., Psalms, Job, the Chronicles) eventually comprised the Tanakh, or what Christians call the Old Testament. Israel's post-exilic leadership used these Scriptures for everything from law to education to national songs, just as the Lord had intended.

Finally, the Jewish people were returning to become a kingdom of priests, dedicated to walking differently in obedience to God's way. Surely now they would see Yahweh's promised blessings. Surely Israel would be restored as the envy of all nations. Surely now the long-awaited Messiah would come to make everything right.

WHAT ISRAEL AWAITED

In Hebrew, messiah (*mashiach*) means "anointed one." In ancient Middle Eastern cultures, anointing someone with oil was practiced in everyday life and in special ceremonies.[2] The Old Testament mostly highlights the latter, such as when a king, priest, or prophet was set apart by and for God to serve in that respective role. Samuel consecrated Saul as mashiach (1 Sam. 12:3, 5), for example, and Solomon referred to himself by the same title when dedicating the temple to the Lord (2 Chron. 6:42). When Israel's exiled prophets frequently described a "chosen one" who would redeem the nation and reestablish God's kingdom on earth, it's not surprising that many Jews began associating this kingly figure with the Messiah.

Although the word *mashiach* does not mean savior, its connection with the idea of someone coming to save people from their enemy runs long before Israel was on the map. The concept of a redeeming, divinely appointed mashiach appears within the first chapters of the Hebrew Bible, as God promised an "offspring" who would eventually crush the head of the serpent that enticed humans to fall into sin (Gen. 3:15). God told Abraham that He would bless all nations through this offspring of his (Gen. 12:3; 18:18; 22:18; 26:4; 28:14). Later Jacob prophetically declared over his son Judah that among his offspring would come a king to rule over all nations (Gen. 49:10). The Gentile prophet Balaam called this king a "star," "scepter," and "ruler [who] will come out of Jacob" and destroy the enemies of this offspring's nation (Num. 24:17–19).

More than five hundred years later, Israel, the nation of this promised offspring, entered its golden age under the rule of King David, yet even he was aware of a far greater King and kingdom still to come. God promised that one of David's offspring would be "over my house and my kingdom forever; his throne will be established forever" (1 Chron. 17:14). According to Psalm 72:4–5, this ruler would "defend the afflicted," "save the children of the needy," "crush the oppressor," and "endure ... through all generations." (Notice the connection between this Messiah-King and those who suffer—it's important!) Indeed, the Messiah would bring God's justice to all nations, and through Him all nations that chose to submit to His leadership would be blessed (Ps. 2, 72, 89, 110, 132).

Such promises would have provided much-needed hope for the Jewish people while suffering in exile. During this dark season the Lord sent multiple prophets to remind His people of a Messiah who would eventually rule with perfection and restore life to the way He originally intended—in followership. Their words undoubtedly raised Israel's hopes and expectations to an all-time high. Who wouldn't be excited when these prophets added so many details to the overall picture of this glorious Savior? For example:

- He would institute a new covenant with God (Jer. 31:31–34).
- He would rescue Israel and bring peace in the land (Jer. 33:15).
- He would judge and rule over all nations (Zech. 9:10; Isa. 2:4).
- He would establish global peace and understanding of God (Isa. 11:6–9).
- He would rule with perfect wisdom, justice, and righteousness (Jer. 23:5; 33:15–16).
- He would reign forever (Isa. 9:7).
- He would ensure justice for the poor and marginalized (Isa. 11:4).
- He would restore God's favor upon Israel and make it a shining light for the Gentiles (Isa. 49:6; 61:1–3).

The promised King sounded too good to be true. HaMashiach ("the Messiah") was everything they hoped for, yet those hopes were left hanging in the air with the closing of the Hebrew Bible.* When Israel's savior didn't show up for four centuries and God seemingly went silent, doubt and confusion crept in. Israel had repeatedly turned away from their Maker in the past; had God now finally abandoned them for good? Were the prophecies about HaMashiach nullified because of Israel's unfaithfulness? Or did the people maybe misinterpret the words of God's prophets? Was HaMashiach really still coming?

As the Jewish people pondered these questions, their culture shifted dramatically during the intertestamental period. I have already mentioned the unprecedented devotion to knowing and following the Torah; because of this, local synagogues grew in importance, as did the influence of synagogue leaders. With the restoration of the Jerusalem temple, spiritual devotion—and division—arose. Religious sects and sociopolitical extremist movements sprouted up throughout the land, producing groups such as the Zealots, Hellenists, publicans, Pharisees, Sadducees, and Essenes. Each emphasized a different aspect of what God's restoration of Israel would look like and how it would come, and this, in turn, confused the ideas surrounding HaMashiach.†

In generations prior to the exile, Jews believed their Mashiach would be a single person sent and anointed by God, as proven in examples such as the prophetic prayer of Hannah (1 Sam. 2:10) or David's Messianic Psalm 2. But amid four centuries of silence from God, new ideas about HaMashiach emerged, including the belief in two Messiahs.[3] Some Jews began to believe the Messiah was merely a human agent sent by God (most still believe this today). Yet the extrabiblical book of Enoch, written during the exile years, clearly described the Messiah as "no mortal. Without beginning or end, he comes down from heaven to reverse the processes of history by segregating good and evil."[4]

Most Jews expected the Messiah to come in their lifetime, and when He didn't, they began to explain away and distort the prophecies. Some placed human preconditions on His arrival (ideas that modern Judaism still carries), such as that He would not come until all Israel repented in a single day or until Israel properly observed two Shabbats in a row.[5] Others believed there was a

---

* The modern Christian ordering of the Old Testament differs from the Tanakh, and they conclude with different books. In its original order, the Old Testament ends with 2 Chronicles 36, not Malachi 4—though by no coincidence, both texts point to a coming Messiah.
† Many Jewish scholars today allege that Christians hijacked the idea of the Messiah and have distorted the Tanakh's Messianic passages to fit the life of Jesus. Yet first-century writings indicate a definitive expectation among Jews during Jesus' time of a messiah who would rescue their people. In addition, even non-Christian scholars argue that the Jewish concept of HaMashiach changed during the exile, as evidenced by the difference between pre-Talmudic and post-Talmudic writings.

Messiah candidate in every generation; whether he was *the* Messiah depended upon a generation's readiness. One rabbi in second-century BC even taught that Mashiach had already come in Hezekiah's time.[6]

What is clear during these four hundred years is that the purpose for the Messiah's arrival began to shift further toward purely a national salvation. When Rome conquered Israel in 63 BC and the empire's oppression and taxation upon the Jewish people grew heavier, the promised Mashiach became far more of a political savior than a spiritual one. Ironically, in an era when Scripture served as a centerpiece to Jewish society, the nation seemed to overlook massive elements of Messianic prophecy.

MESSIAH CHECK

It's not by mistake that God sent Jesus precisely into this muddied period of Israel's history. Scripture says, "When the fullness of the time had come, God sent forth His Son" (Gal. 4:4, NKJV), and obviously this was a *full* time! The various popular-yet-distorted notions of what the Messiah would look like, act like, do, and say—in addition to when, why, and how He would come— are part of why so many questioned whether Jesus was *the* Anointed One. Remember, the Jewish people of Jesus' day were far from scripturally ignorant. They understood the stakes, which is why they felt it crucial to know who this rabbi from Galilee really was. After all, if He was the Messiah, then it meant the following:

- Jesus would deal with the Jewish people's seemingly ageless suffering.
- Jesus would lift up Israel's oppressed—including the widows, orphans, foreigners, and poor, whom God cared for so much.
- Jesus would bring hope to the hopeless.
- Jesus would establish peace in Israel and throughout the world.
- Jesus would initiate a new covenant between God and Israel.
- Jesus would reunify Israel's divided population, bringing them back to the Lord.

Those are all things the Messiah would *do* (and there are many more). But if Jesus was HaMashiach, then certain monumental truths concerning who He *was* had to also be true. This namely includes the following:

- Jesus was Israel's eternal King.
- Jesus was Israel's "greater prophet" promised back in the days of Moses.[7]
- Jesus was Israel's true High Priest.
- Jesus was Israel's ultimate Passover Lamb, who would remove their sins.
- Jesus was God incarnate living among Israel: "God with us."[8]
- Jesus was God's own Son.‡
- Jesus was Israel's counselor who would perfectly guide them in God's way.

Obviously, recognizing someone as *the* Messiah was huge, as it involved virtually every aspect of Jewish life. Can you see why Israel's leadership was so bent on investigating the claims surrounding Jesus? The religious leaders of Jesus' time believed they were protecting the nation from yet another false messiah, and they quickly became Jesus' main source of conflict. By the time Jesus was publicly known, messianic expectations were so distorted that the Jewish leaders felt more threatened by than hopeful over the growing popular notion that this Nazarene might be the Messiah. They did not enjoy Rome's rule over them, but some relished the power Rome (and the people) gave them—and Jesus' popularity could affect that.

PROOF IN POWER

Rome-appointed prefects may have technically governed the Jewish people during Jesus' time, but in reality Israel's religious leaders held the greatest sway. Their regulations governed everyday life, as they imposed on the people what they saw as the acceptable way to follow God. So when Jesus began to challenge

---

‡ The Messiah's divine sonship has long been a major point of contention with Jews because it seemingly goes against God's own words of being one (found in the Shema—Deuteronomy 6:4–9—a core tenet of Judaism). In their view, because God is one, He cannot have a son and thus be divided. Unfortunately, they overlook two major proofs validating the notion of a Son of God: their own Tanakh (e.g., Ps. 2:7, 12; 110:1) and numerous extrabiblical Jewish writings preceding Jesus' time (which prove Judaism hasn't always rejected the idea of God having a son). The Book of Enoch (written 170–64 BC) describes the Messiah as "the Son of God" (105:2). The Talmud and Midrash both include quotes and commentaries directly linking the Messiah and the Son of God. Finally, the Dead Sea Scrolls' "Son of God" fragment 4Q246 shows an undeniable correlation between the singular Messiah and God's own Son. It's worth mentioning that Jews did not begin rejecting the Messiah's sonship until Rabbinic Judaism emerged after the temple's destruction and amid the growing Christian movement.

the Pharisees, chief priests, scribes, and teachers of the Law early in His ministry regarding what walking in God's way *actually* meant, it was understandable why they reacted. (Imagine their frustration when this countryside preacher told the masses, "You have heard that it was said, but I tell you …") The religious leaders were used to deciding all matters related to Judaism, especially when it came to interpreting Scripture. They presumed to be God's appointed leaders, chosen to represent Him. Yet here was a carpenter with no apparent religious credentials who, from the beginning of His ministry, taught "as one who had authority, not as the teachers of the law" (Mark 1:22).

To have such authority required more than just popular opinion. In the rabbinic culture of the day, you were recognized as a rabbi only after you had gone through the ceremony of semikah (ordination), in which your rabbi laid hands on you and commissioned you with the same authority he had (also called semikah) to interpret and give advice regarding the Hebrew Bible. This is why the Pharisees asked Jesus when He taught in the temple, "By what authority [semikah] are you doing these things? … And who gave you this authority?" (Matt. 21:23). Their system prevented commoners from spreading heresy and kept them in control.[9]

The problem was that while Jesus' authority was undeniable, the Jewish religious leaders couldn't figure out where He got it. While most Torah teachers simply cited various rabbis' interpretations, Jesus offered His own explanation that not only awed everyone but, more importantly, couldn't be refuted! His semikah came straight from God (unlike the religious leaders') and had been confirmed at His baptism when He had been commissioned into ministry with both an audible endorsement from the Father and a visual empowerment of the Holy Spirit! (See Matthew 3:13–17.)

Jesus' teaching authority went even deeper when we consider that the Jewish understanding of "interpreting" the Law was not merely mental but also experiential. Stated another way, Jesus was presenting a new way to think Torah *and* live Torah, and He could only offer this if He had personally walked out this "interpretation." It was obvious, then, that Jesus taught from His life, not just from others' theories.

Furthermore, Jesus backed up His words with supernatural power fit for a Messiah-King. He healed the blind, deaf, mute, lame, and diseased as if impairments and infirmities were nothing. He multiplied food. Demons and evil spirits begged *Him* not to destroy them, rather than the opposite. Jesus walked on water, calmed storms, and commanded nature as if it were His servant. He even raised people from the dead as if He reigned over life and death itself. Now *that's* the kind of might people expected from the Messiah!

Jesus' power may have threatened Israel's leadership, but the crowds loved it, while the religious leaders could not deny it. The Pharisees disagreed on whether such power came from Satan (Matt. 12:24) or God: "Rabbi, we know that you are a teacher who has come from God. For no one could perform the signs you are doing if God were not with him" (John 3:2). Their internal dispute didn't stop the masses from connecting the dots. Jesus' power was unmatched and His authority obvious. His Nazareth upbringing confused the religious leaders, but even they were uncertain where the Messiah was supposed to come from (John 7:27, 41–42). (It's possible only a few knew that Jesus was born in Bethlehem, into David's family, therefore fulfilling the royal lineage criteria for the Messiah.) With suspicions swirling, it wasn't long before a single question rose to the surface among everyone: "Could it be that Jesus is the Son of David, the Messiah?" (Matt. 12:23, NLT).

JUST (NOT) AS EXPECTED

Despite Jesus' Messiah-like authority and power, the Jewish people still faced some serious obstacles to believing He was the one. Things just didn't add up for them. If Jesus was Israel's long-awaited King, why was He spending time with societal outcasts and those considered too lowly for His company? Why all the talk about serving others and being the last or the least? None of that seemed very kingly. If He was Israel's righteous Redeemer, why was He content to meet with tax collectors and sinners, much less defile Himself with Gentiles and lepers? That didn't seem very holy or priestlike. Wouldn't the Messiah be above such things? Most importantly to the Jews at that time, if Jesus was the Messiah, why wasn't He concerned about Rome? Wouldn't HaMashiach deliver His people from all oppression? Jesus seemed oblivious to what they believed was Israel's main enemy. On one occasion, He even praised a Roman centurion's faith above everyone else's in Israel! What kind of national hero would do that?

As we've seen, most Jews expected a Messiah-King who would come primarily in power and might. Jesus fulfilled that but not in the way they thought. Their national suffering caused them to long for a forceful deliverer who would bring vengeance on Israel's enemies and elevate the Jewish people above everyone else. Instead, Jesus talked about loving your enemies, lifting others above yourself, and turning the other cheek. Rather than alleviate His people's sociopolitical suffering, Jesus suffered with them under Roman oppression while speaking about an infinitely greater kingdom. They wanted top-down power, yet He exemplified power from the bottom up.

Jesus was far kinder to the Gentiles than the Jewish people, including His closest disciples, wanted anyone to be. He seemed to go out of His way to reach the unclean foreigner (even the despised Samaritans!). Had His people paid attention, however, they could have seen from the very start of Jesus' ministry that their Messiah was coming in a different way than expected and with a different kingdom—one that welcomed people from every nation, not just Israel.

Jesus made one of His first public declarations in a tiny synagogue in His hometown of Nazareth when, by divine orchestration, He was assigned the week's reading from Isaiah 61. "The Spirit of the Lord is on me," Jesus read, "because he has anointed me to proclaim good news to the poor. He has sent me to proclaim freedom for the prisoners and recovery of sight for the blind, to set the oppressed free, to proclaim the year of the Lord's favor" (Luke 4:18–19).

As people steeped in Scripture, almost everyone in the synagogue that day would have recognized not only the passage Jesus read but also His stopping point. Why didn't Jesus finish the sentence? Didn't He realize there was more to Isaiah's prophecy than what He read?

Of course Jesus knew. His stopping point was intentional—it was a message to all humanity, delivered in the boondocks. (How typical of Jesus!) As Messiah, He was here to proclaim the year of the Lord's favor—period. One day, as the same Messiah, He would return to earth and complete the sentence—namely that He would come announcing "the day of vengeance of our God" (Isa. 61:2).

But vengeance and wrath were not the objectives of this mission. Instead, Jesus was offering spiritual salvation to all who needed it, which is everyone. His offer crossed cultural boundaries, and this is what incited the crowd's hatred that day in the synagogue. When He talked about Israel's blessing and favor, they loved Him: "All spoke well of him and were amazed at the gracious words that came from his lips," Luke records (4:22). Yet as soon as Jesus began speaking of God's past record of blessing foreigners instead of Israel, the fickle hometown crowd instantly turned on Him and even tried to kill Him.

That's not normal, is it? There must be serious underlying issues and spiritual forces at work for people to switch opinions so quickly and react with such violent hatred. Indeed, Jesus had hit a nerve in Nazareth. His words uncovered the Jewish people's racist view of spiritual exclusivity: "God wouldn't dare show favor on those other cultures as well, would He? Aren't *we*

His chosen people?" Jesus' statements threatened their worldview and their view of God. But under the surface, Jesus was also hitting the core issue that would continue throughout His ministry: *Will you be offended at how I choose to lead? Or will you follow Me only when I lead the way you want?*

WHAT KIND OF MESSIAH SUFFERS?

If people doubted Jesus' messiahship and His way of doing things, their concerns seemed more than validated when He died after only three years on the national scene. No one—not even His closest disciples—expected the Messiah to hang on a Roman cross, humiliated before all Israel. His abrupt finale seemed to confirm the obvious: This surely was *not* the King of the Jews.

Oh, but He was. Jesus had merely come another way. Not an unpredicted way, mind you—simply an unexpected way. Had Israel known their Scriptures the way Jesus interpreted them, they would have noticed all along a surprising truth: Their Messiah would not just come as a powerful, conquering King; He would also come as a suffering, sorrow-filled servant who could identify in every way with their pain. Israel's true leader, its glorious King, would lead *through* suffering and serving. But would they accept such upside-down leadership?

David offered a hint of the Messiah's strange way centuries before, even as he sang in first person: "I am ... scorned by everyone, despised by the people. All who see me mock me; they hurl insults, shaking their heads. 'He trusts in the LORD,' they say, 'let the LORD rescue him. Let him deliver him, since he delights in him" (Ps. 22:6–8). Even those reading David's psalm years later must have found it odd when he wrote, "A pack of villains encircles me; they pierce my hands and my feet. All my bones are on display; people stare and gloat over me. They divide my clothes among them and cast lots for my garment" (vv. 16–18).

The more recent prophets also spoke of a grief-stricken Savior. Daniel said the Messiah "will be put to death and will have nothing" (9:26). Prophesying in the voice of HaMashiach, Zechariah said, "The house of David and the inhabitants of Jerusalem ... will look on me, the one they have pierced, and they will mourn for him as one mourns for an only child, and grieve bitterly for him as one grieves for a firstborn son" (12:10). And, of course, the Book of Isaiah contains a few references to a rejected and scorned servant (e.g., Isa. 50:6), though none as broad and descriptive as the famous Isaiah 53 passage.

It would take an entire chapter of this book to give due justice to explaining Isaiah 52:13–53:12, which offers descriptions of "the servant" such as:

He was despised and rejected by mankind, a man of suffering, and familiar with pain. Like one from whom people hide their faces he was despised, and we held him in low esteem. Surely he took up our pain and bore our suffering, yet we considered him punished by God, stricken by him, and afflicted. But he was pierced for our transgressions, he was crushed for our iniquities; the punishment that brought us peace was on him, and by his wounds we are healed.

—ISAIAH 53:3–6

Isaiah 53 has long been a major dividing line between Jews and Christians, with much debate over who is "the servant." The passage's context clearly speaks of Israel—Isaiah chapters 52 and 54 reference the people's return from Babylonian captivity. At the same time, specific parts are extremely difficult to explain within a national context, no matter how much poetic license you apply.

It's also fascinating to track Judaism's history in dealing with the text. Not until a thousand years *after* Jesus do records indicate rabbis interpreting Isaiah 53 in a nationalistic way. Even as Christianity arose, we don't know of a single rabbi who tried to debunk the Christology of Jesus by saying the passage *wasn't* about the Messiah, even though doing so would have been optimal for Judaism.[10] Both the Talmud and Midrash contain a Messianic view of the passage, and both were completed during Rabbinic Judaism's earliest stages and centuries before the nationalistic view emerged.[11] Since then, however, modern Judaism continues to find new ways to refute any Messianic connections, including omitting Isaiah 53 from synagogue readings.[12]

For the unbelieving Jews of Jesus' time and those today, it's difficult to reconcile a suffering servant with their version of the Messiah—and understandably so. We have the luxury of reading the Hebrew Bible—including Messianic prophecies—two thousand years after its canonization and can therefore make connections that would have been difficult to see back then. In addition, remember that even Jesus' closest disciples initially did not believe the Messiah would suffer. Only moments after Peter acknowledged that Jesus was indeed HaMashiach, the disciple "took him aside and began to rebuke him" when Jesus told the group how He "must suffer many things … and that he must be killed and after three days rise again" (Mark 8:31–32).

If Peter missed it, I imagine we would have too. No one awaited a suffering Savior in those days. Why would they? They already had enough suffering; they wanted a King to come to the rescue.

And He did. Jesus came with a salvation greater than they could have ever imagined and rescued them from a problem deeper than they ever knew. He came to save them from their own sinfulness and an eternity away from God. If they would turn from their own way and believe in Jesus as the Messiah, they would enter an everlasting kingdom. This was infinitely bigger than just a political salvation from Rome, and it extended to all humanity.

Sadly, almost all Jewish people both then and now refuse to accept anything other than a Messiah who will restore Israel to global prominence. Since the temple's destruction in AD 70 and subsequent rise of Rabbinic Judaism, their Messianic "checkpoints" have remained entirely physical, thus bolstering a firm resistance to the possibility of Jesus' messiahship. Countless generations of Jewish children have been raised to believe that being Jewish inherently means you do not believe in Jesus. As a Messianic Jewish friend (a Jewish follower of Jesus) explained to me, "We grow up and are told that believing in Jesus is 'un-Jewish.' We don't know why, and if we dare ask, we get the same answer: 'Because that's what we do as Jewish people—we simply don't believe in Jesus.'"[§]

Israel at large remains in what the Bible calls a time of "hardening" to the truth (Rom. 11:25). As Paul describes, "Their minds [are] made dull, for to this day the same veil remains when the old covenant is read. It has not been removed, because only in Christ is it taken away. Even to this day when Moses is read, a veil covers their hearts. But whenever anyone turns to the Lord, the veil is taken away" (2 Cor. 3:14–16).

We can rejoice that today the veil is being taken away from more and more Jewish people in a way not seen since the days of Acts. In 1948, when Israel became a state, only one hundred fifty Messianic Jews lived there.[13] Today, around thirty thousand live in Israel, and estimates of the global Messianic Jewish movement run as high as three hundred fifty thousand.[14] These are exciting days as we see the veil being lifted!

Eventually, Israel will be saved spiritually and physically. The Bible's end-time descriptions indicate that the Jewish people will once again face tremendous suffering, possibly a genocide worse than the Holocaust, as

---

[§] To better understand the Jewish perspective on Jesus, I recommend Rabbi Kirt A. Schneider's book *The Lion of Judah* as a starting point.

unimaginable as that is. (See Jeremiah 30:4–7; Zechariah 13:8–9; and Revelation 12:13–17.) Jesus will return then to physically rescue His chosen people, Israel. He will come not as their suffering servant but as their King with such terrifying power that all the earth's leaders will wish for death rather than face His vengeance. (See Revelation 6:15–16.) And on that day, "*all* Israel will be saved" as they recognize Jesus as their one, true Messiah (Rom. 11:26, emphasis added).

HOW COULD THEY MISS IT?!

It's common to assume the Jews of Jesus' time missed seeing Him as Mashiach because they refused to believe in Him. But if we examine the Gospels closely enough, we'll see that isn't the case. Scripture clearly indicates many thousands believed in Jesus, recognizing Him as the long-awaited Messiah (John 2:23; 4:39; 7:31; 8:30; 10:42; 11:45). Even many among the religious leadership believed (John 12:42), though most followed Him to bring charges against Him.

How, then, were only one hundred twenty called believers after His crucifixion? What happened that caused so many to fall away and ultimately reject Jesus? I believe the answer is crucial for us today if we want to avoid the same path as the overwhelming majority in Jesus' time.

You would think the more Jesus revealed of Himself, the more people loved Him; but, in fact, His three years of ministry prove the opposite. Almost everyone loved the Jesus who came in power, especially when they personally benefitted from that power. Mass miracles and healings were crowd-pleasers, as was Jesus' authoritative teaching. But the more Jesus talked about who He really was, what it cost to follow Him, and what the road ahead would be like, the more His followers dwindled in number.

For some, Jesus' words were too challenging or offensive. For others like the Pharisees, it was His disregard for the traditions of the day. For many, however, I imagine it wasn't what Jesus did as much as what He *didn't* do that caused them to stop following Him. Maybe they didn't get healed. Maybe He didn't meet them the way they expected He would. Maybe He didn't stop the suffering the way they wanted Him to. Or maybe He didn't rescue them like they thought He should. Each person who left Jesus ultimately had a choice: *Do I continue following Him even when I think He should have said or done something differently? Or do I stop and just go my own way because I think my way is better?*

I hope you're seeing how this hits home for all of us. At some point in our journey with the Lord we will face a time when we're not sure that what He's doing is actually best. At that point, something in us rises up to challenge His way and tells us, "Wait a minute. Shouldn't I be the one leading here?"

That something is pride, and it's the powerful force that uses disappointment, offense, and hurt as fuel to think: *I would do this better. I would protect myself better and not let this happen. I would change this. I should be God.* Of course, we don't say this out loud, nor do most of us consciously think this way. But pride is what ever-so-subtly gets us to start thinking and acting like we believe we're God—often without even knowing it.

Do you recall how Ezekiel 28 described the reason for Satan's downfall? "In the pride of your heart you say, 'I am a god; I sit on the throne of a god'" (v. 2). Notice how pride is a matter of the heart. Pride allows us to act humbly on the outside while we seethe on the inside. Pride keeps us smiling as we say, "God bless you" to the neighbor we just helped, all while thinking we're the ones really providing the blessing. Pride is what caused thousands in Israel to stop following their Messiah, thinking He should have come a better way. And pride is what hardened the hearts of Israel's religious leaders, resulting in such spiritual blindness that they crucified the very Messiah who could save them.

Christians love to highlight that last one, and we often read the Gospels in such a way that we might as well have Darth Vader's theme playing in the background every time the Pharisees are mentioned. We've turned the religious leaders of Jesus' day into cardboard villains, for obvious reasons. At times Jesus blasted the Pharisees, scribes, and teachers of the Law for their hard hearts, pride, hypocrisy, and spiritual blindness. (See Matthew 9:4; 12:34; 13:15; 15:8; Mark 3:5; 6:52; 10:5; Luke 16:15; and John 5:42.)** He had a righteous anger for how these religious leaders, whose role was to help lead people toward God, were instead *preventing* people from walking in His way.

If we're not careful, however, we can miss the point just as they did. The sobering reality is that I'm never too far away from being a Pharisee. I want Jesus to show up and do things my way—when I want and how I want. That's my sinful nature that routinely tempts me to lean into my pride and play God. And if He doesn't lead the way I think He should, I'm left at the same crossroads of followship as all Israel was: Will I trust God's way of leading even when it's not what I expected or wanted?

** It's worth noting that Jesus also publicly honored the Pharisees (Matt. 5:20; Mark 2:16–17; Luke 15:7) and ate with them multiple times (Luke 7:36; 11:37; 14:1).

What happens if I'm not healed today? What if the Lord doesn't give me the direction I think I need? What if He never confirms what I think He has called me to do? Or here's a tough one: How will I respond when I'm faithfully pressing in to feel His presence, and yet He still seems light years away?

In all these situations, the question remains the same: Will I lay down my own expectations, desires, and assumptions and trust the Lord's leading? It's not easy to do so, but if I can, I give Him His rightful place. He may not alleviate my "suffering" like I would prefer, but He remains God. And as with Israel—and all those who call upon Him—I know someday His salvation will be complete.

CHAPTER 9

A DIFFERENT KIND OF KING

IF YOU LIVE in the kingdom of Jordan, beware: You may be standing next to royalty without knowing it. Apparently, the nation's kings fancy going undercover to occasionally mingle with commoners. The late King Hussein embarked on a few adventurous stunts during his forty-six-year reign, though his disguise involved little more than covering his face with the ends of his headdress. But since his son King Abdullah II assumed the throne, the undercover schemes have grown far more elaborate.

Only months after becoming king, Abdullah disguised himself as a white-bearded television reporter and spent five hours interviewing unsuspecting businessmen and traders on how the kingdom's duty-free zone was operating. His reason? He wanted to see for himself how things in his kingdom were actually running. When area officials showed up demanding to see a filming permit for the TV crew, the monarch was forced to pull off his fake beard and headdress, shocking all those around. Not surprisingly, a crowd quickly swelled of those hoping to catch an up-close glimpse of royalty.[1]

Since then, the king has visited hospitals, border crossings, tax offices, land and survey departments, and other public-service utilities, all while going incognito under such guises as a taxi driver, elderly man, or common businessman. King Abdullah II says going undercover is the best way to get honest feedback from citizens without his royal identity getting in the way of his attempts to improve government services.[2]

Jordan's king certainly isn't the first to shock his people by appearing as an average Joe in average settings. Various royalty throughout history—from Nero to Mary, Queen of Scots to Princess Diana—have all masqueraded as commoners to gain access to the everyday world.[3] But when Israel's Messiah-King, Jesus, appeared two thousand years ago in mundanity, His entry to this world wasn't just shocking; it was scandalous.

As we saw in the last chapter, the Jewish people awaited a Messiah who would come in royal fashion, with strength, power, and authority. They wanted a mighty king who would liberate them from Roman oppression and restore Israel to its glory days. Instead, Jesus was born into such humiliating circumstances—a shameful birth, an embarrassing lineage, a rustic upbringing—that even when He showed supernatural authority and power, they doubted His kingship.

WELCOME TO YOUR WORLD

The beginning of Jesus' life on earth proves how willing He was to confront our idea of what a king should be—and this is key to recognize for those wanting to embark on the followership journey. Kings are typically born in luxury and fanfare, with multiple servants attending their every need and entire nations celebrating their arrival with joy and pride. For Jesus, His birth may have come announced by heavenly choruses, but those on earth mostly perceived it with disdain.

Mary, a teenager pregnant during her betrothal, likely endured months of scornful looks, hateful comments, and condemning lectures wherever she went in public. Jewish culture in that day was brutal for unwed mothers. (Can you imagine the Pharisees' responses?!) Joseph wrestled with the shame of his fiancée's pregnancy, as Scripture says he "had in mind to divorce her quietly" so as not to expose her to more public ridicule (Matt. 1:19). Although Mary's family may have treated her with compassion, it's possible Joseph's extended family in Bethlehem did not, forcing her to deliver Jesus in less-than-ideal conditions.˙

Of course, a handful of people welcomed Jesus like a king. (Here's looking at you, wise guys from the east!) Others came out of shock and amazement and quickly spread the word. (That's you, shepherds!) But other than that, Jesus' welcome party consisted of strained family relations, a cultural stigma, and a paranoid King Herod issuing a death warrant for Him that led to mass infanticide. Not exactly how you'd expect Israel's true King to be welcomed.

FAMILY PICKS

It's important to remember that the Lord planned this arrival—how, when, where, and to whom. Jesus' coming to earth was not a surprise or an accident. But why would the Lord design such a lowly entrance, filled with scandal? For

---

˙ The oft-misunderstood "inn" where there was no room (Luke 2:7) wasn't a Holiday Inn, a cave, or even an exterior animal stable; it was a single-room, upstairs living area (Greek: *kataluma*) common among houses in Israel at the time. Jesus was likely born in an extended family member's house packed with so many out-of-town relatives coming for the census that the only area large enough for Mary to deliver a baby was downstairs, where animals were brought in at night. Still, in most Middle Eastern cultures, there is always room for family—no matter how "inconvenient" to the host—because hospitality is a matter of honor. So regardless of how crowded the house was, what host wouldn't offer their best to a teenager in labor unless shame and disdain weren't part of the picture?

the same reason His lineage was filled with scandal, as we will soon see. Paul described it this way: "God chose the foolish things of the world to shame the wise; God chose the weak things of the world to shame the strong. God chose the lowly things of this world and the despised things—and the things that are not—to nullify the things that are, so that no one may boast before him" (1 Cor. 1:27–29). Jesus was about to prove not only that He was King but that His kingdom was infinitely higher than—and different from—all others.

Make no mistake: Jesus was Israel's rightful King, whether He came in the way people wanted or expected. It didn't matter whether people recognized Him. Jesus submitted Himself completely to the Father's plan, which included being born into a family loaded with purpose yet far removed from its days as royalty. For Jesus to be King and heir to the throne of Israel, He had to come through David's line, as Scripture foretold. God had made David an incredible promise: "I will raise up your offspring … and I will establish the throne of his kingdom forever. I will be his father, and he will be my son. … Your house and your kingdom will endure forever before me; your throne will be established forever" (2 Sam. 7:12–14, 16).

It was no fluke, then, that both Mary and Joseph could trace their heritage through David's line. Proving Jesus' royal lineage was exactly why Matthew and Luke include detailed genealogies of Jesus in their Gospel accounts. Jewish culture is known for its meticulous historical record-keeping, and certainly we would expect such detail when talking about the most important figure in the nation's future. Although how Matthew and Luke prove Jesus' biological link to David differs, both were successful enough that their distinctive genealogies survived the scrutiny of the all-Jewish early church (which certainly would have wanted to get the facts about Jesus right!) and the generations that followed.

Still, I wonder if those first Jewish believers wished they could change Jesus' genealogy to make things smoother with some of their fellow, unbelieving Jews. Why would that matter? Because if Jesus was fully God and fully man as they claimed, then He would be the only person in history who handpicked His own lineage. Whoever He chose as His descendants would therefore say something about God Himself—about His character and the kind of people He wanted to be associated with throughout history.

With Jesus' genealogy serving as critical proof of His messiahship to the Jewish people, you'd think Jesus would ensure His lineage was full of royal "thoroughbreds"—pure, wholesome types who reflected the best of humanity. Instead, among His descendants are murderers, prostitutes, liars, schemers, and drunkards. Jesus' family line includes incest, murder, sexual abuse, and human trafficking. Equally as scandalous, Matthew goes out of his way to include women (which Jewish genealogies never did) and foreigners (which would have been seen as corrupting a Jewish family line). The Gospel writer actually left out plenty of righteous people in Jesus' lineage and instead featured individuals with not-so-stellar records. The following are just a few examples:

- Jacob habitually lied, swindled, and manipulated people—including family—and was one of the Bible's worst fathers.
- Judah trafficked his own brother into slavery and slept with a temple prostitute who ended up being his daughter-in-law.
- Tamar, out of desperation and honor, seduced her father-in-law, Judah, and gave birth to twins by him.
- Rahab ran a brothel and, by the way, was a Canaanite.
- Ruth, as a Moabite, was an enemy of Israel and therefore forbidden to enter God's house.
- David made several major mistakes, which we've already highlighted. (If you've forgotten them, re-read chapter 7.)
- Solomon broke God's law by taking *seven hundred* wives and *three hundred* concubines, most of whom were foreigners.
- Jehoram murdered all his brothers and many royal officials once he took the throne and, like countless other Jewish kings, "did evil in the eyes of the LORD" (2 Chron. 21:6).
- Speaking of evil kings, Rehoboam, Abijah, Ahaz, Manasseh, Amon, and Jeconiah (also called Jehoiachin) all fall into that category, yet they made it into Jesus' genealogy.

Clearly, if Matthew was trying to appeal to the Jewish notion of a pure and royal bloodline, he did a horrible job. And if this is how he wanted to "prove" Jesus' messiahship, he apparently needed a coach. But it's obvious he—and Jesus—had another purpose.

The King of kings came announcing a different kingdom, one unlike any since the days of Eden. He was restoring the kingdom of heaven on earth. And based on those He intentionally included as part of His past, it's clear Jesus was opening the doors of His kingdom not only to scoundrels and sinners but also to outcasts and those who *expected* to be excluded—the poor, oppressed, broken, and weary. It's as if Jesus were saying, "I don't just want My chosen people; I want *all* people. I want as many as possible to be saved into My family. Let it be clear that as King, I don't just desire the 'good' and noble. I want the deeply spiritual and the deeply flawed. I want the obedient ones and the rebellious. I want nobles and peasants, insiders and outsiders."

Jesus is the most inclusive King in history. Many people in the world today love to champion inclusivity; it's pushed by groups on every side of the social and political spectrum. But Jesus' version of inclusivity isn't like the world's. In fact, His type of inclusion bothers the world because it comes on *His* terms and only His terms. As King, He has the right to invite whoever He wants to be part of His kingdom. He gets to set the conditions on whom He calls family. And as the kindest King the world has ever known, He has invited into His kingdom people most of us would never want included if we were king. In fact, He is so generous in His kindness and mercy that it actually offends us.

Why would we be offended? After all, everyone loves that Jesus invites the poor and needy, the broken and hurting. That's a wonderful thing, isn't it? Of course it is—until we begin to realize exactly who the poor, needy, broken, and hurting actually are, especially in relation to how perfect Jesus is as King.

Think of it this way: How many of us would think it right for a king to let a prostitute sit next to him at a royal banquet? What would you think if a queen welcomed a rapist and murderer into her palace, showered him with expensive gifts, and gave him VIP treatment? Or what if a president invited a terrorist into his office and began sharing national secrets with him? What would we think of these leaders? We'd think they had lost their minds! We would question their discernment, their leadership skills, their capability as rulers, not to mention their sense of justice. It offends our minds to think of kingly figures stooping to such an extreme for such lowlifes.

Yet this is what Jesus does for us. It's what He did for the misfits in His lineage. And it's what He did while on earth as He revealed the kind of heavenly Father who throws a banquet and invites "the poor, the crippled, the blind and the lame" (Luke 14:21), or who, like a shepherd owning a hundred sheep, leaves behind the ninety-nine sheep to seek the one that's lost. This should be good news to us; it's the truth of the gospel, after all. And, of course, this gospel of grace demands that we not remain the same; it's the good news that we *get* to be changed. So whether someone is a mass murderer or a soccer mom, we're all called to "repent and believe," as Jesus said in Mark 1:15, so we can enter His kingdom.

But why is this level playing field for everyone so disturbing? Why are we bothered when Jesus invites *everyone* into His kingdom? Because it just doesn't make sense. It doesn't logically add up that someone so holy would invite someone so filthy into His presence and then share everything He has with that person. Isn't it interesting how Jesus' mercy can offend our sense of justice? (But not when that mercy is directed toward us, of course!) His kindness, when we're not the recipients of it, can take us to the limits of understanding grace. We may think we know what's just and right, but then we encounter someone who has done something far worse and yet received even more forgiveness from the Lord. For most of us, we react to this kindness with gratitude. "How great that he turned his life around!" "Wow, it's fantastic that the girl with such a troubled past has met the Lord." We love this kind of mercy from Jesus.

But then there's the *one*. We all keep this one deep in our hearts, often buried to an extent we don't even realize. It's the one person who represents to us the limits of Jesus' mercy. That person is the difference between kindness and foolishness, at least in our minds. "Wait, Lord. You're forgiving *that person*? Don't You know he has abused children? Don't You know she repeatedly cheated on her husband? Don't You know he scammed people out of billions of dollars and ruined countless lives?" I don't know who it is for you: Hitler, Osama bin Laden, your father, your ex. And here is the harsh truth that brings us to the limit: Jesus would still leave behind those who are safe to go after that one. And yes, He would invite even that one into His kingdom.

Jesus' kingship tests us. He is so outrageous in His generosity to those who don't deserve it that it can bother us. It seems unfair. It just doesn't seem right. And often, He allows this irritation to rise to the surface—to be exposed—so we're forced to come to terms with what is already in our hearts. More specifically, we are forced to deal with our mistrust of His way of leading or ruling. What kind of King pardons the guilty so easily? What kind of ruler pays the penalty Himself so that prostitutes and pastors, tax collectors and teachers, scoundrels and social workers all have the same chance for freedom?

As many preachers and Bible teachers have stated, Jesus offends the mind to reveal the heart. He purposely challenges what we *think* so we come face-to-face with what we actually *believe* in our hearts. When there is a gap between the two, we're forced to come to grips with the deeper issue—which, most often, is that we want to rule rather than allowing Him to do so (at least in the area of our life that's been revealed). We'd rather decide who is granted mercy and who isn't, or what is fair and what isn't. We'd rather be king.

This sounds harsh, extreme, and maybe even a little cynical. "I don't want to rule anything," you may say. "I'm just having a tough time believing it really works this way. I know Jesus forgives even the worst of sinners, but aren't there consequences to our sins?" Yes, there are. There are countless examples where the Lord grants mercy and forgives, yet a person still must deal with the repercussions of his wrongdoing. But what if the Lord decided to intervene and not allow a person to bear the brunt of his sin? What then? Would we be OK with that? Or would we question the Lord in our hearts?

WHO GETS THE FINAL WORD?

Years ago I desperately needed God to intervene in a situation at my job. I had earnestly tried to serve my boss at the time and thought I'd done what he had asked, but instead he blamed me for something I didn't do. Every bone in my body seemed to cry out, "This isn't fair!" And it wasn't. I did not do what I was being accused of, but I could not defend myself, even while I was being humiliated in front of others. During those days and weeks, I frequently prayed something like: *Lord, You are my defender. You've seen my actions, and You know my heart. You're the only one who can make this right.*

Guess what? He didn't make it right. God did not intervene, and to this day many of the people involved probably still blame me. But before you start to pity me, it's important that I mention something else I had to consider during that time, even as I prayed. Years earlier, I had also needed the Lord to intervene in a situation at my job, only this time, I wasn't innocent. I was completely in the wrong and deserved to face the consequences, yet I still prayed that the Lord would come to my rescue and defend me.

Once again, He didn't. He allowed me to face the repercussions, which were severe, and rightfully so. Yet those consequences actually ended up changing the course of my life, setting me on a new path that I would not trade for anything. I believe it was actually God's mercy that He *didn't* intervene; I am convinced that otherwise things would have never changed for me.

Job is undoubtedly one of the Bible's most challenging books. A righteous man suffers greatly under a divine "test" of sorts, and even as Job calls out for God to intervene, the only reply he gets is silence. His friends offer an assortment of theological positions, all of which do no good. Job is crushed and confused, yet throughout the test he refuses to curse his Maker. As believers, we love the perseverance and commitment Job displays when he famously says, "Though he slay me, yet will I hope in him" (Job 13:15). But one of the reasons I have always loved the Book of Job is because of the final act in this complex story. Job and his friends never get an explanation. His life is restored, but that's secondary to the main point: God is God. He doesn't give Job a reason for his suffering because He doesn't have to. He is Master over everything He has created. Why should He give an explanation?

And yet God's character is to redeem. He can't help it because that is who He is. Job's suffering is eventually redeemed and his life restored because the Lord is the Lord, but even if those things hadn't happened, He would still be the Lord. Regardless of the outcome, Jesus the Lord is King over all. He's the supreme ruler over everything in this earth, and He is ultimately the King over your life and my life, whether we want that or not.

The question is not if He is King. The question is: Will we submit to this King's ways when He offends us with His mercy, grace, and kindness? Will we allow Him to rule His kingdom and decide who is part of it, or deep in our hearts will we think we know better?

Often in our lives the Lord allows situations that challenge or even mess up our nice, organized theology, and in the process we discover what's really inside us. He allows persecution or tragedy to be the cleansing tool for our hearts. He permits, even repeatedly, hardships to unfold that press the deeper, internal issues. Will we accept that? Will we trust Him as King and trust His decisions? If not, we will always struggle to follow Him, much less *enjoy* following Him.

ENTERING THE KINGDOM

Any king has the right to determine the conditions for entering his kingdom. You may be welcome to come into that kingdom, but it's up to him if and what requirements must be met to actually enter and experience the unique elements his kingdom offers. It's no different with Jesus, and as I have already mentioned, His invitation extends to everyone. But He does have qualifications for entering and, despite popular opinion, those are not simply a matter of self-evaluation. Today, half the population believes they will enter God's kingdom if they are "good enough" or do enough good things, while a slightly smaller percentage think they don't even need to believe in God to enter.[4]

Let's look at what King Jesus actually set as His conditions. As we'll see, there are only two—repenting and believing—and yet both have become vastly misunderstood.

Just as a king would send messengers out to declare the arrival of his kingdom, God sent John the Baptist to announce His kingdom and prepare the way for its King. John's radical lifestyle and fiery messages didn't deter crowds from flocking to see him out in the Judean wilderness, where he declared, "Repent, for the kingdom of heaven has come near" (Matt. 3:2).

As John emphasized, Israel's repentance couldn't be just lip service. Most Jews in John's era understood this because offering God empty words was one of the reasons for their exile. God had spoken through the prophet Isaiah during the Assyrian exile, saying, "These people come near to me with their mouth and honor me with their lips, but their hearts are far from me" (Isa. 29:13).

True repentance, on the other hand, was to experience such remorse from opposing God and walking away from Him that you completely turned around and walked toward Him with your whole life—your thoughts, words, and actions. Such a transformed life would naturally yield different results, which is why John instructed people to "produce fruit in keeping with repentance" (Luke 3:8). Later, he added, "Every tree that does not produce good fruit will be cut down and thrown into the fire" (Luke 3:9). Without true repentance the people didn't have a chance to enter the kingdom that had come near.

Today many Christians preach a different gospel message that is devoid of repentance and focuses merely on believing in Jesus (the other prerequisite, which we will address next). That's somewhat understandable, as the word *repentance* can be both offensive (it requires us to turn) and misunderstood. Because of its association with street preachers screaming through megaphones and toting "Turn or burn!" signs, many believers avoid the topic of repentance out of embarrassment or fear of being labeled judgmental and narrow-minded.

Maybe that's why repentance is often described as the "lost doctrine of the twenty-first century," though it used to be a core message of the church.[5] As the late David Wilkerson said, "Whatever happened to repentance? You rarely hear the word mentioned in most churches today. … Pastors nowadays seldom call for their congregations to sorrow over sin—to mourn and grieve over wounding Christ by their wickedness."[6]

The key to reclaiming an accurate view of repentance is to understand what Jesus actually preached. When the Lord began His earthly ministry, He "went into Galilee, proclaiming the *good news* of God. 'The time has come,' he said. 'The kingdom of God has come near. Repent and believe the *good news!*'" (Mark 1:14–15, emphases added). Let's keep in mind how the Bible relays what Jesus shared; we know He preached *good* news because that's exactly how both Jesus and the Gospel writer Mark described it. Therefore, Jesus wasn't talking about something bad that you didn't want; He was talking about a *good* thing!

I don't know about you, but I've never heard of someone having to threaten people with good news. It would be absurd if I walked into my sons' bedrooms and threatened them with, "If you clean your rooms, we'll go get ice cream!" That's not a threat; that's good news to them. Likewise, if I told my wife, "I'm surprising you with a romantic getaway this weekend, but before we leave, we have to clean out the car or we'll be traveling in a smelly vehicle"—that's not a threat or any sort of bad news; it's music to her ears! (And you better believe we'd be cleaning that car together as fast as we could!)

Jesus' message was verbatim to John's. (See Matthew 3:2 and Matthew 4:17.) Both directly linked repentance with the gospel (good news) of the kingdom. If the heavenly kingdom's nearness was good news, then so was the fact that people could repent!

What specifically was the good news? That people could now be reconciled to God. That His kingdom was open to *all*. That there was a way for true salvation—a rescue that went beyond the physical realm. Not only was God's kingdom coming, but they could be part of it.

Was this good news conditional? Of course it was—Jesus was the King, this was His kingdom, and He had the right to put whatever conditions He wanted on who entered His kingdom. The good news would be *good* only to those who adhered to the King's conditions to enter. But those conditions most certainly did not overshadow the good news; in fact, the conditions made it even better news. Now God's people knew *how* they could enter the kingdom!

Can you see how this makes the repentance that brings us to salvation a joyful privilege, not a depressing burden? Although sorrow may rightfully be part of the process—don't get me wrong, true repentance isn't a light matter—the bottom line is still that we *get* to repent. We have been given the opportunity to turn from our hopeless way of self-rule and enter a kingdom of heaven, where the King generously offers an abundant, *eternal* life of fellowship.

Such life begins with our initial salvation—our entrance into the kingdom—but it continues as we walk the way of becoming more and more like our glorious King, which is what followship is all about. When we are citizens of His kingdom, we have the privilege of living a *lifestyle* of repentance. That sounds strange if we view repentance as an arduous, one-time ordeal. But, in fact, repentance is an everyday part of our ongoing sanctification as the Lord, by His Spirit within us, continues to fashion us into His image. He does the work, but we get to be part of it. As He purifies us, He works out the impurities in us just as dross comes to the surface when gold is refined. When our sin is revealed—

those areas of our lives where we still oppose God—we repent (that's our part), knowing that "if we confess our sins, he is faithful and just and will forgive us our sins and purify us from all unrighteousness" (1 John 1:9).

Notice how even in repentance the Lord calls us into an ongoing partnership with Him. The more we turn from our sins and toward Him, the more we discover the fruit He grows that is found only in His kingdom—fruit such as true freedom, joy, and purpose. This is incredible news! And I believe the more we walk with Jesus in followship, the more we will appreciate that repentance is an invaluable key to His kingdom.

BELIEVING THE KING

If repentance is a key to God's kingdom, then faith is a keyhole. The two fit together like a hand in a glove and always have. Jesus immediately followed up His announcement of a nearing kingdom with a twofold command: "Repent and believe the good news!" (Mark 1:15). These were the King's two requirements to enter His kingdom. As His ministry progressed, He would continue to clarify what each meant. At times He spoke purely of repentance:

- "I have not come to call the righteous, but sinners to repentance" (Luke 5:32).
- "Unless you repent, you too will all perish" (Luke 13:3).
- "This is what is written: The Messiah will suffer and rise from the dead on the third day, and repentance for the forgiveness of sins will be preached in his name to all nations, beginning at Jerusalem" (Luke 24:46–47).

Other times the Lord only mentioned believing in Him:

- "Whoever believes in the Son has eternal life, but whoever rejects the Son will not see life, for God's wrath remains on them" (John 3:36).
- "Very truly I tell you, whoever hears my word and believes him who sent me has eternal life and will not be judged but has crossed over from death to life" (John 5:24).
- "I told you that you would die in your sins; if you do not believe that I am he, you will indeed die in your sins" (John 8:24).

- "I am the resurrection and the life. The one who believes in me will live, even though they die; and whoever lives by believing in me will never die" (John 11:25–26).

So which is it: Are we to repent or believe? Both, just as Jesus first preached! The two are inseparable when it comes to entering the kingdom of God. You cannot have saving faith without repentance, and repentance means little if it does not lead to faith in Jesus. Many would say they are two sides of the same coin. Theologians often explain that repentance is about a person in relation to sin (moving away from *sin*), while faith is about that person in relation to Jesus (moving toward *Him*). "The individual who trusts in Christ simultaneously turns away from sin," writes Scottish Reformed theologian Sinclair Ferguson. "In believing he repents and in repenting [he] believes."[7]

Sadly, we live in an era when God's love and grace are so overemphasized—and His justice and holiness underemphasized—that today's modern gospel has separated the seemingly inseparable. Countless churches and ministries offer a soft, easy gospel that has been neutered of anything costly on our part. Theirs is a Disney-like gospel that's purely about believing something exists and—*poof!*—all your wishes come true: *Just believe. Just have faith. Anything is possible if you just believe.* (Cue the princess song.)

This was not the good news Jesus preached, nor was it the kingdom He described. In the next chapter we will examine what He specifically said about His kingdom, but for now we must remember that Jesus' first message to the masses was for them to repent and believe. (And don't forget, both were part of the *good* news!) Their turning away from sin and being baptized revealed hearts prepared for His kingdom. To actually enter that kingdom required more than repentance, though; it also required faith in Jesus. This was not faith that simply believed Jesus existed. (Of course He existed; He was right in front of their eyes!) No, the more He spoke about this kind of believing, it was clear that it involved a deeper element of *trust*.

At this point the people faced a dilemma: They now had to trust in this man who seemed to be claiming He was sent by God. John the Baptist testified that Jesus was "God's Chosen One" (John 1:34), and Jesus was certainly showing all the signs of being the promised Messiah. But would they actually choose to believe someone who said things such as, "I am the way and the truth and the life. No one comes to the Father except through me" (John 14:6)? Or, "I am the gate; whoever enters through me will be saved" (John 10:9)?

BELIEVING VS. FOLLOWING

The choice was easy for many, as we've already seen. The more Jesus performed miracles, healed the sick, cast out demons, and spoke with unprecedented authority, the more people believed He was the Messiah-King. It wasn't difficult to believe when they witnessed supernatural signs firsthand. But the more the crowds of believers swelled, the more Jesus talked about not just believing in Him but actually *following* Him.

Jesus' first invitation for His disciples to follow Him sounded positive and hopeful, albeit a little strange: "Come, follow Me," He told the fishermen brothers Peter and Andrew, "and I will send you out to fish for people" (Matt. 4:19). If you were a disciple, you already knew that following Him would involve serving Him. As we learned in Chapter 2, any disciple at that time was expected to serve his rabbi through everyday tasks such as cooking his meals, carrying his belongings, and even paying for his supplies.[8] So it made sense when Jesus said, "Whoever serves me must follow me; and where I am, my servant also will be. My Father will honor the one who serves me" (John 12:26).

So far so good—Jesus' invitations to follow Him weren't so startling when He stuck to the basics. Even when He made profound statements about Himself while inviting people, still He was relatively understandable, such as when He said, "I am the light of the world. Whoever follows me will never walk in darkness, but will have the light of life" (John 8:12). As long as the crowds got past Jesus calling Himself the light of the world, then they could grasp the concept—namely, that if you followed Him, you would be walking in light. Most would have immediately linked His words to Psalm 119's famous metaphor of the Torah: "Your word is a lamp for my feet, a light on my path" (v. 105). In their minds, then, Jesus was saying that if you followed His teachings of the Torah (God's Word), then you would walk in the light.

Sometimes even the "easy" statements Jesus made about following Him could cause confusion. Other times they were, well, simply weird: "Then he called the crowd to him along with his disciples and said: 'Whoever wants to be my disciple must deny themselves and take up their cross and follow me. For whoever wants to save their life will lose it, but whoever loses their life for me and for the gospel will save it'" (Mark 8:34–35).

Huh? What was He talking about? Deny yourself? Take up your cross? How can you save your life by losing it? I would guess many in the crowd that day heard Jesus' words with a glazed look in their eyes and never understood what He meant. They continued to believe in Him—yes, this was the Messiah—and they followed Him alongside the masses, who were awed by this King's power. Yet despite being near Jesus and surrounded by His fans, they never grasped His invitation to *truly* follow Him.

Sadly, not much has changed in two thousand years. Countless people still hang around the activity of King Jesus yet never take to heart His personal yet conditional invitation. They sit in church services, attend all the right Christian functions, and say all the right Christianese words, but they never understand that following Him means denying their fleshly desires by refusing to click on that seedy link or killing their desire to humiliate a coworker just to impress their boss. Somehow, real followship—the kind that affects every area of life—always seems to apply to someone else, just as many in the Jesus-following crowds thought as well.

It's not as if Jesus' requirements got any easier. To the rich ruler who wanted to follow Him, Jesus said, "You still lack one thing. Sell everything you have and give to the poor, and you will have treasure in heaven. Then come, follow me" (Luke 18:22). Is it any surprise that this young man left saddened?

When Jesus explained to His closest disciples what following Him meant, He said, "Anyone who loves their father or mother more than me is not worthy of me; anyone who loves their son or daughter more than me is not worthy of me. Whoever does not take up their cross and follow me is not worthy of me" (Matt. 10:37–38).

And maybe the most blatant example of the heavenly King making it difficult for the masses to follow Him is in Luke's account: "Large crowds were traveling with Jesus, and turning to them he said: 'If anyone comes to me and does not hate father and mother, wife and children, brothers and sisters—yes, even their own life—such a person cannot be my disciple. And whoever does not carry their cross and follow me cannot be my disciple'" (Luke 14:25–27).

Again and again Jesus spoke of His followers carrying their crosses. The analogy was crystal clear: They had to die, not a physical death but a death of self that, by Luke's recollection, had to occur *daily* (9:23). Instead of leading, they had to follow. Rather than preserving their "self," they were to die to all it entailed—identity, career, family, future—so they could experience true life in Jesus. They would give up a life of being their own god and exchange it for a life yielded to the one true God.

Why would anyone willingly do this? What would make following Jesus so worth it that you would kill your own dreams, desires, and will *every single day,* much less one time? For people to even remotely consider this, there had to be some serious incentive. And this is exactly why Jesus spoke so much about what His kingdom was like, as we'll cover in the next chapter. The world needed to hear that this heavenly kingdom—and its King—really was worth giving up everything for.

CHAPTER 10

A KINGDOM FIT FOR ITS KING

I DON'T KNOW any leaders who would amass a following of thousands of people, only to increasingly give those followers reasons to turn away. Yet that's exactly how Jesus responded to His rising popularity. In John 6 we see a fascinating example of His ministry's odd, seemingly backward progression.

The chapter begins with one of Jesus' most famous miracles: feeding five thousand men—probably a crowd of fifteen to twenty thousand in all—with only two fish and five small loaves of bread (John 6:1–13). Jesus then topped this unfathomable act with two others: walking on water and teleporting a boat full of His disciples across a lake (vv. 18, 21). At this point, Jesus' supernatural power was apparent to all. Finally, the Messiah had arrived and was making Himself known! In fact, John even highlights how the masses "intended to come and make him king by force" (v. 15). All hail Israel's Messiah-King, right?

Not so fast, because then Jesus began teaching.

The more Jesus spoke, the more He lost the crowds with His challenging words. Sadly, it wasn't just the strangers, hangers-on, or casual followers who began to leave. John specifically mentions that "from this time many of his *disciples* turned back and no longer followed him" (v. 66, emphasis added). These were ones who believed Jesus was the Messiah and had signed up for a lifestyle of closely following Him, mimicking His every move, and learning how to be just like Him. Yet the more Jesus revealed about Himself and what it meant to *truly* follow Him, the more these disciples fell by the wayside.

The mass exodus prompted Jesus to ask the twelve closest to Him, "You do not want to leave too, do you?" (v. 67). Peter answered with one of my favorite responses in the Bible: "Lord, to whom shall we go? You have the words of eternal life. We have come to believe and to know that you are the Holy One of God" (vv. 68–69).

There was no other option, no one else they would want to follow. Peter and the other disciples knew Jesus not just from a distance, but up close. They didn't just believe He was from God; they knew and trusted Him through intimate relationship. They would follow Jesus because of who He was, not for what they would get out of the journey. This is key for any disciple who longs to continue following the Lord despite facing great challenges. Lasting followship is based on intimate fellowship with Jesus.

But there's another foundational element to lasting followship. As inspiring as Peter's words were, they did not prevent him or any of the other remaining disciples from one day abandoning Jesus just as everyone else had. In His worst hour, when Jesus needed them the most, the disciples left their rabbi. Judas betrayed Him. Peter repeatedly denied ever knowing Him. And the rest hid for fear they would be caught by authorities. At that point things were just too difficult for them.

The truth is, we need the Lord's help to follow Him—and to continue following Him. Without His intervention, we will succumb to our old nature of self-preservation, doubt, and unbelief. Without His help, we will fall away, just like the rest. But it's not as if Jesus doesn't know this. He is not surprised by our being prone to weakness or unfaithfulness, and somehow, in His extreme kindness, He accredits our tiny seed of faith in Him (which He gave us to begin with!). He promises to be with us, just as He promised His disciples. They were full of fear following Jesus' crucifixion, and yet, upon receiving the Holy Spirit, they were radically transformed to follow Jesus even to death. In the same way, we who have "the Spirit of Jesus Christ" living within us can be encouraged that He will guide us in ongoing followship (Phil. 1:19).

Simply put, it takes Jesus to follow Jesus. This seems a bit backward, doesn't it? Why would God require something from us that necessitates His own help? How is it that we must repent and believe to enter God's kingdom, and yet God is involved in both? How can it be that He calls us to not only believe in Him but also follow Him, and yet we can only continue in such a way with His guidance?

Welcome to the nonlogical, higher ways of God.

Welcome to His upside-down kingdom.

THE KINGDOM IS LIKE …

God's kingdom is unlike any on earth. Because of this, Jesus spent much of His public ministry speaking about His kingdom, explaining it, and describing it in ways that could help those following Him relate to it. As history's greatest teacher, He used word pictures and parables, each packed with a slightly different glimpse of this multifaceted kingdom. In Matthew 13, for example, we get an entire series of parables on how "the kingdom of heaven is like":

- seed scattered on four different types of ground, each yielding different results (vv. 3–8; 18–23);
- weeds and wheat growing together and then being separated at harvest time (vv. 24–30; 37–43);
- a mustard seed that, despite its size, grows to become a massive tree (vv. 31–32);
- yeast working its way through a huge portion of dough (vv. 33);
- treasure discovered in a field that, when found, is worth selling everything to get (vv. 44);
- a fine pearl that, when discovered, is also worth giving up everything to buy (vv. 45–46); and
- a fishing net that brings in a mixed catch, which is then separated into good and bad (vv. 47–50).

Elsewhere, Jesus described the kingdom as a king settling accounts with his servants (Matt. 18:23–35), or like ten virgins with lamps waiting for the bridegroom (Matt. 25:1–13), or like a man entrusting his servants with his wealth while he goes away (Luke 19:11–27). Each of these kingdom parables contained a disturbing exclusivity, where some were brought into blessing and favor, while others missed out. The difference was what those individuals did—specifically, how they responded to the challenge they were given.

Every parable about Jesus' kingdom sounded wonderful for those who had "ears to hear," and He certainly *wanted* people to be able to hear the deeper truths of His kingdom (which is why He repeatedly said, "Whoever has ears to hear, let them hear" throughout His teachings; see, for example, Matthew 11:15 and Mark 4:9, 23). But for those who couldn't or wouldn't hear, the language of this kingdom seemed mysterious to the point of being indecipherable, like a door that refused to open, no matter how hard they pushed. Sadly, Jesus predicted this, telling His disciples there would always be those who, "though seeing ... do not see; though hearing ... do not hear or understand" (Matt. 13:13). The reason, He explained, was their "calloused" hearts (Matt.13:15).

Isn't it interesting the Israelites of Jesus' day could not escape the same hard-heartedness that plagued the previous generations led by Moses, by Samuel, or by Rehoboam or any of the numerous other kings the people asked for? Even after four hundred postexilic years of seeking to follow God's instructions, and even with their true leader, the Messiah, standing before them, most Israelites still had such calloused hearts they could not or would not hear their King's call.

Are we any different today? I know far too many people whose hearts have become so hardened they cannot see or hear the truth of Jesus' words. Many of those people never received His words in the first place. Some claimed to be Christians before, only now they blame Him. "If Jesus wants everyone saved," they argue, "then why did He make the way of salvation so narrow?" In other words, how can the same King who came to open His kingdom to everyone be so excluding?

If these people were king, I am certain their kingdom would not be so inclusive as Jesus'. Their standard of entrance probably wouldn't be denying self and taking up your cross, but it would be something that undoubtedly excluded a type of people such as racists, bigots, rapists, murderers, Republicans or Democrats (depending on their own leaning), Yankees fans, people who eat at McDonald's—you get my point. We all at some level would rule differently from Jesus, and the hardness of our own hearts would be exposed by whom we exclude.

Jesus, as the ultimate King, has every right to exclude whomever He wants. He has all authority and power; therefore, He can set the standard for His kingdom to include or exclude whatever types of people He wants. Whether we think the standards of His kingdom are inclusive or exclusive makes no difference; He is King and therefore has the right to decide.

But it's important that we get our facts straight. Jesus actually *hasn't* excluded anyone—yet. One day He will (more on that in the next chapter). But for now, the good news of His kingdom is that everyone still has an opportunity to enter it, and this is what Jesus came announcing. His conditions for entering may seem hard, narrow, or exclusive to some, yet in truth they are simple—even childlike—and outlandishly generous. And His descriptions of the kingdom reflect a King so willing to welcome and befriend His natural enemies that any earthly king would call Him foolish.

So I would ask anyone today who questions Jesus' authority as King the same thing: *Have you considered all of what Jesus taught about His own kingdom?* I ask because it seems clear to me that this King has turned the tables: It's actually *we* who choose whether we want in or out of His kingdom, and the decision starts within our own hearts.

That, tragically, is our main problem—the same timeless problem that has haunted all who would prefer to lead themselves rather than follow God.

Once again, the crucial deciding factor boils down to a single question: *Will you follow?*

THE INSIDE-OUT, UPSIDE-DOWN KINGDOM

If Matthew's Gospel has one continuously beating drum, it is the reverberating theme of who's in and who's out of the kingdom. As his account goes from story to story, we repeatedly see the same question posed: Who will follow Jesus as King and enter His kingdom, and who will not? And surprise!—each group includes people we would never expect.

The kingdom Jesus described to the masses sounded glorious, but it also seemed offensive and threatening to those accustomed to being in control. In His kingdom, the weak became strong, the poor got to be rich, the last were put in first place, and the least were made the greatest. For those who were accustomed to being "out" on the margins, this was good news—fantastic news, to be exact. How else could you describe suddenly being given another chance at life when life itself had almost finished you off? The poor, oppressed, and destitute were now welcomed into a kingdom with a completely different value system.

For those who thought they were "in"—the religious leaders, political authorities, wealthy, and powerful—Jesus' parable descriptions of His kingdom were simultaneously perplexing and haunting. The more you chewed on them, the more you realized just how intrusive and radical this King was. The kingdom He described wasn't just different from all others; it was opposite. It was strange and seemingly backward. It was upside down.

That Jesus' heavenly kingdom was now "upside down" from what was on earth shows how far humanity had gone in twisting God's original plan for the planet. Virtually anywhere humans lived they produced not the peace and blessing God desired but instead fruits of another kingdom—fruits such as pride, domination, violence, deceit, and hatred. As the ultimate King, Jesus continued to drive out this satanic kingdom throughout His ministry with supernatural power. He could heal sicknesses and deliver people from demons. But the values of His kingdom still had to be reinforced through His teaching for "those with ears to hear."

For example, His kingdom honored those who were weak—thus, Jesus said it belonged to the likes of little children, the poor in spirit, and the persecuted, among others (Matt. 5:3, 10; 19:14). The greatest masters would be those who stooped the lowest to serve, reflecting Jesus' posture of constantly submitting to His Father and the Father constantly glorifying His Son.

In Jesus' kingdom, you were to go to extreme lengths to love your enemies, bless those who persecuted you, and forgive wrongdoers instead of retaliating. If you were despised, poor in spirit, or a peacemaker on earth, you would actually be blessed in this heavenly kingdom.

The desire for wealth and material things could not rule people in Jesus' kingdom, which is why He warned that it was virtually impossible for the rich to enter without God's miraculous intervention (Matt. 19:23–26). (It also explains why He mentioned selling all your possessions on a handful of occasions.)

Jesus also went to great lengths to warn those who prided themselves on being holy. "Truly I tell you, the tax collectors and the prostitutes are entering the kingdom of God ahead of you," He told the chief priests and elders. "For John came to you to show you the way of righteousness, and you did not believe him, but the tax collectors and the prostitutes did. And even after you saw this, you did not repent and believe him" (Matt. 21:31–32).

Can you see how the good news—repent and believe for the kingdom has come near!—had suddenly turned into bad news for these religious elite? Jesus' emerging kingdom meant theirs would be diminishing. If they were not humble enough to submit to Jesus' authority and leadership, they would suffer the consequences.

It is no different today, and not only for the religious elite but for all those who pride themselves on being more like God (or closer to Him) than others. When we begin admiring our own holiness and beauty, we would do well to remember who also started down that path. If you recall from chapter 5, Satan's pride was what launched his eternal descent. His desire to be like God consumes him to this day, and he is obsessed with seeing as many as possible destroyed along with him. One of the greatest traps he lays for us, then, is tempting us to do what he did and take God's place on the throne of our lives. The devil loves it when we refuse the Lord's perfect leadership and instead act as our own god.

We were not made to be God, however. We were made to partner with Him in perfect followship, not to attempt to supplant Him as supreme leader (which, by the way, not a single being has ever succeeded in doing throughout history). Jesus came to earth announcing the good news that despite our sinful hearts that continually reject God's leadership, He has made a way for perfect fellowship to be restored. We can follow once again! We can follow the King into His kingdom!

It is no coincidence, then, that the ultimate key to Jesus' kingdom was also His most common teaching. It's the only thing He taught that's found in all four Gospel accounts, and it's mentioned six times. In fact, based on what we know about Jesus' travels, we know He taught it in at least four different settings, but given how much of His teaching we *don't* have recorded, it's likely far more than that.[1] So what was the key to Jesus' kingdom that was so important it's highlighted in every Gospel?

If you want to live, you have to die.

The writers present slightly different variations of the wording, but the essence is the same. (See Matthew 10:39; 16:25; Mark 8:35; Luke 9:24; 17:33; and John 12:25.) It's only when we give up everything that we can gain everything. Only by losing control of our lives can we find a far greater freedom. And it's only when we die to ourselves that we can be resurrected to true life—life in Jesus.

The apostle Paul explained this beautifully in the latter part of his own life: "For to me, to live is Christ and to die is gain. … Whatever were gains to me I now consider loss for the sake of Christ. What is more, I consider everything a loss because of the surpassing worth of knowing Christ Jesus my Lord, for whose sake I have lost all things. I consider them garbage, that I may gain Christ and be found in him" (Phil. 1:21; 3:7–9).

There it is! The key to the kingdom is not only our dying so we can "be found in Him," but it's also that Jesus *is* worth it! Knowing Him is worth losing everything. Being back in relationship with Him—following Him in fellowship—really is worth the price of dying to our self-delusional independence where we think we have control of our lives. If following Him ultimately means dying to self, then we're back at the same fundamental question: *Will you follow?* Only now, we can rephrase it more accurately according to the kingdom: *Will you die?*

THE ROMAN TRIUMPH

You have to die to live.

What a crazy, upside-down principle. It's illogical, sounds like absolute foolishness to this world, and doesn't make sense unless you have "ears to hear." But foolish or not, it is the truth of Jesus' kingdom. And there is no greater evidence of this upside-down kingdom principle than Jesus' own death.

Indeed, to gain a deeper understanding of just how inverted Jesus' kingdom is, I want us to examine the details surrounding His death. As we do, we'll discover that only in His kingdom can the seemingly worst defeat become the greatest victory ever. What should have been the most humiliating, horrific hours of Jesus' life are in fact His most triumphant. Keep in mind, however, that only those with kingdom vision perceive this as victory. Just as Jesus' kingdom is upside down, His actions can seem to be as well, and they challenge us to the core with what we think is kingly.

Long before Jesus' time, the Roman Empire would honor a victorious military general's success in battle by staging a "triumph" for him. These elaborate celebrations lasted all day and involved multiple elements, symbolisms, and ceremonies as part of parading the general through the heart of a city for the public to honor him like a god. During Jesus' lifetime, triumphs were reserved for the emperor (and on rare occasion, a member of his family) and became far less frequent. A triumph not only was the means for the emperor to pronounce victory over a significant enemy but also served as his deification ceremony. Because Romans believed the emperor to be appointed by the gods, his triumph was the focal point of the entire empire and was expected to culminate in a supernatural sign affirming his divinity.[2]

When Mark wrote his Gospel account of Jesus' death, he knew his Roman readers would be well acquainted with the emperor's triumph, including each phase of the procession. He also knew they might struggle to see how Jesus' death on a Roman cross, enforced by Roman soldiers under Roman rule, was in any way victorious for the one who claimed to be King of a greater, heavenly kingdom. Mark's purpose, then, was to portray Jesus' final hours through a spiritual lens for those who had "eyes to see" it as a triumph.

As Bible scholar Thomas E. Schmidt says, "Mark presents the crucifixion as an 'anti-triumph'—with Jesus mocked and killed—to show that the seeming scandal of the cross is actually an exaltation of Christ."[3] Let's take a look at how the Roman emperor's coronating procession serves as the contextual backdrop for Mark's account of the "victory march" that culminated in a Jewish King dying on a cross.[*]

---

[*] Credit needs to be given here to Thomas E. Schmidt, whose work comparing Mark's account with the Roman triumphal procession is fascinating and has been commended by many respected Bible teachers.

In the Roman emperor's triumph, his entire army of personal bodyguards, called the Praetorian Guard, would gather en masse in the courtyard of the palace. (For some emperors, this could mean thousands of men.) Soldiers would then clothe the emperor with two special items taken from the temple Jupiter Capitolinus, where there stood a statue of Jupiter, the king of the gods (Rome's equivalent of the Greek god Zeus). The first item was a purple robe decorated with gold embroidery (it was illegal for anyone other than royalty to wear purple); the second was a gold laurel wreath. Both signified the emperor being clothed in royalty and divinity. As their final act in the praetorium, soldiers would shower the emperor with shouts of praise, hailing him as lord of all and the one sent by the gods. In some cases, the emperor would then distribute gifts among his bodyguards as they essentially worshipped him.[4]

After being adorned with clothing and praise, the emperor would sit in an elevated chair in his chariot or a litter carried upon the shoulders of his soldiers. He would then be led out into the streets by his Praetorian Guard in a royal procession that paraded him before the "adoring" public (who were usually forced to attend). Some sources indicate there would be incense altars set up along the way to continue the worship and adoration of this "heaven-sent" ruler. Certainly, the crowds were expected to continue the shouts of honor and praise as he passed.

Many artistic renditions of the triumphal procession depict a sacrificial bull as part of the parade. The bull would be dressed and crowned to signify an association with the emperor. This was no average bull, however. The Romans (and triumph-staging Greeks before them) saw the bull as a divine symbol of the gods that played a key part in the climax of any triumph. An imperial official walked beside the bull carrying a double-bladed ax—the instrument of death for the sacrifice.

The triumphal procession would always end at Capitoline Hill, Rome's famous hill upon which stood the most important temple in the empire, Jupiter Capitolinus. Legend held that while laying the foundations of the temple, workers found a man's severed head, prompting the name (*caput* means "head" in Latin) and a prediction that this place "shall be the head of all Italy."[5]

Next would come the triumph's key stage: the sacrifice to the gods. As the altar was prepared, the emperor would be offered a cup of wine mixed with myrrh. This was no cheap drink; the mixture was an expensive delicacy, fit for royalty. To prove his opulence and authority, the emperor would reject the precious drink and instead pour it onto the altar or upon the bull being sacrificed. But his response wasn't impulsive; it was full of tradition and meaning. The Romans believed the slaughtered animal took on the form of a god, who would inhabit the emperor and further affirm his divinity. The wine, then, represented the precious blood of a god-like victim poured out to transform.

According to some historians, at this point the emperor would perform his first act as a now-deified ruler. To demonstrate that he possessed power over life and death itself, the emperor would randomly decide from among a group of prisoners which ones would be executed. He would then ascend the steps of Jupiter Capitolinus and sit on a throne with the temple's high priest on his right and his chief commander on his left, signifying his preeminence over all other royal and imperial figures. The crowds would once again sing his praises, only now as lord *and* god. And in some cases, they would even wait for a sign from heaven to show the gods' further approval.

THE KING'S TRIUMPH

Keeping the details and progression of the Roman triumph in mind, let's now take a step-by-step and verse-by-verse look at how Jesus' final moments, as recorded in Mark 15:16–33, compare.

1. Roman triumph: The entire Praetorian Guard is called together.

Jesus' triumph: "The soldiers led Jesus away into the palace (that is, the Praetorium) and called together the whole company of soldiers" (v. 16). Because it would have been highly unusual for even a hundred men to gather just for the sake of a single Jewish prisoner, it seems likely that Mark is intentionally using this language—even specifying the location as the praetorium—to trigger his Roman readers' association with the triumph process from the very beginning of this section.

2. Roman triumph: Soldiers clothe the emperor in a purple robe and gold crown.

Jesus' triumph: "They put a purple robe on him, then twisted together a crown of thorns and set it on him" (v. 17).

3. Roman triumph: Soldiers praise the emperor.

Jesus' triumph: "And they began to call out to him, 'Hail, king of the Jews!' Again and again they struck him on the head with a staff and spit on him. Falling on their knees, they paid homage to him" (vv. 18–19).

4. Roman triumph: Soldiers parade the emperor through the streets before an "adoring" public.

Jesus' triumph: "And when they had mocked him, they took off the purple robe and put his own clothes on him. Then they led him out to crucify him" (v. 20). It's interesting to note the connection here between the afflicted one (Jesus) willingly carrying His cross upon His shoulders and the so-called "adored one" (the emperor) essentially forcing his soldiers to carry him upon theirs while parading him through a crowd that had little choice but to praise him. While the emperor of Rome elevated himself to be reluctantly worshipped by all, the King of kings lowered Himself to serve all.

5. Roman triumph: An official carries the instrument of death for the sacrificial bull.

Jesus' triumph: "A certain man from Cyrene, Simon, the father of Alexander and Rufus, was passing by on his way in from the country, and they forced him to carry the cross" (v. 21). Although other Gospel writers mention Simon of Cyrene, it is no coincidence that Mark mentions him at this very point in the procession. Jesus' march toward death continues to be uncannily ordered in line with the sequence of events in the emperor's triumph.

6. Roman triumph: The procession ends at Capitoline Hill, the place of the "dead" head.

Jesus' triumph: "They brought Jesus to the place called Golgotha (which means 'the place of the skull')" (v. 22). Just to recap: The emperor ascends a hill as his final stop to the place of sacrifice specifically named after a severed head. Jesus ascends to "the place of the skull." Mere coincidence? I doubt it.

7. Roman triumph: The emperor refuses wine mixed with myrrh and then pours it out on the altar as part of the transforming sacrifice.

Jesus' triumph: "Then they offered him wine mixed with myrrh, but he did not take it. And they crucified him. Dividing up his clothes, they cast lots to see what each would get" (vv. 23–24).

The parallels are almost too many to comprehend here. First, notice how the emperor pours out the refused wine, just as Jesus poured out His blood. More figuratively, He "poured out" His life, which was rejected by the world to such an extent that they slaughtered Him like the bull. As Bible scholar Thomas E. Schmidt spells out, "The bull is the god who dies and appears as the victor in the person of the triumphator. ... At the crucial moment of a triumph, the moment of sacrifice, expensive wine is poured out."[6]

It's hard to not make another parallel between the wine of the Roman altar and the wine of the Last Supper, about which Jesus said, "This is my blood of the covenant, which is poured out for many" (Mark 14:24).

In addition, we see yet another connection in the blood of the bull that, when taken in by the gods as an acceptable sacrifice, supposedly transforms the emperor into a god-like figure. Likewise, Jesus' shed blood was the acceptable sacrifice on behalf of all humanity that made a way for each of us to be transformed into His divine image.

8. Roman triumph: The emperor ascends to his throne with two lesser figures on his left and right.

Jesus' triumph: "It was nine in the morning when they crucified him. The written notice of the charge against him read: THE KING OF THE JEWS. They crucified two rebels with him, one on his right and one on his left" (vv. 25–27).

Jesus ascended not to sit on a throne but to hang on a cross. His placard could not have been more truthful and yet it hung in ironic jest, an attempt to mock the man on whom the Jews had once hung their hopes. And flanking Jesus' sides were not two men of rank but two political criminals. This humiliating mockery was the upside-down coronation of not only the true King of the Jews but, in fact, the King of the universe.

9. Roman triumph: The people praise the emperor, seeing him now in his exalted state.

Jesus' triumph: "Those who passed by hurled insults at him, shaking their heads and saying, 'So! You who are going to destroy the temple and build it in three days, come down from the cross and save yourself!' In the same way the chief priests and the teachers of the law mocked him among themselves. 'He saved others,' they said, 'but he can't save himself! Let this Messiah, this king of Israel, come down now from the cross, that we may see and believe.' Those crucified with him also heaped insults on him" (vv. 29–32).

Just as the Roman crowds would shout praises and adore their exalted emperor as he sat on the throne, the Jewish crowds (now comprised almost entirely of religious leaders) showered Jesus with insults and vitriol as He hung on the cross. "This Messiah, this king of Israel" could have come down at any second. He could have forced His point and instantly humiliated His mockers by releasing Himself from the cross. Instead, He suffered so that they too could possibly enter His kingdom. Even with every heavenly being on command, longing to come to the aid of their King, Jesus resisted the temptation to exalt Himself—all for us, all for a humanity that He loved unto death.

10. Roman triumph: The people await a sign from heaven to indicate the gods' response.

Jesus' triumph: "At noon, darkness came over the whole land until three in the afternoon (v. 33). When the Pharisees told Jesus to silence His disciples for praising "the king who comes in the name of the Lord," He responded by saying, "I tell you … if they keep quiet, the stones will cry out" (Luke 19:38, 40). Here at Jesus' upside-down triumph, the heavens could not refrain from a response of grief. Upon His death, Luke's Gospel explains that "the sun stopped shining" (23:45). Matthew adds that the "earth shook, the rocks split and the tombs broke open" (Matt. 27:51–52). Indeed, the earth wailed, wept, and groaned as its King suffered and died. But …

BUT …

That was not the end. As we know, there was more to this triumph than a coronation that ended on the cross because unlike that for a Roman war hero or emperor, the King of kings' triumph had a greater purpose than self-exaltation or being approved by the gods. Jesus *was* God. He did not need to hear others tell Him that. Instead, He needed to rescue the citizens of earth so they could enter His kingdom of heaven to eventually restore heaven on earth as He had wanted to do all along. And to complete that rescue mission, He had one last enemy to defeat. It wasn't Judas, His betrayer. Nor was it the mocking religious leaders gloating at the cross.

No, Jesus' last enemy was death itself. The King of life had to venture into the uncharted territory of hell. As He died and descended into hell—the real enemy's territory—Jesus faced His last real fight.

It wasn't even close.

As Peter told the Jewish crowds on the day of Pentecost: "It was impossible for death to keep its hold on him" (Acts 2:24). Satan was no match for Jesus— he never has been—and neither was his ultimate weapon, death. On the third day, Jesus rose from the grave, never to die again. And through His eternal resurrection, the Messiah-King did what the prophets from hundreds of years before had already said He would do: "I will deliver this people from the power of the grave; I will redeem them from death. Where, O death, are your plagues? Where, O grave, is your destruction?" (Hos. 13:14).

Only a perfectly upside-down King like Jesus would be willing to descend into hell so He could raise everyone else out the pit of sin and death. And only an upside-down kingdom like His triumphs over all others by turning the ultimate sign of weakness and domination—the cross—into the ultimate sign of power and love.

The cross is what we cling to as believers. It is our saving grace—the living symbol of God's love for us, poured out through the precious life of Jesus. We cling to it because it assures us of what Jesus has done for us that no one else could do: restore us to God.

Yet the cross is also what continually calls us to die, to venture the same narrow way as our Savior. It is still an instrument of death. And when Jesus called us to take up our cross and follow Him, He was not joking. His cross challenges us daily with the same penetrating questions: Will you follow? Will you endure the same "triumph" as Jesus? Will you walk the road paved with hardship, suffering, pain, insults, persecution, and a thousand other things we think will kill us?

From a distance, that path doesn't seem so triumphant, does it? It seems like weakness. It seems like foolishness. In fact, Paul said the exact same thing in 1 Corinthians 1:18: "For the message of the cross is foolishness to those who are perishing." Can I get an amen? We can expect the world to mock us as weak and mark us as idiots when we cling to the cross.

"But ..." Paul wasn't finished: "But to us who are being saved it is the power of God" (1 Cor. 1:18). *To us who are being saved.* To those who have heard the good news, who have repented and believed, who are walking in the kingdom because we continue to follow the King—to those the cross is the power of God. This is why we not only treasure the cross, but we *choose* the cross just as our Lord did. The cross is true victory, true freedom, and true life—life in the resurrected Jesus who has defeated death! So what seems like weakness is actually power. And what seems foolish is actually wisdom. As Paul puts it: "God chose the foolish things of the world to shame the wise; God chose the weak things of the world to shame the strong" (1 Cor. 1:27).

Once again, this sounds like the traces of an upside-down King and an upside-down kingdom, doesn't it? While Jesus' procession to the cross seems like the ultimate display of weakness for a King, He turned everything upside down. The insults became praise. His injuries became our healing. The cross became His throne. Death became life.

When you think about it, how else could it be in His upside-down kingdom? Jesus' crucifixion was not a defeat but instead the way to the greatest triumph. But still, what a mysterious, glorious way for a kingdom to come!

CHAPTER 11

THE RETURN OF THE KING

ISRAEL'S RELIGIOUS LEADERSHIP rejected Jesus as the long-awaited Messiah-King and had Him killed to preserve their own power and status. The public, though they once believed in Jesus as the promised one, increasingly rejected Him the more He spoke about Himself and the cost of following Him. And today most Jews reject Jesus as their Messiah because such a response has sadly become inherent to modern-day Judaism.

None of these things changes the fact that Jesus is the rightful King of Israel. He is their long-awaited Messiah and the one whom God appointed from the beginning of time to show Israel—and the world—what perfect followship is. Just because Israel today rejects Jesus as their King and Savior does not mean He isn't. As mentioned briefly before, one day Jesus will return to save His people. On that day, He will finally be recognized by everyone as King of Israel and King of all.

Although all people—Jews and Gentiles—will acknowledge Him, I believe most of the world's population will still be shocked when Jesus comes back to earth as its returning King. Many will be in disbelief out of ignorance—because they didn't expect Him to return or didn't think He existed. But I believe countless others will be in shock because of how different He is from what they expected. What they thought He'd be like will be nothing like who He really is.

Today Jesus is often presented as everyone's buddy. With the message of grace so predominant these days, many believe that no matter what you do, no matter how much you continue to sin, Jesus will always be your best friend—the pal who overlooks your flaws and loves you no matter what. Of course, there is some truth to that; Jesus' love reaches out to us again and again, despite our sinful nature. But when love is one of the only aspects of the Lord people perpetually hear about in sermons and songs, is it any surprise the kind of Jesus this generation believes in? When the Barna Group asked American believers to describe Jesus, the most frequently used words were *accepting, warm, brave, strong, practical,* and *fun-loving*. (Interestingly enough, the same study found that only 59 percent believe He will return to earth someday.)[1]

Over the last few generations, we've increasingly developed a "nicer" image of Jesus. He's seen as soft and fuzzy, warm and kind, like a velveteen figure on an old felt Sunday school board. He's gentle, patient, and oh-so-loving. He's like Santa Claus—the children love climbing in His lap, and the adults all smile at Him. What a nice, cute, likeable guy.

I never want to make light of Jesus' extreme love, His gentleness, or any of His wonderful characteristics. At the same time, I shudder to think how shocked people will be when Jesus comes back and they see Him face-to-face for the first time. I am convinced many, including those who say they know Jesus, will hardly recognize Him as the most powerful King ever because they don't know what the Bible says about His return. They base their image of Him on their ideas rather than on what He's actually told us. Not only is that frightening, but it will also be the ruin of many.

When Jesus returns He will not come as a giant, soft teddy bear. He won't come singing "Kumbaya" as He tip-toes through the tulips. In case you have not read the Book of Revelation or any of the Old Testament's end-time prophecies, let me give you a spoiler alert: Jesus will come in awesome, terrifying power to judge the nations. He will return as history's mightiest warrior and King, and the scene of His arrival will not be pretty for any of those remaining on earth.

I know many Christians who mostly ignore these parts of Scripture, yet by doing so they're missing out on seeing a more complete picture of who Jesus is and how He leads. Understanding the Lord's leadership in the future can strengthen our followship journey with Him today. So while we have spent the last few chapters looking at various aspects of who Jesus is as the perfect Messiah-King, let's now see what we learn from His imminent return.

WHAT A DAY!

Scripture refers to the time surrounding Jesus' return as "the day of the Lord" (1 Cor. 5:5), "the day of God" (2 Pet. 3:12), or "that day" (2 Thess. 2:3, 2 Tim. 4:8). Sometimes the Bible presents this as a literal day, while at other times it is a season or longer period. Either way, it's important for us to understand what will occur on this "day," particularly since hundreds of scriptures connect to this point in history—what we call the end times. Some of these scriptures been partially fulfilled; others remain open-ended. While I challenge you to study the end times for yourself, let me offer a brief overview of how I believe the Bible describes what happens during this season. You may disagree with me on various eschatological points or their timing—people have argued for centuries over how much of the Bible's end-times language is to be taken literally. Regardless, I hope you can still see what a major factor Jesus' leadership—and the world's yielding to it—will be on the day of the Lord.

In Daniel 9, the angel Gabriel gave the prophet a timeline of future events related to Israel and the Messiah's return. In this, Gabriel mentioned a "ruler who will come" (not Jesus) and "confirm a covenant with many for one 'seven'" (vv. 26–27). I believe that is a literal seven-year period in which the forces of evil will increasingly rise to power and govern the world. During this period, Satan's supernaturally empowered puppet, the Antichrist (literally, the anti-Messiah), will be adored by the nations as the leader who brings peace and unity to the world. After three and a half years of ascending to global power, this man will demand to be worshipped and reveal his true intentions: to kill all Jews and followers of Jesus. This point marks the beginning of the day of the Lord (the longer "day"), when God will begin to pour out His wrath on earth in what we call the great tribulation.

The word *tribulation* means tremendous distress or suffering, but I doubt we'll ever truly understand the depths of this word until we see the horrific events of the great tribulation before Jesus' return. During that three-and-a-half-year period, God will allow various increasing expressions of judgment to change the face of the earth and its inhabitants. John refers to these judgments in his Book of Revelation as the seven seals, seven trumpets, and seven bowls. What is God's purpose with these twenty-one portions of wrath? He wants to restore earth to what He originally planned for it. Essentially, the Lord will do another reboot of the planet because of humanity's utter defilement of it, just as He did with Noah. Only this time there will not be a flood; this time the Lord will cleanse the earth using judgments such as global famine, earthquakes, hail, fire, toxic water, plagues, darkness, and demonic creatures.

During this season of intense judgment, the number of homicides around the world will skyrocket (Rev. 6:4). Economies will collapse under the strain of food shortages, wars, and disease (Rev. 6:5–8). An oceanic disaster will destroy a third of the world's sea creatures and ships (Rev. 8:8–9). Global pandemics will become the norm (Rev. 9:13–21; 16:2). And the earth's protective atmospheric layers will apparently diminish, causing direct sunlight to scorch the planet's inhabitants (Rev. 16:8–9).

God's wrath is a challenging idea to grasp. Many people respond by getting frustrated at God or accusing Him. It's natural to have questions when we read accounts of the Lord pouring out His wrath on the world like the judgments described in Revelation. How can a God who's supposed to be full of love not just allow but *inflict* so much suffering and pain on His own creation? Isn't this the same God who loved the world in such a way that He sent Jesus to save it?

I cannot do justice to all the questions involving God's wrath without veering far off the thread we are tracing throughout this book regarding Jesus' leadership and our followship. Let me encourage you to ask the Lord Himself and dive into His Word both alone and with others to see how He answers those questions. But in light of understanding Jesus' leadership and our invitation into followship, it is important for us to at least address one all-encompassing question regarding God's wrath in the end times: *Why?*

A DAY OF RECKONING

What if there were no consequences for any of our actions in life? Sometimes it can seem like the world operates this way when we look at the injustice all around us. I'm not just referring to the global corporation that received a mere slap on the wrist after committing a billion-dollar crime or the country that regularly dumps massive amounts of toxic waste into the ocean but is never penalized.

Those are certainly frustrating examples of injustice, but let's bring the issue closer to home. What about the job you didn't get because the company opted to hire someone you know lied on his résumé? Or what about the girl awarded an academic scholarship, even though there's proof that she cheated on multiple tests? Or what about the mechanic whose business is booming but who makes racist remarks and seems to always charge you more than customers who have the same color skin as him?

We know life isn't fair. But it seems even worse when people doing wrong things end up ahead, especially if you're doing all the right things and still are floundering.

The Bible is full of people asking the same type of questions you've probably had. Jeremiah asked, "Why does the way of the wicked prosper? Why do all the faithless live at ease?" (Jer. 12:1). A suffering Job cried out to God with a similar question: "Why do the wicked prosper, growing old and powerful?" (Job 21:7, NLT). And the psalmist was honest enough to ask, "How long, LORD, will the wicked ... be jubilant?" (Ps. 94:3).

The day of the Lord puts an end to those questions. It is the "day" of reckoning—the concluding period in human history when the world's ever-growing account of sin and evil will be dealt with. To be clear, this is not the final judgment, nor is it the final time evil will appear on earth. (We'll address both at the end of this chapter.) But the day of the Lord does include an initial judgment in which the wicked who hate Jesus will receive their just recompense (at least in part).

This brings up a secondary question that's often asked by those skeptical about the fairness of God's wrath: Why is all this judgment necessary? In other words, why does God go to such extremes to inflict pain and suffering on people? Isn't one round of His wrath enough?

It's easy to read about the seven seals, seven trumpets, and seven bowls and assume God is going overboard. In fact, the easiest thing to do is to hear about these judgments and accuse the Lord of being sadistic. For some people, the sum of the judgments seems too harsh, especially if the earth's inhabitants in that day are having to suffer for humanity's cumulative sinfulness throughout all history.

Let me stop you before you go down that path and remind you of the bigger picture. Let's quickly review God's story with humanity: God created a perfect world. Humans messed up and, instead of partnering with their perfect leader, decided to lead themselves, which put them in partnership with the one in constant opposition to God—Satan. This harmful decision and partnership set them on a new path of ongoing sin, a path of walking away from God instead of with Him. Even when God repeatedly made a way for humanity to walk with Him in followship, people continually chose their own way—and paid for it with the consequences of sin (e.g., pain, suffering, death, and so on). In the process, the entire planet also suffered from these ramifications.

God sent His Son to make another way for people, but this way required them to die to their sinful nature and follow Him in the opposite direction. Some chose this, others rejected it, yet God has since left the way open for as long as possible. Meanwhile, the effects of people's sin continue to expand and spread like a virus ruining everything—and this will only get worse until the last days. Only the Lord knows when those days will culminate and when no one on earth (apart from His chosen people, Israel) will choose His way. When that time comes, He will pour out His wrath to cleanse the world of evil. Even then—in the middle of this great tribulation—God will still offer a way for people to repent, yet they will refuse. To conclude this great cleansing, Jesus will appear in person to rid the world of its rebelliousness and establish a world of perfect righteousness that reflects the Lord, just as it was originally supposed to.

If people have continually gone against God since the Garden of Eden and continually ruined the earth with the fruits of sin, is it unfair for the Lord to finally put a stop to that? Certainly not! If He alone knows what measure of judgments are necessary to complete the cleansing, then is it unjust for Him to release those? I don't think so—especially not when we consider who will be left on earth during the great tribulation.

Imagine you gave me the keys to your brand-new car and on my very first drive out, I crashed it. Somehow, you not only forgave me, but you paid for the car's repairs. Because you still trusted me, you continued to let me drive it. But you also noticed that often I would return your car with a ding here, a busted taillight there … until eventually I crashed your car again. And again. And again.

The car started having bigger problems. Each time you would repair it, but you noticed that I no longer felt bad about damaging the vehicle, nor did I offer to fix it. In fact, even after crashing it a few more times I began to blame you for the accidents.

If this story were true, tell me: How long would it take you to stop giving me the keys to your car? Probably not long at all. I don't know many people who would let *anyone* drive their car again if that person had already crashed it twice—for the car's sake and for the sake of keeping the person alive!

God's love for people has extended far, far past the point it should have. In His mercy He has continued to offer us the keys to His kingdom, and in His faithfulness to His own commitment, He has withheld from destroying us, even while we destroy ourselves and all creation around us. Older Bible translations tell of the Lord being "longsuffering," and I think that's a good way to describe His dealings with us. He has certainly suffered a long time with humanity's persistence to reject Him and rule ourselves, and yet as Peter said, "He is patient with us, because He does not want any to perish, but all to come to repentance" (2 Pet. 3:9, MEV).

The Lord's end-time judgments are part of His perfect leadership. Those who remain true to Him, who continue to follow Him even through history's greatest time of peril, He will lead into eternity, where they'll walk in perfect followship with Him.* However, those who refuse His leadership will face a far different outcome—one that is in no way excessive or unjust.

---

* I am intentionally avoiding any discussion of the rapture to keep our focus on the purposes for Jesus' return as they relate to His leadership. Of course, one of the primary reasons for Christ's return is to "gather his elect" (Matt. 24:31), and this is not only a hope we carry as believers but also a key event to know about. However, I have found that often when Christians discuss the end times, they quickly focus on the timeline of events and, more specifically, different eschatological positions (i.e., Are you premillennial? Postmillennial? Amillennial? Pre-tribulation? Post-tribulation?). Although I believe such viewpoints are important, each requires further explanation, and my purpose for this chapter is not to discuss these stances but instead highlight the challenge of Jesus' return for us as believers and for the world at large.

UNWELCOME BACK

The Lord's judgments will throw the world into complete chaos during the great tribulation. Daniel described these years as "a time of distress such as has not happened from the beginning of nations until then" (12:1). God will shake "the nations in the sieve of destruction" (Isa. 30:28).

If that again sounds unfair, let me remind you who will be on earth at this point. Jesus, the King of kings, will return to a planet filled with people who despise Him and His way of leading. These aren't people who don't know Him and are just mad about Him causing chaos in the world. No, these people will have such hardened hearts that they will have rejected the Lord again and again at every opportunity in which they could have turned to Him. For example, the Bible says the cosmic disorder of the sixth seal will result in such massive earthquakes and geological shifts that those left will wish they were dead so they could avoid "the wrath of the Lamb" (Rev. 6:16). Amazingly, these people will feel no remorse nor beg God to relent. In John's vision, he saw how they repeatedly "cursed the God of heaven" after many of these judgments, "but they did not repent of their evil deeds and turn to God" (Rev. 16:11, NLT).

Even amid the great tribulation, humanity will still shake its collective fist at God while being unable to escape His increasing judgments. It's no wonder why Paul indirectly described those remaining on earth during these days like this: "They refused to love the truth and so be saved. For this reason God sends them a powerful delusion so that they will believe the lie and so that all will be condemned who have not believed the truth but have delighted in wickedness" (2 Thess. 2:10–12).

The Bible also tells us that people from around the world will conspire and plot against the Lord (Ps. 2:1). They will compare living under His leadership to being in "chains" and "shackles" (Ps. 2:3). Out of this hatred, "the kings of the earth [will] rise up and the rulers band together against the LORD and against his anointed"—specifically Jesus (Ps. 2:2). The global leaders and the masses who follow them won't be alone in their rage but will gladly be accompanied and even empowered by the satanic forces that create a unified opposition to the Lord. These same demons, rulers, authorities, powers, and principalities have partnered with fallen humanity to stain this world for thousands of years with sin, unrighteousness, and countless other fruits from the kingdom of darkness.

During the last days, deceiving spirits, operating through false teachings, false prophets, and false messiahs, will dupe millions of people, maybe even billions, into the wrong kingdom—including "even the elect" who will fall away from their faith, as Jesus warned (Matt. 24:24; 1 Tim. 4:1). These evil forces, under the leadership of the Antichrist, will convince the world that the Jewish people are the problem. As the intensity of God's judgments increase, so will the world's hatred for His people.

God will supernaturally protect Israel for a season (Rev. 12:6), but eventually all nations will assemble at Armageddon with a united goal: to wipe the already diminished Israel—especially Jerusalem—off the map (Zech. 14:2). The kingdom of darkness—now a mixture of humans, demons, and spiritual beings—will unite not only to destroy Israel but also to challenge Jesus to a physical battle.

This is the setting for Jesus' return. These are the ones He will face upon His re-entrance to planet Earth—a fallen spiritual kingdom that has despised His authority from the beginning, a people created to be partners who refuse to submit to His leadership, and a world that looks nothing like the one He made.

So let me ask you: Is it right for Jesus to be more than a little angry? Does His wrath make more sense now? Even if it does, I wonder if any of us are truly prepared for what He will do when He sets foot on the planet again.

TRUE TERROR

For those who hate Jesus, nothing will be more terrifying than seeing Him return to earth. Think about it: These people will have endured the torment of demonic creatures—a horrific blend of locusts, scorpions, horses, lions, and humans (Rev. 9:1–11). They will have seen every form of evil join them at Armageddon and probably stood side-by-side with the most hellish ghouls imaginable. Yet still, Jesus will be more terrifying to these rebels than all those creatures combined.

Why will the Lord be so terrifying? Scripture doesn't hold back in its R-rated descriptions of what Jesus will do to those who oppose Him. Zechariah speaks of people's eyes, tongues, and flesh rotting instantly from a plague the Lord unleashes upon them (14:12). Isaiah depicts Jesus trampling the rebellious and staining His robes with their blood (63:1–6). John notes that "they were trampled in the winepress outside the city, and blood flowed out of the press, rising as high as the horses' bridles for a distance of 1,600 stadia" (Rev. 14:20). That's about three hundred kilometers covered in blood running almost two meters deep! Can we even fathom such mass slaughter? As terrible as the Holocaust and Cambodian genocides were, this will be even worse.

John continues describing Jesus' terrifying yet triumphant return:

> I saw heaven standing open and there before me was a white horse, whose rider is called Faithful and True. With justice he judges and wages war. His eyes are like blazing fire, and on his head are many crowns. He has a name written on him that no one knows but he himself. He is dressed in a robe dipped in blood, and his name is the Word of God. The armies of heaven were following him, riding on white horses and dressed in fine linen, white and clean. Coming out of his mouth is a sharp sword with which to strike down the nations. "He will rule them with an iron scepter." He treads the winepress of the fury of the wrath of God Almighty. On his robe and on his thigh he has this name written: KING OF KINGS AND LORD OF LORDS.
>
> And I saw an angel standing in the sun, who cried in a loud voice to all the birds flying in midair, "Come, gather together for the great supper of God, so that you may eat the flesh of kings, generals, and the mighty, of horses and their riders, and the flesh of all people, free and slave, great and small." ... The rest were killed with the sword coming out of the mouth of the rider on the horse, and all the birds gorged themselves on their flesh.
>
> —REVELATION 19:11–18, 21

Does this look like the pacifist guru Jesus, the stained-glass, somber Jesus, or the best-buddy Jesus? No, this is warrior-King Jesus, revealed in all His power! He is not the Jesus the world expects, nor is He the one the world prefers. Unbelievers don't mind the Jesus who's a wise teacher and does good for the poor because then He can be evaluated, admired, or dismissed if you don't agree with Him. As believers, however, we too often tend to keep the Lord in a similar box. We like the Jesus who's friendly and full of unconditional love because that way we can handle Him. We can fit Him nicely into our lives or worldviews without Him bothering us too much, and that way He won't be too forceful or demand too much. It's easy to keep Jesus tame when we keep Him caged like a pet—a nice mascot to have around when we need Him.

But Jesus is none of these things. The King of kings shatters every box we try to put Him in, just as He will shatter every sword at Armageddon. That day,

His mere presence will exterminate every enemy on earth. Paul says Jesus will "overthrow [the Antichrist] with the breath of his mouth and destroy [him] by the splendor of his coming" (2 Thess. 2:8). One word from Jesus and Satan's greatest warrior will be toast! Think about it: Jesus will defeat the massive conglomeration of history's mightiest forces of evil by simply showing up. This is how unfathomably powerful our Savior is.

A LOVE FOR JUSTICE

Just as Jesus' power astounds us, so will His zeal for righteousness. The King of kings is returning to set things right, and He is passionate about restoring the planet to how it should be by cleansing it of evil. He has more passion for true justice than anyone, which is why throughout Scripture He is known as the defender of the poor, vulnerable, and oppressed. If we think social justice is important now, wait until we see Jesus at His return! He will come with a vengeance against injustice that comes purely from His righteous, perfect love for people. And that vengeance will lead Him to eradicate all who do not represent His kingdom.

Now, will Jesus' actions seem loving? Of course not—especially not to those He destroys! His ferocious retribution and righteous anger will shock the world on that day, just as it confounds the world now. People who are not part of His kingdom cannot understand Jesus' perfect love. They are offended by it, especially by how exclusive and intolerant it is. If we as believers succumb to seeing Jesus through a worldly perspective, defining Him by our own standards, then we too will be offended to the core. His love will appall us.

Today's world says love is essentially whatever you want it to be, as long as it doesn't hurt anyone else. This is a twisted love that essentially revolves around "me" and what makes me happy. It's also a love that comes judgment-free, as reflected in the bumper-sticker-ready words of the Dalai Lama XIV: "Love is the absence of judgment."[2] Yet if perfect love really was without judgment, there would be no justice. God's "love" would forbid Him from ever setting wrongs right. This kind of loving God would never nor *could* ever convict a serial murderer—which means evil would be allowed to have the final say.

Thank God, the Lord's love is infinitely higher than the world's version. God's love is absolute, selfless, righteous, and perfect. It is *because* of His love that He will judge right from wrong. His love compels Him to judge the wicked. Without both His love and His justice, what hope would those who suffer injustice have?

God's love and justice—which include His righteous judgments—are two sides of the same coin. You cannot have one without the other in a just world, which is exactly what Jesus' return will usher in. The King is coming to cleanse the world of the filth of sin and evil so His perfect kingdom can be restored—a kingdom full of the love, righteousness, and justice that accurately reflects Him. He wants to restore what He originally intended: a world where humanity follows its perfect partner in fellowship. One day, the righteous, loving God will re-establish this relationship with His people, even if it takes Him doing what we think is offensive to remove those who refuse His leadership.

THE RIGHT FEAR

Nothing can diminish God's immeasurable love, which "surpasses knowledge" and is revealed to us in the person of Jesus Christ (Eph. 3:19, Rom. 8:39). At the same time, such love cannot allow evil to go unchecked forever. In His love, God has given people the free will to choose to follow Him, and in His love, God has determined a set "day" to cleanse the planet of everything that opposes Him, as only He knows when no more people on it will follow Him.

This is exactly why we fear the Lord. He is the only one worthy to sit in such a place of distinction and the only one capable of wielding such power without corrupting it. We fear Him because He holds all power and justice in His hands, and as humans whose nature is to oppose Him, that puts us in a vulnerable position. The good news for those who are born again is that we are no longer bound to our natural condition and can live in the righteousness of Jesus. That doesn't mean we should no longer fear God—quite the opposite. As we fear Him, we learn to love Him even more!

Unfortunately, many of us misunderstand what it means to fear God. We think of it only as being scared of Him. But fearing God biblically means to honor Him as the highest authority who wields matchless power. Proverbs 9:10 says, "The fear of the LORD is the beginning of wisdom," and it is certainly wise to not take someone's power for granted. For example, if I saw a grizzly bear moving toward me in a forest, it would be wise of me to not run up and try to shake the bear's paw. Wisdom says I should honor the bear for the power it has—namely, its ability to maul me to bits in a second. According to the psalms, God is to be feared (Ps. 76:7, 11; 96:4), and Proverbs 19:23 says fearing Him actually leads to life.

But did you know fearing the Lord also helps us *love* Him more? The two are supplemental, not contradictory. The more I fear God, the more I love

Him, and the more I love Him, the more I fear Him. For example, I personally fear God for His power to judge my sinfulness and end my life with a single thought, but because I know He is righteous yet withholds judgment when I am alive in Christ, then I willingly love Him even more. My gratitude deepens my love, which also deepens my reverence for Him.

On a larger scale, we not only fear the Lord's ability to purge this world of everything that is evil, but we also fear Him because we know that, left on our own, we too are evil and would be removed. With this in mind, doesn't it make us love Him more for making a way for us to be saved through Jesus, despite us doing nothing to deserve such an offer of salvation? To top it off, the Lord doesn't want us to love Him from a distance. He actually *invites* us into deeper intimacy with Him because He longs for us to know Him in the same way the Father knows the Son. (See John 17:22–23.) What a mystery!

God is to be feared and loved. He asked this of the Israelites more than three thousand years ago, and He asks this of us today: "And now, Israel, what does the LORD your God ask of you but to fear the LORD your God, to walk in obedience to him, to love him, to serve the LORD your God with all your heart and with all your soul, and to observe the LORD's commands and decrees that I am giving you today for your own good?" (Deut. 10:12–13).

To love God means we obey Him. (See 1 John 5:3; John 14:15, 23–24). Therefore, we show that we love Him not just through our words or thoughts but also through our actions. The Book of Ecclesiastes, one of the Hebrew Bible's premier books of wisdom, concludes: "Fear God and keep his commandments, for this is the duty of all mankind. For God will bring every deed into judgment, including every hidden thing, whether it is good or evil" (12:13–14).

Eventually, the Lord will bring everything into the light for judgment. The good, the bad, the ugly—it will all be revealed one day. In the last days God will release His wrath upon the earth as judgment for its evil, and Jesus will return to pronounce judgment upon those who will not submit to His leadership. The wickedness of the world will be exposed and dealt with.

But what about those who do submit? What about those who fear, love, and obey the Lord? Scripture is clear that on that day they will be rescued by Jesus: "For the Lord himself will come down from heaven, with a loud command, with the voice of the archangel and with the trumpet call of God, and the dead in Christ will rise first. After that, we who are still alive and are left will be caught up together with them in the clouds to meet the Lord in the air. And so we will be with the Lord forever" (1 Thess. 4:16–17). What a glorious meeting!

So where does that leave us now? How do we encounter Jesus today, regardless of when He physically comes back to earth? He has called us to follow Him, so how do we submit to His leadership? I know many who don't want to just submit to Jesus; they want to enjoy Him—in fact, that probably describes you and is why you're still reading this book! So what does that look like in your life? What does it look like to not grin and bear Jesus' leadership in your life but to actually *enjoy* it?

These are the questions we'll deal with in the final section of this book. Before we address them, let me offer some encouragement—it's often needed after dealing with such an intense topic as the end times. For those of us determined to fear, love, and obey the Lord for as long as we live, let me offer some extra incentive to keep going, even as we see more and more people falling away. Our motivation is found in the last part of the end-times story.

UNDER JESUS' REIGN

After defeating all who oppose Him, Jesus will toss Satan into a bottomless pit for a millennium so he cannot "deceive the nations anymore until the thousand years [are] finished" (Rev. 20:3, NLT). With evil completely removed from the planet, Jesus will begin His millennial reign on earth, during which we will get to see up close what perfect leadership is like. Remember, this planet has not fully experienced perfect leadership since Adam and Eve partnered with the Lord in Eden. As it was at the beginning of this world's history, the Lord's kingdom will be "on earth as it is in heaven" (Matt. 6:10).

Jesus will begin His reign by taking His rightful place on the "judgment seat of Christ" (2 Cor. 5:10; Rom. 14:10). Whether this is the same "glorious throne" Jesus mentioned in the parable of the sheep and goats is uncertain (Matt. 25:31); what is certain is that Jesus will serve as the world's greatest judge, and He will "separate the people one from another" based on whether they have called upon His name for salvation (Matt. 25:32). Some will expect to enter His kingdom but will not; others will expect to receive punishment but instead will be welcomed into the kingdom.

After judging the nations, Jesus will then reward believers according to what they have done on earth. We will each "receive what is due us for the things done while in the body, whether good or bad" (2 Cor. 5:10). That alone should give us incentive to live every moment of our lives in service to Him, knowing that "nothing in all creation is hidden from God's sight. Everything is uncovered and laid bare before the eyes of him to whom we must give account" (Heb. 4:13).

This can be good news or bad news. For some, the truth that God is watching elicits a response of "Yikes! You mean *everything*?!" Yes, everything. Every click online. Every whispered word after someone cuts you off in traffic. Every thought about your coworker or boss. For others, it's wonderful news that God sees you. It means He notices when you bite your tongue and don't retaliate when your wife issues verbal attacks. He sees when you tell the truth about a mistake at work, even though it may cost you your job. And yes, He knows it's you writing those anonymous notes of encouragement to others.

Under Jesus' perfect leadership, even the smallest acts done "to the least of these" can take on great significance. A cup of water. An invitation inside. A coat or a shirt. Heaven's exchange rate is ridiculously in our favor. Not only is everything we do on earth seen, but everything can be done unto Him— washing dishes, picking up after our kids, or putting down the phone to resist temptation. Our lives are lived before Him, and in light of what awaits us in eternity, this changes everything.

But being credited for our actions and gaining eternal rewards are not the only things we can look forward to under Jesus' perfect leadership. When the King of all kings ascends His throne to rule again, He will do what no other king with His kind of power would do: He will share His kingdom.

Jesus doesn't want to rule alone. He actually prefers to reign in partnership with His bride—and that's us, His redeemed people! Revelation 5:9–10 says Jesus "has ransomed people for God from every tribe and language and people and nation. And [He has] caused them to become a Kingdom of priests for our God. And they will reign on the earth" (NLT). Daniel foresaw this picture hundreds of years earlier: "Then the sovereignty, power and greatness of all the kingdoms under heaven will be handed over to the holy people of the Most High" (Dan. 7:27). Paul understood this when he said, "Do you not know that the Lord's people will judge the world?" (1 Cor. 6:2). And John gave the clearest description of our ruling with Jesus when He described a heavenly courtroom scene:

> Then I saw thrones, and the people sitting on them had been given the authority to judge. And I saw the souls of those who had been beheaded for their testimony about Jesus and for proclaiming the word of God. They had not worshiped the

beast or his statue, nor accepted his mark on their foreheads or their hands. They all came to life again, and they reigned with Christ for a thousand years. … They will be priests of God and of Christ and will reign with him a thousand years.

—REVELATION 20:4, 6, NLT

Jesus is unlike any ruler in history. He is the most generous King ever. He wants to rule with us, eagerly awaits it, and has already established that we will reign with Him for a thousand years. The fact that He wants this is remarkable considering our lousy track record of leading upon the earth. And it's even more remarkable when we understand what will happen at the end of our millennial reign with Jesus.

Revelation 20 says that after a thousand years Satan "must be released for a little while" (v. 3, NLT). Why would God allow such a horrible thing? Wasn't everything going so perfectly with evil unable to ruin the world?

Not so fast. As wonderful as this thousand-year reign will be, there is still one issue that must be dealt with. In fact, this element may be the most telling evidence of humans' true nature in all history. Even in a perfect environment of Jesus' total rule, we *still* will eventually prefer to lead ourselves rather than partner with Jesus and His generous way of leading. Even in the vacuum of evil, with Satan bound, we *still* will choose to walk opposite God at some point. Even after being redeemed, we will sin.

How do I know this? Take a look at John's description:

When the thousand years come to an end, Satan will be let out of his prison. He will go out to deceive the nations. … He will gather them together for battle—a mighty army, as numberless as sand along the seashore. And I saw them as they went up on the broad plain of the earth and surrounded God's people and the beloved city. But fire from heaven came down on the attacking armies and consumed them. Then the devil, who had deceived them, was thrown into the fiery lake of burning sulfur, joining the beast and the false prophet. There they will be tormented day and night forever and ever.

—REVELATION 20:7–10, NLT

Humanity will experience Jesus' flawless leadership for a thousand years, during which there will not be a *single* wrong judgment. Every decision will be made from perfect love and in perfect justice, and with His government working in complete harmony to reflect God's character. Yet even in such a paradise, people will still be so easily deceived that as soon as Satan is allowed to tempt them, *billions* (technically, "numberless") will opt to rebel against Jesus again (Rev. 20:8). Their pride will rise so quickly they will repeat the same idiotic challenge as on the day of the Lord. Their hatred will blind them, and they will gather for battle to once again try—pointlessly—to defeat Jesus, His people, and His holy city, Jerusalem.

If this sounds familiar, it's because it is. And the outcome will be just the same as a thousand years earlier. With a flash the Lord will consume the opposition—this time with fire from heaven. He will put a final, once-and-for-all end to Satan by throwing him into the fiery lake where his torment and punishment will never end.

Why would God allow this again? How is it possible for paradise to be ruined yet again?

The answer lies in what Adam and Eve learned the hard way in the first paradise and what Jeremiah revealed years later: "The human heart is the most deceitful of all things, and desperately wicked. Who really knows how bad it is?" (Jer. 17:9, NLT). Within that heart is a love for sin that, even under optimal conditions, will eventually cause mankind to rebel against God's leadership and try to elevate "self."

At the end of Jesus' thousand-year reign, humans will once again be exposed. We will not be able to blame Satan this time; it will be obvious that evil can be birthed in our hearts without his assistance. The great deceiver will simply be the match to light the fuel that already simmers inside us. Once again, the depth of our depravity will show why God's righteous judgments are justified. But it will also show another thing: Even when we are offered a ruling partnership with Jesus, *He* must still be the ultimate leader. We were meant to follow Him in fellowship, and if that purpose gets twisted, our own nature will *always* rise to the surface. If there is one hope we can cling to for eternity, it is Jesus and Jesus alone. He is our *living* hope, both now and truly forever.

PART IV

... OF ENJOYING HIS LEADERSHIP

What does following Jesus actually look like? How do we go from simply enduring His leading to enjoying it? In particular, how can we find joy when He seems to lead us in ways we don't naturally like? In the following chapters, we'll dive into what joyful follow ship looks like practically on an everyday basis—yes, even through the tough, uncertain terrains of life.

CHAPTER 12

FROM FELLOWSHIP TO FOLLOWSHIP

MY WIFE AND I first met in a roomful of mutual friends, all of whom had attended the same college except me. She was the bold one, approaching me with a handshake and a "Hi, I don't think I've met you before." Though we connected quickly and soon knew we were interested in each other, all our early meetings were in group settings. I couldn't wait to get to know Amber one-on-one, so you can imagine how excited I was when she agreed to meet me alone at a restaurant one evening.

That Thursday after work I rushed from the office to meet her for what could technically be called our first date. After more than four hours, neither of us was ready to leave the other—and the rest is history.

But what if on that first date, before we had even placed our drink orders, I turned to Amber and asked, "So what should we name our first child?"

Or, "What kind of a house should we buy?"

"Which housecleaning duties will you expect me to do?"

"How much money should we save each year?"

Or how about, "Should we live close to my parents or yours—or neither?"

I'm almost certain I would have scared off Amber had I been so direct. When you're getting to know someone, especially in a dating relationship, you don't jump into questions like these so soon. You first get to know the person better, of course; then, eventually, you may reach a point down the road where you discuss details of a future together. But it's only when you've established trust and have a history with each other that it makes sense to do so.

Why, then, do so many of us approach God the same way? I have met many people who seem to spend much of their time with God peppering Him with questions such as: "So what do You want me to do?"; "Is this Your will, God?"; "Where do You want me to go now, Lord?"; "What do You want from me?" Because my wife and I work with many young adults, most of whom are single, we have walked with countless individuals seeking God for direction in life. They ask us for counsel, wanting to know God's will for what job they should take, if they're in the right career, if they should go back to school, whether they should date a certain person, where they should live, what church community they should be a part of, whether they should buy a house or apartment, who they should marry, *if* they should marry, how long they should date someone before thinking about marriage, and on and on. The questions typically come from a sincere heart of wanting what God wants for their lives.

The first question I usually ask these people is this: "How do you think the Lord feels about this?" Often, I will then get a long, usually frustrated response of either how difficult it's been to hear the Lord's voice or how ambiguous He has been.

"I keep asking Him—every time I pray," they'll say with exasperation. "But I get nothing. I don't understand it. Why can't He just be clear with what He wants?"

It's a good question—if God were a robot with no emotions or desires. But He isn't. He values one-on-one time with us, just like I valued first getting to know my wife in a more exclusive setting, and just like I still value our alone time today. The Lord enjoys us, and He loves it when we enjoy Him.

The problem, however, is that so many of us don't really know *how* to enjoy Him. Many of those who come to me for advice say they are frustrated by God's lack of guidance, yet they're so busy seeking answers from Him that they overlook simply being with Him. Some have never taken the time to really get to know the Lord in the first place. Their relationship with the Lord started with them immediately jumping into asking Him major life questions, and they haven't stopped asking since. I wonder what the Lord thinks about those kinds of first dates.

The truth is, God is a person—a real being—with feelings and opinions. Although He is infinitely above us in every respect, we were still made in His likeness, which means we share some similarities. The Bible's overarching storyline proves that one of those similar characteristics is a value for intimacy and relationship. The Lord is not a formula or an equation waiting to be solved. We can't just push a button here and expect a certain outcome with Him. Now, most of the people who come to me wanting to know God's will for their lives aren't intentionally trying to control the Lord or turn Him into a formula. But without them realizing it, their actions and attitudes say otherwise.

Often in our eagerness to serve the Lord or in our zeal to do something for Him, we skip the relationship and jump right into tasks and details. Even with a pure desire to follow Him, sometimes we can overlook what Paul considered the greatest goal in life: knowing Jesus. I want that to be my highest goal too. Not knowing a lot *about* Jesus. Not even knowing what He wants me to do. I mean really, truly *knowing* Jesus in a way that even surpasses the way I know my wife or my best friend.

WHO DO YOU KNOW?

If anyone would have appeared to know God, it was Paul. His zeal for God was undeniable. As a Pharisee, he would have spent much of his young life committed to loving the Lord with all his heart, soul, and strength, in obedience to the first part of the Torah's Shema (Deut. 6:4–9). He learned under one of Israel's most well-known rabbis, Gamaliel, and his training included studying the Hebrew Bible virtually all day long, every day (except Shabbat, of course). He spent hours in prayer, talking to Yahweh; he spent hours talking about Yahweh with others, discussing and debating His Word; and in the hours between, he spent much of his time meditating on Yahweh's words.

Yet it wasn't until a radical encounter with the Word Himself, Jesus, that Paul discovered He didn't know God like He thought He did. Paul had spent his whole life trying to know and serve God; he had even persecuted the first followers of Jesus in the name of Yahweh, truly believing he was helping God. One encounter with Jesus changed everything, however, and Paul became an entirely new man. (See Acts 9:1–19.)

Think of what an absolute crisis this must have been for Paul. This was a man far more devoted to God than you or me. His entire life had revolved around knowing God and serving Him. While the Jewish culture of his time became increasingly influenced by Hellenism and other foreign ideologies, Paul had committed himself to the Pharisaical way of staying separated and pure for God.

Jesus popped Paul's balloon with one life-deflating question: "Why do you persecute Me?" (See Acts 9:4.) I believe the Lord's words weren't just about Paul hunting, harassing, and imprisoning believers; otherwise, He could have simply said, "Why do you persecute My followers?" Jesus was asking a bigger yet more personal question about Paul's life: Why is your life going against Me? You think you're walking with Me, and yet you're not just opposing Me—you are *hurting* Me.

How often in our lives do we assume we're walking with God when we may not be? More than a few times I have caught myself drifting down the stream of ministry life, doing good things and assuming that what I was doing pleased

God. I was teaching His Word, leading people in worship, making disciples for Him, and living my life for Him; therefore, surely I knew Him well. It's by God's grace that in those times He shook me awake by reminding me that I can do the most incredible things for God and even see amazing fruit, and yet still never really know God.

In Matthew 7:21–23, Jesus spoke what I believe is one of Scripture's most haunting truths: "Not everyone who says to me, 'Lord, Lord,' will enter the kingdom of heaven, but only the one who does the will of my Father who is in heaven. Many will say to me on that day, 'Lord, Lord, did we not prophesy in your name and in your name drive out demons and in your name perform many miracles?' Then I will tell them plainly, 'I never knew you. Away from me, you evildoers!'"

It's chilling to think that we can live with the honorable intention to know God and serve Him and yet still miss Him, just as Paul did. We can surround ourselves with good things: Christian fellowship, biblical teachings, amazing worship services. We can do wonderful, fruitful things like feeding and clothing the poor, taking care of widows and orphans, or maybe even transforming communities with long-term service projects. We can even do supernatural things like healing the sick, casting out demons, and calling dead things to life with our prophetic words. Surely God would approve of us if He were to give such divine endorsements, right?

Not necessarily. Jesus said we can do all these great things—yes, including miraculous things—and yet *never* be known by Him.

Are you kidding me? *Never*?

Jesus said it, not me. The original Greek for *knew* in Matthew 7:23 indicates personal recognition rather than intellectual knowledge. We may do things that look like we are following Jesus, yet He doesn't "recognize" us because there was never real relationship. We can produce the very fruit of His kingdom and yet have no relationship with the King. In fact, notice that Jesus even called these strangers "evildoers." Why so harsh? Because in Jesus' kingdom, if we are not for Him, then we're against Him (Matt. 12:30). If we don't have real relationship with Him, we can appear to produce the fruit of God's kingdom and yet actually be living for Satan in the kingdom of darkness.

That idea haunts me. It puts the fear of God in me. More than anything, it compels me to set aside everything and really *know* Jesus. Matthew 7:21–23 challenges me to daily ask myself: Is knowing Jesus still my top reason for living today? Am I willing to throw away everything to keep my relationship with Him as my number one priority?

It's important to point out that knowing God and serving Him are not mutually exclusive. We can do both. We can know the Lord while serving Him without our "doing" getting in the way. The issue is whether our actions stem from true relationship or mere religious activity. And between those two— relationship or religion—there is truly no comparison. One is full of life; the other kills life in the long run. Paul said it best when he compared the greatest things in his own life—those things he could boast about—to knowing Jesus.

> But whatever were gains to me I now consider loss for the sake of Christ. What is more, I consider everything a loss because of the surpassing worth of knowing Christ Jesus my Lord, for whose sake I have lost all things. I consider them garbage, that I may gain Christ and be found in him, not having a righteousness of my own that comes from the law, but that which is through faith in Christ—the righteousness that comes from God on the basis of faith. I want to know Christ—yes, to know the power of his resurrection and participation in his sufferings, becoming like him in his death, and so, somehow, attaining to the resurrection from the dead.
>
> —PHILIPPIANS 3:7–11

Paul considered all the things he could boast in to be garbage compared to knowing Jesus. The word he used for *garbage* is equivalent to dung—it's worthless and even detestable. That's radical speech, especially for someone who did so much. Other than Jesus, few people in the New Testament match Paul's contribution to the Christian movement. He planted churches, preached the gospel, pioneered new missionary work, taught theology, encouraged believers everywhere, wrote thirteen of the twenty-seven books in the New Testament—the guy did a lot! Not only that, but even after two thousand years his work continues to impact every believer today. So Paul's work was *really* significant. And yet he went to such an extreme in comparing the accolades of his life to simply knowing Jesus that he would say his accomplishments were as worthless as excrement. What the world called positive Paul considered negative because knowing Jesus was worth infinitely more to him.

What kind of knowing is Paul referring to in that passage? This time, the original Greek word (*gnōnai*) isn't about recognition but about sharing intimate experiences with someone. Elsewhere the word is used for sexually knowing someone; it's that intimate! Paul obviously wasn't using the word in a sexual way, but he longed to know Jesus with a closeness that surpassed any other relationship. And now that Paul had experienced the "surpassing worth" of this kind of knowing, everything else seemed like utter waste.

I don't know about you, but I'm not always at a place in life where I can echo Paul's sentiment. I wish I was, of course; I want to consider everything worthless except for knowing Jesus. But the reality is, some days I put many things above knowing Him: my family, my work, my ministry, my future plans, my enjoyment of life. All those areas of life can seem so important that I end up devoting more time and attention (great indicators of what we value) to knowing them than I do to knowing Jesus. Other times my thought life can reveal how low of a priority knowing Jesus has become. It's amazing how many minutes of the day I can spend thinking about myself!

Even in good seasons—those times when Jesus is the object of my affection and I'm placing Him first in what seems to be every area of life—even then there's a ditch I can fall into. I've found it's possible to spend lots of time thinking *about* Jesus and yet not actually spend any time being *with* Jesus. Have you found that to be true as well? We can spend hours studying His life or learning things about Him—wonderful things—and yet when we take a step back, we can't remember the last time we just enjoyed His presence.

I love thinking about my wife. If I'm away from her too long, I will still catch myself daydreaming about her eyes, her smile, her voice, or simply her presence. (I'm glad it's still that way after almost twenty-five years of marriage!) But as much as I love thinking about her, it's infinitely better when I am actually with her. There is no comparison between the two.

The same is true with Jesus. Nothing can replace being with Him—basking in His presence and enjoying His fellowship with no agenda other than savoring the relationship. Just being. I believe that's the kind of *knowing* Paul was talking about.

Paul lived out what it meant to be in constant fellowship with Jesus. Yes, he was a busy guy who did many great things for the Lord. But all of Paul's actions stemmed from a deep intimacy with Jesus. Paul would have gladly traded in all those ministry successes for simply being with His Lord. That was the kind of *knowing* they shared.

It's impossible to experience that kind of knowing without also enjoying the Lord. We cannot separate knowing Jesus from enjoying Him. Likewise, we can't expect to enjoy being with Jesus if we don't first enjoy Him. I realize that sounds obvious; if you want to be with someone and get to know him or her, of course it means you enjoy being with that person. But if that's true, why do we so often say we want to be with the Lord, and yet many of us don't enjoy Him when we are with Him? Instead of enjoying His perfect love, for example, we continue to ask Him how much He loves us. Rather than enjoying His perfect peace, we're busy praying for Him to calm all the storms in our life. Instead of enjoying His perfect provision—that He has promised to supply all our needs—we pepper Him with petitions to supply all those needs. And rather than enjoying His perfect leadership, we spend our time asking Him how He will lead us—what He wants us to do next, where we're supposed to go, how He's going to get us there, and what we're going to do once we get there.

Do you see the difference? I hope so, because it's big.

Jesus longs for us to know Him through enjoying Him. More than a husband and wife enjoy each other in a great marriage. More than two lifelong best friends can sit in complete silence and still love the moment. We enjoy Jesus when there are no strings attached to our time with Him. We enjoy Him when we take our eyes off ourselves and focus on Him, with no goal other than to love Him. As we love Him, actions will naturally follow, just as He said they would. We obey and fulfill His commandments out of love. But if our eyes stay fixed on Him, then those actions will always be secondary to the joy of simply knowing and being with Him.

Amid the busyness of my life, even as I've been doing things in Jesus' name, the Lord has often stilled me and called me into this deeper fellowship, saying: *Rest in Me. Be in Me. Know Me. Enjoy Me.* This is the foundation of my relationship with Him. It's the foundation of followship. If we want to truly follow Jesus, we will know Him through enjoying Him. And enjoying Jesus starts from a place of resting in Him—simply being in Him. This is the true key to enjoying Jesus' leadership in our lives. We were made for fellowship with the Lord, and that fellowship was never intended to begin from a place of doing but simply being. As we get to know Jesus in the deepest way possible, we can delight in a relationship that's always living, growing, expanding, and making all other things seem worthless in comparison.

ABIDING FELLOWSHIP

We won't ever truly enjoy Jesus' leadership until we enjoy Jesus Himself. I'm not talking about enjoying what He can do or where He can take us, but simply enjoying Him. As we just saw, enjoying Jesus is about resting in Him. This is where our journey of following Him really gets, well, *enjoyable.*

One of Jesus' most fundamental teachings came on the night of His arrest, and it was given to only eleven disciples. (Judas had already left.) Jesus said much that night—so much that Scripture even highlights that some of it went over His disciples' heads. John's transcription of all Jesus said that night spans five full chapters (John 13–17). But at the core of Jesus' teaching was the key to how His disciples could continue following Him through the uncertainty of the future. They had no clue what lie ahead for them, nor that in the next few hours they would face the toughest time of their lives. So what was this crucial key? What was the one element to keep them holding fast to everything Jesus had taught them?

Abide in Me.

Jesus used the word translated "abide" ten times within a mere seven verses (John 15:4–10, NKJV), emphasizing it like a drum getting louder with each beat. *Abide in Me. Abide in Me.* Between His different uses of the phrase, you can almost see the flashing message: *This is really important, guys. Let this sink into you. Let this become your heartbeat. Abide in Me.*

Some Bible translations use the phrase "remain in Me," which certainly helps put it in everyday language. Few people use the word *abide* today, and yet it holds a powerful meaning when used in the way Jesus did. To abide is to live in something; it's to make a home and continue to dwell there. The emphasis isn't on a one-time entry point but in the ongoing staying. When we abide in something, we are content to establish ourselves in that place for the long haul.

This is what Jesus commands us to do *in Him.* He used the perfect analogy of a vine and branches. If a branch has any hope of producing fruit, it must remain connected to the vine; it must continue being in the vine.

Do you want to bear fruit? "Live in Me," Jesus said. "No branch can bear fruit by itself; it must remain in the vine. Neither can you bear fruit unless you remain in me" (John 15:4). You want to do something worthwhile and meaningful with your life? "Dwell in Me," Jesus said: "When you're joined with me and I with you, the relation intimate and organic, the harvest is sure to be abundant. Separated, you can't produce a thing" (John 15:5, MSG).

Did you catch that last part? Without remaining in Jesus, we can't produce a thing. Given the context of what He says elsewhere, we find this to be any *lasting* fruit—anything that will remain throughout time. Talk about leaving a mark on this world! That desire to do something significant has been the cry of many generations—certainly today's—and yet here we find Jesus giving the key to changing the world: *abide in Me.*

This is the essence of fellowship with Jesus. After all, how much closer can you get in a relationship than to be within someone? Jesus didn't use that phrase in a sexual way, but there most certainly is a degree of intimacy when we abide in Him. Our taking up residence in Him must start with the foundation of enjoying Him, *knowing* Him.

If we hope to follow Jesus, we must be in fellowship with Him. And if we long to remain in fellowship with Him—to abide—then He must be our first love. Our priceless pearl. The treasure we find that's worth selling everything for. The one we'll willingly give up everything—including life itself—to be with.

This kind of relationship is what Jesus is after when He invites us into followship. He wants us to enjoy Him and the way He leads us through life, but that requires knowing Him in the deepest way. Maybe that has been difficult for you. Maybe you've done many things for Him in your life and been around a lot of Christian activity, and yet you're starting to realize you barely know the Jesus you are supposed to be following. Or maybe you've come to see that His call to follow Him requires more than you originally thought. Or maybe you've done your best trying to get to know Him, but it seems the relationship never really grows.

If any of those describe your situation, don't lose heart. Abiding in Jesus is ongoing. Yes, the journey must have a starting point, but once begun, it is still a journey, filled with ups and downs, faster seasons and slower seasons. As with any journey, it's possible to get stuck while we are on the way. We can unintentionally set up camp in one of the phases of followship mentioned earlier in this book and never move forward. That was many chapters ago, so let's review those seasons of the journey in light of us now better understanding Jesus' different way of leading.

THE FOUR PHASES

As we reexamine the four phases of followship, keep in mind that often we can be in different phases in different areas of our life. For example, we may enjoy the way Jesus leads us in our finances, having surrendered, submitted, and trusted Him to guide us with our money however He wants. Yet at the same time we may be having a hard time surrendering some of our past emotional wounds to Him, and we're not sure how we will ever be able to forgive those who hurt us.

Don't be discouraged if you find yourself in different places in your life. That's how it is for everyone! Thankfully, Jesus can handle us being all over the map. Even though our lives may seem inconsistent, He is not. If we continue to hand over those different areas of our lives, He will continue to rule them. He will not force Himself to be Master over those areas; His lordship comes with our free will. But as the most patient leader ever, Jesus is the only one who knows how to graciously deal with our dissonance. He is determined that we not remain the same, and it's *His* transforming work that will change us—not ours. Our job is first to simply surrender, which is the beginning phase of followship.

Surrender—*Will we surrender to Jesus' leadership?*

The starting point of real relationship with Jesus is surrender. This is typically the greatest obstacle for most people, mainly because the Lord is not shy about His conditions of surrender: He requires everything. "Those of you who do not give up everything you have cannot be my disciples," He told the crowds following Him (Luke 14:33).

Giving Jesus all authority and control in our lives can seem like death to us, and for good reason. Surrender is dying to our own desires, preferences, rights, and ways of doing things. We are to crucify those parts of our "self" daily and surrender control over our own lives to His lordship. Obviously, this isn't easy. Surrender is a battle of wills: our will versus God's. In his classic devotional *My Utmost for His Highest*, Oswald Chambers wrote, "True surrender is not simply surrender of our external life but surrender of our will. … The greatest crisis we ever face is the surrender of our will. Yet God never forces a person's will into surrender, and He never begs. He patiently waits until that person willingly yields to Him."[1]

We do not surrender our will easily to God. Throughout this book we have seen how the nature of humans is to call our own shots and master our lives. We've walked through the biblical timeline using the followship lens and observed the same issue repeated infinitely: We want to lead instead of following. Although Jesus calls us to follow Him, which begins with surrendering, the *last* thing we naturally want to do is hand over the reins to Him.

Thankfully, the Lord is gracious, gentle, and patient with us in this transfer of authority. He starts with our will—are we *willing* to surrender to Him?—

and then gradually helps us through the process of giving up one thing at a time. He knows we won't relinquish everything to Him all at once because we're unaware of how much control we actually have. Our self-mastery runs deep, and it can take a long time for the Lord to uncover all the areas of our lives where He really isn't Master, even though we call Him that. Thankfully, His Holy Spirit can guide us, gently helping us to surrender more and more, so we can look more like our Master.

Surrender is indeed a process, and at the core of each stage of that process lies the same question: Will I surrender to Jesus' way? Stated another way: Will I give up leading my life and allow Him to lead?

What is in your life that you know remains to be surrendered? Maybe it's one of the same areas we've seen in this book. For example, have you surrendered your reputation to the Lord as Noah did? A righteous man in a completely sin-consumed world, Noah willingly gave up all control over what others thought of him. He was willing to be a fool in the eyes of others just to obey the Lord.

Or maybe the issue for you is surrendering your doubts and fears, just as it was for Moses. When God met Moses at the burning bush and asked the former prince to follow Him on a journey unlike any human had been on, Moses immediately thought of why he wasn't qualified and questioned God's choice. He eventually surrendered his skepticism and his right to determine if he was fit for the task, instead trusting that the Lord knew best.

Whatever area of life you need to surrender, let me remind you that Jesus is trustworthy as a Master. It is safe to trust Him, not because His way will always be easy but because He desires the absolute best for you, even more than you do. His ways are perfect, even if we disagree with them. His leadership is still flawless after thousands of years of leading humans. He has all authority and power, and therefore He's the only one who has the right to demand your life—yet He promises to care for it like no one else. He doesn't hold a gun to your head or ransom your family as He awaits your answer. But He does ask the same question day after day: *Will you surrender everything to Me?*

Submission—*Will we submit to Jesus' leadership?*

Just because *submission* is a dirty word in today's Western culture, evoking images of police brutality and marital abuse, that doesn't mean God's definition has changed. Sadly, the church has been just as involved in distorting submission's true meaning. Previous generations, under the influence of male chauvinism, turned submission in Christian marriages into the very thing God abhors: domination of the husband over his wife. Wives became servants instead of partners, and husbands got away with "ruling" their households instead of leading them like Christ did, with humility and a servant's heart.

I thank God that submitting to Him is nothing like these examples. Even if believers have misrepresented godly submission throughout history, Jesus hasn't. His example remains perfect, and it is still the model we are to follow.

Submitting to Jesus' leadership means not only giving Him the right to have all authority in our lives but also following through with action that proves our yielded position to Him. For example, Jesus continually submitted to His Father's will in perfect humility. He had supreme authority and power. Jesus rightfully could have entered every town with a hyped-up, angelically produced smoke-and-fireworks pre-show, then walked through the streets like a supernatural rock star—raising all the dead to life with David Copperfield-like showiness and commanding the rocks to sing His praises as background music. He could have waltzed into Jerusalem (or Rome, for the matter), overthrown whoever was in charge—Caesar, schmeezer—and shown everyone how powerful He was.

Jesus really could have done these things if He had wanted to. He had every right to, but He didn't because He was perfectly submitted to the Father in every moment—to such a degree that He was willing to be humiliated, misunderstood, mocked, and despised. "Very truly I tell you, the Son can do nothing by himself," Jesus explained. "He can do only what he sees his Father doing, because whatever the Father does the Son also does" (John 5:19).

What kind of powerful leader willingly submits like this? Jesus does. He did during His time on earth, and He continues to do so in the eternal posture of perichoresis as He revels not in glorifying Himself but in exalting His Father.

So will we submit to Jesus? Maybe it's easier when we realize the one we are submitting to is constantly submitting Himself to the Father. He doesn't ask us to do what He hasn't already done—that's why we are called to *follow* Him. He doesn't take us places where He hasn't already been. He is our experienced leader.

Yet it's His leadership that typically presents the more difficult challenge for us. Are we willing to fully submit to His way of leading, even when we don't like or agree with it? Will you lower yourself and yield to His decision-making? Will you relinquish your "right" to challenge where He leads you in life? Will you give up your pride and accept that He knows what is best for you?

His way of seeing things may not line up with yours. In fact, I'm positive it won't. He is God, after all, and you are not! His ways are infinitely higher than yours, as are His ways of thinking. (See Isaiah 55:8–9.) Will you submit to both? Or will you rise up in pride like so many of the examples we've seen in our biblical overview—from Satan to Saul to the running roster of wicked Jewish kings. Notice what they all had in common: They thought they knew better than God.

Do you too? Maybe the more precise question is this: In what areas of your life do you think you know better than the Lord? Those are the exact areas that need to be submitted to Him. Without doing so, it is a contradiction to call Him Lord and Master. In fact, Jesus even questioned those in His day who referred to Him as their Master but didn't live like He was in control over everything: "Why do you call me, 'Lord, Lord,' and do not do what I say?" (Luke 6:46).

Jesus was not a fan of hypocrites. He didn't use that term lightly with the religious leaders who said one thing but did another. And I am positive He doesn't want you or me on the roster of hypocritical followers—those who call Him Master but never submit to Him. Let's commit to being true with our surrender by showing it through our submissive actions. Let's let Him lead.

Trust—*Will we trust Jesus' leadership?*

When we have surrendered to following Jesus on His terms, it becomes easier to submit to His lordship. We then can prove we are both surrendered and submitted through our active faith demonstrated as we allow Jesus to lead. That active faith is simply called trust.

Trust is not trust unless there is an action behind it. For example, I may say I trust you with taking care of my children, but until I've actually left my children alone with you, I am merely holding to a belief. Or think about a trust fall, which shows us the differences between hope, faith, and trust. In a trust fall, I hope my friends will catch me as I consider falling backward from a height into their linked arms. But until I act on that hope, it's not faith. The Bible defines faith as "confidence in what we hope for and assurance about what we do not see" (Heb. 11:1). I don't have faith in my friends catching me until I actually fall. And what does it take to have such faith? Trust!

The writer of Hebrews described this attribute as "confidence" and "assurance," and when you assign those elements to a person, then you have trust. In a trust fall, I have confidence and assurance that my friends will catch me. Even though I can't see them catching me, I am confident enough in them catching me that I act upon my blind assurance. I can't say I trust them until I take the "leap of faith" by falling backward into their arms.

In our journey with Jesus, neither can we say we trust Him until we have put that trust to action by stepping out in faith, confident that He will lead us. Following Jesus will always require blind, active faith. The Lord has a track record of consistently leading His people into situations and seasons of life where we must trust Him—and only Him. Remember Noah building an ark for a flood that hadn't yet come? Remember Gideon whittling down his troops from thirty-two thousand men to a mere three hundred—and then facing an enemy army "thick as locusts," with camels that "could no more be counted than the sand on the seashore" (Judg. 7:12)?

Those were impossible situations, as were all the times Israel went into battle with worshipping musicians on the front line, just as the Lord instructed. Likewise, it was almost an impossible situation when Paul's ship was being torn apart by a storm. Yet he assured all those on board that "not one of you will lose a single hair from his head" because of God's promise (Acts 27:34).

The Bible is full of powerful examples of normal people like you and me facing do-or-die situations and their trust in God being put to the test. Why does the Lord allow these kinds of circumstances? There are many reasons. First, it builds our faith in Him when we see Him come through. The next time we face a similar situation, we won't just believe He can come through; we'll act upon that belief and have assurance that He *will* come through. That's the very definition of faith, and it's built upon trust.

Conversely, we only develop such trust in the Lord by experiencing situations where we *must* rely on Him. Without having to act, it's just theory. But when we have seen His faithfulness and reliability up close, it leaves an impression. I believe Jesus allows us to be in tough spots to mature our relationship with Him. Scripture tells us that "without faith it is impossible to please God" (Heb. 11:6). That means if we are to grow in our relationship with Him, then our faith must also grow. The Book of James says it's through trials that our faith is tested, which then produces the perseverance to stay true to the Lord and deepen our relationship with Him. (See James 1:2–4.)

If this sounds too challenging, let me assure you: God is faithful. That doesn't mean walking in faith is easy; it's not. But the more you see God's faithfulness firsthand, the more you love Him. And the more you cherish Him, the easier it is to trust Him.

When my family left the United States and moved to Norway as missionaries, I knew we would have to trust God more for our provision. Some friends had committed to help support us financially, but the total amount we raised was nowhere close to covering our costs for living in what was then the world's most expensive country.[2] For the first few months after moving, I had freelance work that helped provide regular income. Yet admittedly, I felt a tinge of fear in me every time I thought about when those checks would stop coming. We had some savings, but that wouldn't last long. I hoped to find more freelance work before we got to that point.

I don't remember when it was, but during those months the Lord challenged me in that gentle-but-firm way of His. "Are you going to trust Me to provide?" I sensed Him asking me. "Haven't I brought you this far and opened every door for you to step through? And have I ever let you down?"

He hadn't. Not once.

"OK, then trust Me. Stop trusting in your safety net—trust Me. Trust Me beyond what you can do. Watch Me lead you and provide for you in every way."

The next month we totaled our income and compared it to what we had spent. The numbers matched—like, exactly.

Wow, Lord! You're amazing, I thought. And my faith rose a notch.

A few months later, many of those who had supported us financially suddenly dropped off. I was all but certain we would have to dip into the last bit of savings we had until a woman whom I'd barely met several months before deposited money into our account at the last minute. When we checked our income versus expenses at the end of that month, my jaw dropped. The amounts lined up to the exact penny once again.

The previous time we had laughed, high-fived, and celebrated how cool God was. This time was serious for me. I knew God wasn't joking about His promise to provide.

Something in me shifted that day. I began to rarely worry about our finances, much less think about them. It wasn't automatic, but it was noticeable. I started enjoying a newfound trust in God that whatever He called us to do and wherever He sent us, He would always provide what we needed. For the previous decade-plus, I had tried my best to be a wise steward of our finances and to honor God through everything He gave us. We had been debt-free for years and lived below our means, and God used these things to help transition us into missionary life. But I had formed a habit of always having a self-made plan B, C, and D if plan A didn't work. I had unknowingly trusted more in the safety nets I created than the God who allowed me to create them in the first place.

But that day in Norway changed something deep. I cut my safety nets, obeyed the Lord, and began to trust Him in a far deeper way than I ever had before. A few months later, He again matched our income with our expenses.

"OK, now You're just rubbing it in my face," I told Him with a smile.

My wife and I worry less about money now than when we had plenty. I have settled in my spirit that God will provide for my family, and He has never, ever disappointed us, even before I made that decision. Since we moved to Norway, we have never lacked and instead have received more than what we've needed—all while the cost of living continues to rise. I refuse for my trust to be dependent on whether things are good, because it may not always be this way. Regardless of the amount in our bank account, I believe—no, I *know*—that wherever and however the Lord leads us, He is faithful to "meet all [our] needs according to the riches of his glory in Christ Jesus" (Phil 4:19).

THE TRUST FACTOR

You likely have your own testimonies of God's provision—maybe even miraculous ones. I've known people who experienced food multiplying at an evangelistic crusade and an eleventh-hour anonymous donation that saved an orphanage. Countless believers are inspired by George Müller, who committed to never ask anyone other than the Lord for money while caring for more than ten thousand orphans, helping to establish more than a hundred schools, and running a global missions organization. Müller trusted God for everything, and his life was full of miraculous provisions—from hundreds of children being fed when they had no food to massive orphanages being funded by strangers. An astounding one hundred fifty million dollars (in today's money) passed through Müller's hands during his life, yet he kept none of that for himself and died with only one hundred sixty pounds in his estate.[3]

What trust! Stories like these not only inspire us toward greater faith but can help us trust God on a deeper level—and not only with finances and provision. Are we willing to trust Jesus with our future? Our relationships? Our careers? Our children? What about our healing—whether emotional, physical, or in another area? Healing raises many difficult questions, but the core issue is the same: Will we trust the Lord no matter what our "reality" indicates? And will we trust Him through our disappointments and when He doesn't come through like we think He should?

This is why trust boils down to real relationship. The deeper you know a person, the easier it is to trust because not only do you know her character, but you've also developed a history together. You have a track record that proves her trustworthiness.

So it should be with the Lord. His track record is flawless. Need proof? Turn to virtually any page of the Bible and you will see examples of God's faithfulness, His supreme wisdom, or His power. We've all known people whose track record proves you cannot or should not trust them. But again and again, the Bible shows there is no one more reliable than the Lord, and there is no better leader to trust than Jesus.

Let's be honest, though. The problem is not that we haven't seen proof of this in God's Word; it's that we must put action to what we believe—we have to trust. Having recognized this, then, let's shift from theoretical to practical: In what areas of your life do you need to trust Jesus more? Where do you sense hesitation in trusting His leadership, and why is that? What are some disappointments you've had with the Lord, and are you honest enough to bring those into the light so He can address them? What makes it easy for you to trust the Lord's leading in some areas but not others? Do you detect a common element in those areas of distrust?

Surrender may be the starting point for real relationship with Jesus, but I believe trust is the fuel that keeps us going in it. Trust is as necessary for experiencing real life with Him as blood is for our physical bodies. I am convinced that's why two of our biggest enemies in life are doubt and fear—the tools of mistrust Satan has used since the beginning of human history when he asked Eve, "Did God *really* say …?" (Gen. 3:1).

Adam and Eve failed to trust God when the enemy came into paradise with some clever thoughts, and their relationship with the Lord was never the same. Jesus, on the other hand, defended Himself against Satan's similar attacks of doubt and mistrust by using God's Word. When the "father of lies" tried to tempt Jesus in the wilderness, Jesus used Scripture as an offensive weapon—like a sword slicing apart every seed of doubt that could have sprouted. (See John 8:44; Luke 4:1–13; Ephesians 6:17.) As followers of Jesus, we are to do the same as we protect the critical element of trust in our relationship with Him.

In the next chapter we will cover the last phase of followship: enjoying Jesus' leadership. But as we end this one focused on the challenge of trusting the Lord, let me offer you some scriptures to build up your trust in Him. I encourage you to not just zip through reading these, even if you've heard them many times before. Take time with each one. Meditate on the words. Let the Lord grow that vital element of trust in your relationship with Him as He reveals Himself more through His Word.

> Those who know your name trust in you, for you, LORD, have never forsaken those who seek you.
>
> —PSALM 9:10

> God's way is perfect. All the LORD's promises prove true. He is a shield for all who look to him for protection.
>
> —PSALM 18:30, NLT

> Trust in him at all times, you people; pour out your hearts to him, for God is our refuge.
>
> —PSALM 62:8

> Trust in the LORD with all your heart and lean not on your own understanding; in all your ways submit to him, and he will make your ways straight.
>
> —PROVERBS 3:5–6

> Fear of man will prove to be a snare, but whoever trusts in the LORD is kept safe.
>
> —PROVERBS 29:25

> Trust in the LORD forever, for the LORD, the LORD himself, is the Rock eternal.
>
> —ISAIAH 26:4

> Blessed is the one who trusts in the LORD, whose confidence is in him.
>
> —JEREMIAH 17:7

> I the LORD do not change.
>
> —MALACHI 3:6

> Jesus Christ is the same yesterday and today and forever.
>
> —HEBREWS 13:8

CHAPTER 13

WALKING THE WAY OF UNCERTAINTY

HAVING JUST REEXAMINED the first three phases of followship—surrender, submission, and trust—we now reach the final one: enjoyment. Enjoying Jesus' leadership is the heart of this book, which is why we'll spend the last two chapters unfolding what we have already discovered about it throughout these pages and unpacking more of what it looks like in everyday life.

Notice how these four phases are progressive. Unless you have willingly surrendered control of your life to Jesus, how can you expect to be able to submit to Him, much less to His leading? If you haven't submitted to Jesus and given Him full authority over your life, then I highly doubt you'll be able to trust Him to lead you in life. Of course, you may be able to trust Him with the "smaller" areas of life, but your overall trust will undoubtably be tested once you face situations where you have no control over the outcome. Only if you are able to trust Him in such uncertainties will you then be able to actually enjoy His leadership.

For some, it may help to see the connection between these four phases in reverse order: You cannot enjoy a leader whom you don't trust. You don't fully trust a leader if you're not also willing to submit to his authority and decision-making. And it's not possible to submit to that leader unless you've first surrendered your own rights to leading yourself.

I realize that identifying these phases of followship can sound formulaic. Let me remind you, however, that when we choose to follow Jesus, we are led by a person, not a robot. Jesus is living. He has emotions, and He leads us with compassion. Before we dive into how followship can sometimes feel unnerving, it's crucial that we start from a place of recognizing Jesus' feelings toward us.

One of the foundational truths we can bank on when we surrender our lives to Jesus and follow Him as Lord is this: He *always* has our best in mind, no matter what our circumstance. The Bible proves this again and again. Think of Joseph telling his treacherous brothers: "You intended to harm me, but God intended it for good" (Gen. 50:20). Or Jesus' reminder that the Father cares for us to such a degree that "even the very hairs of your head are all numbered" (Matt. 10:30). Or Paul's frequently quoted reminder to believers: "And we know that in all things God works for the good of those who love him, who have been called according to his purpose" (Rom. 8:28).

If we want to enjoy Jesus' leadership, then we must *know*—in a deep, relational, experiential way—His supreme care. Jesus isn't just all-wise and all-knowing; He's also all-caring. He is more concerned about our condition than we are. He really, truly, perfectly wants the absolute best for us. That truth is crucial for us to not just believe but *know* to the point that we *trust* Him in that belief—because as the rest of this chapter will show, our journey with Him can often be simultaneously thrilling and exasperating, wonderful and frustrating.

FOLLOWING HIM TOWARD ONE THING

My friends Benedicte and Gjermund are living examples of the followship journey. A married Norwegian couple with three children, their roller-coaster ride started in 2005, when the Lord began showing Benedicte how the church is the bride of Christ and how prayer and worship are part of preparing that bride for Jesus' return as the Bridegroom. She believed God wanted to "awaken the bride" of Norway and sensed an urgency from the Lord to call together as many people as would come to seek Him in prayer and worship. The gathering was to be called Onething Europe, named after a conference in the United States for young people committed to making Jesus the "one thing" for which they live (Ps. 27:4). For those who knew Benedicte, the vision was an obvious stretch; she wasn't the type of person to naturally start a conference, nor did she really want to. She preferred ministering to the Lord in her prayer closet and staying behind the scenes. But she submitted her preferences to Jesus and chose to say yes to whatever He asked of her.

Over the next few years, the Lord reminded my friends of this vision through many extraordinary signs and prophetic words. Once during a prayer conference, a leader onstage suddenly singled out Benedicte among the crowd and, without knowing her situation, declared, "Benedicte is carrying a vision that is important for this nation." Later she received two boxes: The first was full of money people gave in response to the leader's statement, while the second contained a wedding dress, a pair of bridal shoes, and fresh flowers. As strange as this second gift might have seemed, Benedicte knew the Lord was confirming His invitation for her to help prepare His bride and that He would provide the resources for whatever He asked her to do.

Each step Benedicte and Gjermund took in faith led to the next, until one day the Lord gave three blatant messages that Onething Europe was to be held in one of Norway's largest stadiums. The couple didn't have the money to book the twenty-thousand-seat venue, but they knew the Lord did; they just needed to wait to see how He would come through. Meanwhile, He continued to refine the vision for the gathering, even expanding it to include a missions element.

By late 2018 it looked like Onething Europe might actually become a reality. The couple felt led by Jesus to step out in faith and book the stadium, although they were still unsure how He would provide the funds. When one organization with deep pockets approached them, it seemed their prayers had been answered—yet Benedicte lacked peace about saying yes. She wrestled with the matter for weeks in prayer and eventually made one of the most difficult decisions she'd ever made: She turned down the offer.

Naturally speaking, Benedicte's choice made no sense, yet in her spirit she felt a joy and peace she could not explain. Five minutes later she received another call from a private donor offering to fund the entire event. The uncanny timing set the course for an exciting season in which Benedicte and Gjermund saw one miracle unfold after another—including God sending volunteer leaders to help at just the right time. Missions organizations soon wanted to partner with the event and send out short-term missions teams as part of its conclusion. Churches began to lend their support. Volunteers wanted to help because they too sensed God stirring the nation into an awakening of bridal identity, prayer, and missions. After more than a decade, Onething Europe was actually happening!

Everything came to a screeching halt when in early spring 2020, only weeks before the gathering, Norway went into lockdown amid the COVID-19 pandemic. Any plans to assemble twenty thousand people—much less twenty people—were completely dashed. For the next two years, my friends faced a seemingly impossible mission: trying to lead a team of volunteers in planning an event amid total uncertainty—including no date.

Benedicte and Gjermund felt like they were staring into a dense fog, with zero visibility ahead everywhere they turned. They did their best to stand in faith, and they trusted that Jesus was in control, but as the months turned into years, carrying what they believed was His vision for Onething Europe wasn't always easy.

Have you ever faced this kind of uncertainty in following Jesus? If you haven't, you will. If there is one certainty about following Jesus, it's that there will be uncertainty! The good news? We can be sure of everything in Jesus. Nothing about Him is shaky. Who He is, what He says, what He does—these are all absolute. The bad news? Jesus calls us on a journey of followship where things will seem questionable, even precarious, at times. He will lead us into situations and seasons where we cannot see ahead, to the side, or maybe even behind us. We will face moments when we're unsure where we are and maybe even why we're there.

I believe these moments define our followship. Will we choose to give into the doubts and fears that sweep in to attack us in the face of uncertainty? Or will we "set our face as flint," as Isaiah said, and continue to trust Jesus' leading through the uncertainty? (See Isaiah 50:7.)

Benedicte and Gjermund did just this—and it's one of the reasons I am so honored to know them. They have lived the call to followship: struggling to surrender at times, occasionally wrestling with submitting to Jesus' seemingly backward way of leading, trying to trust the Lord when the task He gave them felt overwhelming and virtually everything related to accomplishing it seemed unknown. Yet in every phase, I have also seen my friends simply enjoy Jesus. They haven't just trusted Him based on whatever latest miracle He did regarding Onething Europe (though those helped). And they haven't submitted to Him simply because He could provide a better plan. What I admire is that they enjoyed following Jesus through uncertainty because it was *Jesus* leading them, and that's all that mattered to them.

Onething Europe did happen. Just when my friends wondered if they were to lay down the vision, Jesus led them through another faith-stretching adventure that culminated at the stadium they originally booked, with only a fraction of the stands filled. The numbers ultimately didn't matter to them; this was about awaking a nation to prayer, which by nature involves unseen things. More so, the journey was about following Jesus in complete obedience. That obedience cost Benedicte and Gjermund dearly. Not only did they devote years of their lives to the gathering; they risked having to rent the stadium with their own money and were prepared to sell their house if needed. (They didn't, as the Lord provided another miracle *after* the event.) But to say Benedicte and Gjermund's journey *ended* at the stadium would be incorrect, because it was never just about a large gathering. They are still walking the same ongoing followship journey—after Onething Europe, the Lord led them to Kenya for a couple years and then back to Norway—and they are still just as committed to enjoying the same Jesus.

Not everyone is called to follow Jesus through a seventeen-year, roller-coaster journey like my Norwegian friends. But we are invited to enjoy Him, no matter where, when, or how He leads us. When we enjoy Jesus, we can follow Him through things far worse than thwarted plans or unfulfilled dreams. Sure, we may have days when we trust Jesus yet struggle to like the way He is leading us—that's normal. But when we love Him first simply because of who He is, then we can ultimately enjoy the journey He leads us on—yes, even through the darkness of uncertainty.

WHY CAN'T I SEE ANYTHING?

When my family lived in Florida, I enjoyed riding roller coasters at the multiple theme parks there. I was usually excited to try all of them, but two especially stood out: Space Mountain and Rock 'n' Roller Coaster. On both rides, you spent most of your time rising, plummeting, zigging, and zagging *in complete darkness*. In general, I like the harrowing speeds, turns, corkscrews, and loops in a roller-coaster ride. But when you do all those things in the dark with no clue what's ahead, it's a totally different experience. I don't know about you, but I don't enjoy having my stomach end up in my throat after an unexpected twenty-five-meter plunge. I certainly don't like not being able to see anything to determine for myself how safe a roller coaster is.

During my first few rides in the dark I had to remind myself that the roller coaster had been tested, that my car would not suddenly fly off the track, that my seat belt and the lap bar really would hold me in, and that I was more likely to die in a car accident than on that ride. Because I couldn't see anything, I had to trust that those who built and maintained the coaster had ensured it was safe enough to ride. My lack of vision forced me into a choice: Would I hate the experience and spend the entire ride worrying about whether a mechanic had done everything right, or would I trust the engineers and enjoy the ride despite those nagging fears?

I'm proud to say I am now a card-carrying enclosed-coaster enthusiast. I absolutely love them! Does that mean I enjoy the unexpected drops? Not exactly. Do I take joy in not being able to see how safe a roller coaster is? Nope. But I have learned to let go and have fun in the two to five minutes of those rides, even while still being plagued by an occasional thought of falling out and plummeting to my death in some freak accident. The more I have ridden those coasters, the more I've relinquished such fears.

Part of my about-face came through a calculated, logic-based process, but most of it emerged through a deeper change. In my head I could rationalize that the chances of me dying on a roller coaster were so slim that my worries were unfounded. But how many of us know that when fear grips us, it isn't about the head but about the heart? That meant I had to do more than just be convinced in my mind that riding in the dark was fun. My heart needed to believe the ride wasn't just safe but actually enjoyable.

So how did I do that? I let go. I willingly trusted what I could not see. And do you know what? When I did that, I eventually enjoyed the same thrills on enclosed coasters that I experienced on roller coasters operating in the light, even though I couldn't see what was ahead. That helped convince my heart that having full visibility wasn't so necessary to have fun on the ride. When I think back now, I realize I *never* would have enjoyed those roller coasters, no matter how many times I rode them, had I not made the choice to let go.

What are the enclosed roller coasters of your life? In what areas do you have a hard time letting go and following the Lord into the unknown? If you're unsure how to answer, think of it this way: Where in your life do you find yourself white-knuckled and wanting more control? What is the most terrifying thing Jesus could lead you through? Maybe it's giving up a career. I couldn't imagine that at one stage of my life, yet I found more joy when I let God decide my future employment. Or maybe the terror of the unknown hits hardest when you think about never being married. Surely Jesus wouldn't take you down that path, would He? Or maybe what grips you with fear is losing the house you've worked so hard to fix, or the children you've worked so hard to raise, or the reputation you've worked so hard to build.

The Lord is not a killjoy who's constantly conspiring new ways to rob you of the things you enjoy in life. We know from His Word that He is the most loving Father there is, and He delights in giving us good, perfect gifts. (See James 1:17.) But it's essential for us to recognize that our idea of a good journey in life is different from God's. We like smooth rides, whereas He is willing to take us through some bumpy patches if it means we will trust Him more. We prefer a way that avoids pain and suffering, yet if that's what it takes for our relationship with Him to deepen, then what's actually best in the long run? And we definitely like shortcuts, whereas the Lord is patient enough to go the long way with us if it means by doing so we will gain freedom from whatever keeps us from Him.

Jesus is infinitely more reliable than a roller-coaster mechanic. As strange as that sounds, think about it: A roller-coaster mechanic doesn't know every rider personally, and he couldn't care less whether each rider *enjoys* the ride. His only concern is ensuring the ride operates safely. Jesus, on the other hand, is concerned with our well-being—in fact, far more than we are! He doesn't just want to keep us safe; He cares deeply about how we are throughout the journey.

The Lord who knows the number of hairs on our heads and who designed every strand of our DNA is the same God who cares for our emotional health and our relationships. He wants what is good for us. We tend to measure "good" by how something makes us feel or, when we're more farsighted, what future benefits we think we'll gain. But God has an infinitely greater vision for our lives. Our happiness is not His goal, nor is our pleasure always what's best. Those are secondary to what He knows are the deeper elements of life.

Does this mean He doesn't want us to enjoy anything? Of course not! But if we enjoy something at the cost of never enjoying *Him*, the source of all that is permanently good, then what kind of enjoyment is it? It's temporary and fleeting! As Ecclesiastes says, we are then "chasing after the wind" (2:11, 17, 26).

The world's ideal of "good" ultimately revolves around self-preservation. We avoid things that hurt. When we're uncomfortable, we pop a pill. If we're sad, we binge on a pick-me-up. Even in comforting others, we quickly remind them, "Things will get better." I wish these responses rang true only among unbelievers, but I see the same aversion to dis-ease affecting the church. When we buy into a "God wants me happy" gospel, we unwittingly embrace a self-centered paradigm of good. God forbid that He would allow pain or difficulty to bring about good, because that's not our version of good!

Whatever happened to walking the way of Jesus? Whatever happened to "sharing in His sufferings" so we can know Christ and the power of His resurrection? (See Philippians 3:10.) As followers of Jesus, we are called to follow Him through the path of pain, and that should not come as a surprise. Jesus *promised* pain for those who follow Him! "Here on earth you will have many trials and sorrows," He said matter-of-factly. "But take heart, because I have overcome the world" (John 16:33, NLT).

Years later, Peter reiterated this when believers were suffering immensely: "Do not be surprised at the fiery ordeal that has come on you to test you, as though something strange were happening to you. But rejoice inasmuch as you participate in the sufferings of Christ, so that you may be overjoyed when his glory is revealed" (1 Pet. 4:12–13).

Jesus' glory is revealed in suffering. His splendor can be showcased through our pain if we allow Him to work. But do we really believe this? When He leads us into the darkness of pain, do we "rejoice" in our opportunity to join Him, or do we go white-knuckled and screaming all the way?

THE PATH OF PAIN

I have been privileged to interact with many leaders of the global persecuted church. These mighty men and women of faith will never appear on magazine covers or in many megachurch pulpits, yet their impact is profound. One persecuted pastor I met from China has been imprisoned dozens of times yet seen revival break out among inmates in multiple prisons. An Indian pastor returned from a ministry trip to discover the remains of his wife and children after a mob locked them inside their house and burned it to the ground. He not only forgave the murderers, but he preached the gospel to them and led a handful to Jesus. And I'll never forget speaking with a pastor from Egypt during the Arab Spring who was almost certain she would die the next day at the hands of Muslim extremists. In her case, and with every persecuted-church leader I've interviewed, I asked how we in the West could pray. Their answers were always the same: "Do not pray for the persecution to stop; please do not pray for that or that will rob us of the honor God has given us. Instead, pray that we will remain strong in the persecution."

Those words challenge me to the core. Would I see facing life-or-death situations as an honor? Would my prayer be to stand strong in the face of such suffering, or would I ask the Lord to relieve me of it? I complain when a brother in the faith criticizes me; would I rejoice if a stranger threatened to behead me for my faith?

The persecuted church can seem so far away, and their stories can seem like extreme cases we barely relate to from equally unfamiliar parts of the world. But I believe we in the "pampered church" must regain something our suffering brothers and sisters have seized. Again and again, their perseverance in horrific situations produces a church full of believers committed to following Jesus, no matter what the cost. Tertullian's famous statement is true: "The blood of the martyrs is the seed of the church."[1] And I have seen firsthand how that church is full of fruit we in the West are after: true joy, true purpose, true contentment, true peace, and true love.

These are not only fruit of God's kingdom—they are what the Lord is trying to produce in our own lives when He leads us into situations we think are too dark, uncertain, painful, or dangerous. But are we willing to follow Him there? Are we still willing to trust He has our best in mind during these times? We tend to avoid such hard places or seasons, yet Jesus will often lead us *into* them. The first believers encouraged each other with a strange line: "We must go through many hardships to enter the kingdom of God" (Acts 14:22). How many churches do you know today that encourage believers with such a perspective?

I understand why suffering isn't a trending topic. Why would I trust a leader who promises suffering if I follow him? Why would I want to follow him through such a miserable path? I cannot answer that question for you, but I can tell you more about the leader who is calling you to such a journey.

A MATTER OF PERSPECTIVE

I once got a behind-the-scenes look at the Space Mountain roller coaster I mentioned earlier. I had to retrieve an item from an attendant and in the process stepped into the ride's control room. Though small, the room was filled with screens, each showing a different segment of the ride. Cameras placed above the tracks monitored every part, from beginning to end. Though the riders couldn't see anything while speeding through the dark, the cameras picked up everything. If anything were to go wrong, the control room operators would know exactly where to go and what to do, given all the technical instruments measuring and monitoring every aspect of the ride.

Our lives are far more complicated than an enclosed roller coaster, and experiencing a real-life season where we don't know what's ahead is admittedly different than an amusement-park ride. If you are facing uncertainty or suffering, I do not want to minimize what you're going through—believe me, I have been there too. (See Afterword.) Yet I have also found that I'm more likely to let go in those seasons when I discover more about who is actually in the control room of my life.

We have already seen that Jesus cares more about our lives than we do. Yet He also sees infinitely more of our lives than we do. We have a limited scope. None of us can be certain what will happen next year, much less next month. Jesus, however, knows exactly how things will go—both in my life and yours. Figuratively speaking, He always sits in a control room with a bird's-eye view of our lives. In fact, He is incapable of seeing us outside the lens of supreme wisdom and omniscience. He *always* knows where we are in connection to our final destination, and therefore we can be assured that wherever He leads us is purposeful and intentional.

In addition, because of the Bible, we know the Lord is supremely passionate about being *with* us—now and forever. Sharing life together is what caused Him to create humanity, and it's what compelled Jesus to the cross. So while a roller-coaster ride has a final stopping point, there is no end when we "ride" with Jesus on the journey of followship. We can know Him and enjoy Him for eternity.

When we look at our lives from this perspective, can we afford to *not* trust Him? It's incredibly risky! When we venture through life on our own, under our own leadership, we have no idea what the outcome will be. Yet when we follow Jesus, there is true certainty. It does not always feel or look that way. But because the Lord is sure, His way is sure as well.

WALKING THROUGH THE SEASONS

As we continue looking at what enjoying Jesus' leadership looks like in real life, it's valuable to identify different types of paths through which He often leads us. The Bible's wisdom writings tell us, "There is a time for everything, and a season for every activity under the heavens" (Eccl. 3:1). Indeed, those who have walked with the Lord for many years can look back and recognize seasons in their own lives. I believe Jesus will lead us into and through these different seasons to deepen our relationship with Him. Sometimes He leads us into times of triumph, blessing, abundance, and hope, as well as other wonderful, positive seasons. But what about those tougher periods we have been talking about in this chapter? What does it look like when He purposefully takes us through those?

Allow me to highlight three challenging seasons Jesus has used in my life to not only develop my trust in Him but also enrich my enjoyment of Him. On the surface, none of these seems enjoyable, yet when I've been able to let go and trust Him through the process of each one, I have discovered these seasons produce a treasure in me that I would not trade for all the world.

1. Seasons of quietness

Almost every Christian wants to hear God's voice more frequently. Relationships thrive on good communication, and poor communication can cause relational drift. Why, then, does God sometimes take us through seasons of speaking less—or what seems to be not at all?

Much has been written about when God is silent, and I have used that expression in my life as well. The older I get, however, the more I question if the Lord is ever really silent from this side of the cross. Obviously, we have examples like Job and the intertestamental period to prove God *can* be silent. But if we believe the Bible is His living, Spirit-breathed Word, then it would be a stretch to say we can't find Him still speaking to us on every page. In addition, Jesus left us with His Holy Spirit as our Guide and Teacher. I don't know many teachers who stay silent long when their students continually ask for help.

Often when we assume God is silent, we later discover He was speaking to us all along, just not in ways we perceived. What we think is silence can actually be our own inability to hear, see, or understand His way of speaking.

Of course, we may reconcile these truths in our heads, but as usual, our hearts can say otherwise. When we are in desperate need of God's direction and the heavens seem to be like brass, it sure *feels* like God is silent, doesn't it?

I now see in hindsight how God used these times of supposed silence to stretch my faith. Without His response, I was required to step into the unknown and trust that He would come through. Faith often feels like stepping off a cliff, and the higher the height, the scarier the step. Yet everything we do with God requires faith. It is, as many have said, the currency of heaven. He uses our faith, no matter how little we have, to deepen our knowing of Him so we can in turn trust and enjoy Him more. What a deal!

Still, if God isn't necessarily silent, then why must He whisper so much? I believe the Lord's quietness is often a sign of Him maturing us. He desires such trust from us that He is willing to lower the volume of His voice so we will still walk in the confidence of our intimate relationship even when we do not hear Him. I believe this is why you rarely find the Lord being quiet with new believers. Once they discern His voice, they hear Him everywhere and in everything. It's only years down the road when they encounter God's voice being still or quiet.

God's quietness intentionally calls us to press into Him more. The maturing of our faith—our trust in Him—will naturally grow our intimacy with Him. When you are intimate with someone, there is not much shouting, is there? That's an oxymoron! Intimacy, by its very definition, involves closeness and quietness as each person cherishes the other. So it is with the Lord as we grow with Him. Seasons of quietness are opportunities to adore the Lord and, in faith, know He is reciprocating that adoration in an infinitely greater way. As Oswald Chambers wrote, "When you cannot hear God, you will find that He has trusted you in the most intimate way possible."[2]

2. Seasons of trial

Perhaps no other life experience can mature our relationship with the Lord like enduring difficulty. Trials come in many forms—from persecution to

God-ordained tests to ongoing struggles. Some trials are directly from God, while others are from the enemy, yet God allows them. Sometimes the Lord orchestrates a season of trials, and other times He grieves along with us that we must experience such times of pain. For example, a season of quietness from God can be a trial, yet so can an unexpected death.

Such a variety of trials obviously raises many questions, and yet most of those inquiries boil down to a single word: *Why?* Why does God allow such difficulty and pain? We briefly touched on how persecution, suffering, and pain relate to followship earlier in this chapter, and I in no way presume to resolve the issue in just a few paragraphs. I highly encourage you to delve more into the topic, as I believe wrestling with "the problem of pain," as C.S. Lewis called it, is core to every believer's theology.[3]

Answering why God allows pain and suffering is like trying to answer why God gave us free will. Every answer unfolds another series of questions in a matrix of thought. Yet isn't it interesting how all those questions seem almost pointless when God comes near to us? We can wrestle with the theological issues surrounding suffering—I have and will continue to—and yet both we and those burning questions melt in the Lord's presence when the great Who shows up and silences every why.

Job certainly found this to be true. His fascinating account in the Bible includes almost forty chapters of theological gymnastics from Job and his friends, who offered various angles to "solve" the problem of pain in Job's life. Yet all these answers were rendered moot when the Lord "spoke to Job out of the storm" (Job 38:1) and then played the silencing trump card by asking him a series of unanswerable questions that boiled down to this: *Are you God?*

Job responded to the Lord with some of the book's most poignant statements:

> I know that you can do anything, and no one can stop you. You asked, "Who is this that questions my wisdom with such ignorance?" It is I—and I was talking about things I knew nothing about, things far too wonderful for me. … I had only heard about you before, but now I have seen you with my own eyes. I take back everything I said, and I sit in dust and ashes to show my repentance.
>
> —JOB 42:2–3, 5–6, NLT

Indeed, God is God, and we are not. That was reason enough to silence Job's "why" questions. Yet what put him on his face was encountering the Lord up close, not just through hearsay.

I believe that is not only the proper posture for anyone whom God calls into a season of suffering, but it's the only way we get through such pain. Seeking answers to the why questions when my father died of a heart attack was not helpful; throwing myself before the Lord and clinging to His presence was. In suffering we find ourselves painfully human—small, hurting, and with no answers. Yet in our humanness, the presence of Immanuel—God with us— transforms our discomfort.

Crying out for God's presence is the appropriate response to suffering. But how are we to respond to other trials? After all, not every trial is the same.

The Book of James gives a shocking answer that seems like foolishness to the world: "Consider it pure joy, my brothers and sisters, whenever you face trials of many kinds, because you know that the testing of your faith produces perseverance. Let perseverance finish its work so that you may be mature and complete, not lacking anything" (Jas. 1:2–4).

God longs for our maturing—for us to be complete in Him, not lacking anything—and He uses trials to grow us. But it's one thing to endure trials; it's another thing to "consider it pure joy" when we encounter them. Was James off his rocker? How can we be expected to take joy in something so painful?

It's for the same reason Jesus endured the cross "for the joy set before him" (Heb. 12:2): He saw its greater purpose. Despite His own desire to avoid the pain and shame of the cross, Jesus recognized its ultimate gain surpassed His suffering. And what was that gain? Us! *We* were the ones He had in mind. Somehow, *we* were the joy set before Him.

What kind of all-sufficient God takes such joy in His people? The same kind of Bridegroom who delights in His broken-but-becoming-beautiful bride. It is the paradoxical way of Jesus' kingdom that He calls us to turn trials and suffering on their head and take joy in something so ugly. That is indeed foolishness to the world, yet it is the wisdom of the kingdom.

If we are willing to endure our cross just as Jesus did, we too will find our ultimate joy: Christ Himself! For whatever reason, He has chosen pain as the pathway to knowing Him in a deeper way. We find joy in growing closer to Jesus by suffering just as He did. Our joy is made perfect as we willingly walk the same way our Savior did. This is how we *know* Him with an intimacy like no other.

If you want to know Jesus to the point of enjoying Him in followship, then I can assure you, He will take you through seasons of trial and suffering. He doesn't do this to kill you, though He will allow it to kill your flesh, if necessary. He is honoring you in the same way the pastors I've interviewed felt honored to endure persecution.

When the apostles' backs were shredded after they had been flogged with the same thirty-nine lashes Jesus received, Scripture records their crazy response: "The apostles left the Sanhedrin, *rejoicing because they had been counted worthy of suffering disgrace for the Name*" (Acts 5:41, emphasis added).

What would it look like if you faced your season of trial with the same inexplicable joy? What if instead of avoiding difficulties you began to embrace them as opportunities to grow closer to Jesus? This is the invitation He extends to you each time He leads you through seasons of trials. Be honored, because it is an invitation to know Him in the deepest way.

3. Seasons of transition

Some people are born decisive. They walk into a restaurant already knowing what they'll order, and when shopping they don't blink when choosing between the blue outfit or the black one. Not me. I'm the kind of guy who second-guesses his order as soon as the waiter walks away and who takes days of researching to decide which phone to buy.

When Jesus leads through seasons of transition, both personality types face challenges and the opportunity to mature in trusting His leadership. The decisive person will often overlook this opportunity and plow on through the life intersection with only a brief stop, if any. Their danger is missing out on Jesus' leading because of their own drive. The indecisive person, however, will often stop at the intersection so long that they allow doubts, worries, and an endless string of what-ifs to keep them frozen. They too can often miss out on Jesus' leading, only in their case it's because of their own unwillingness to step out in faith.

Transition is always exciting, even if you don't like change. To move from one situation to another means something new is being introduced—a new job, relationship, environment, or opportunity. Obviously, with such transition we also face a new set of obstacles, which is why we must depend on the Lord's guidance even more. If we passively float through a season of transition with a que será, será attitude, letting things "just happen," we will often miss out on the thrill of seeing Jesus direct us in supernatural ways. We need to be intentional about turning to Him, allowing His Spirit to be our Guide, and yielding to His decision-making. As we do this, we can be assured that He *will* guide us.

When Amber and I moved from Colorado to Florida years ago, we were not thrilled about leaving the picturesque Rocky Mountain state. Our oldest son was only a year old. I had just completed a new basement in our house that we loved, located in a dream neighborhood. And we had a strong community of friends we didn't want to leave.

I was offered a job that we both sensed was an opening from the Lord, and yet moving across the country presented several crossroads. If this was indeed Him, He would need to change our hearts. Practically speaking, He would need to help us sell our house and provide a place for us in Florida. But just as important, we needed to know that our move was dictated by Him and not by my career.

So what did Jesus do? We had an offer on our house within fifteen minutes of it going on the market. When Amber took a scouting trip to Florida, she came back full of hope and assurance. In short, the Lord couldn't have been any clearer. So we stepped out, full of faith because of how Jesus had led us.

But not every crossroads has been so easy to navigate in our journey, and I would guess it's been that way in your life as well. I counsel many people facing a junction in life, and among the most common questions they ask are: How do I know if it's the Lord leading? How can I be sure that what I sense is His way and not just mine?

One way I respond is to inquire about any noticeable shifts. In my life, it has usually been obvious when Jesus wanted me to leave something. Often I have lost the strength or will to endure a situation, or I've found myself inexplicably compelled toward change. (To be sure, this is over a long period of time; it's not just after having a bad day, week, or even month.) Those have been some common signs indicating things are about to change in my life.

Yet even when the Lord has obviously led me to an intersection, at times I've still not known which way He wanted me to go. If I made a move, how was I to know if it was actually the Lord? How could I be sure it wasn't just my subconscious desires driving me toward change? How could I trust my decision if I didn't sense the Lord speaking to me?

Can you see what the common thread is in those questions? They all essentially start with me! Often in our sincere desire to know that we are being led by the Lord, we ask questions that are centered on us and our ability to discern God's direction. What if we instead started from a place centered on God's ability to lead rather than our ability to follow? For example, what if our self-talk sounded like the following:

- *God* has said He will guide me; therefore *He* will show me the way.
- *God* has said He will provide for me; therefore *He* will supply all my needs.
- *God* has said He will give me the words to say; therefore *He* will speak through me.

This changes the perspective, doesn't it? It can also change our approach to the seasons of transition to which Jesus leads us. The key to walking through these seasons with Him is getting our eyes off ourselves and *our* sense of hearing or discerning, and instead focusing on the Lord. He is more than able to lead us. The issue isn't whether He can or wants to lead. No, the issue is whether we trust Him enough to step into what we consider the unknown.

As we saw in the last chapter, "Faith is confidence in what we hope for and assurance about what we do not see" (Heb. 11:1). Not only does faith involve stepping out with confidence into the unseen, but we know that "without faith it is impossible to please God" (Heb. 11:6). Put these together and it means anytime we walk in God's way—in accordance with His will, by His leading—it will require faith!

It's wonderful when we "feel" enough faith to trust God is leading us somewhere or to something. But what if we don't sense that? It's still a matter of relationship with God. If we love Him, we will "walk in obedience to his commands" (2 John 6). And if He has called us to step out into the unknown in faith, then our choice is a matter of obedience—which, in turn, shows our love for Him.

I like how bluntly Dietrich Bonhoeffer puts it: "If you believe, take the first step, it leads to Jesus Christ. If you don't believe, take the first step all the same, for you are bidden to take it. ... Then you will find yourself in the situation where faith becomes possible and where faith exists in the true sense of the word."[4]

Too often we fret over figuring out the Lord's will when He is trying to lead us to enjoy Him through obedience. We can get caught up in our actions, while He wants us to get caught up in Him. Our faith is built on a real relationship in which we trust Him. The way we develop this faith is by knowing Him more and taking action out of that trusting relationship; the two work in tandem. This is not a works-based relationship; He is the essence of my faith in the first place. The more I know Jesus, the more I will want to deny myself, take up my cross, and follow Him. In that ongoing process of dying to self, *He* will continue to resurrect me more and more into *His* life, transforming me more and more into *His* likeness. As He does so through the Holy Spirit's work in me, I will begin to think, feel, and act more like Him. My desires will reflect His desires more and more; therefore the actions I take will—in faith—also be more in line with what He wants (His will). Simply put, I will be acting less out of "me" and more out of Him.

This is how we can grow in confidence that He is leading us and that we're not just going our own way. The more we trust Him, the more His ability to lead us becomes the focus rather than our ability to follow in the right way. Our starting place is trusting Him, which can come only through knowing Him. Can you see how it all comes back to the fundamental point of knowing Him? Does it make more sense now why Paul so brilliantly said he would willingly count everything as garbage for the sake of knowing Jesus?

I realize this sounds so simple that it's frustrating. I have had plenty of students ask me to help them discern whether God is leading them to change jobs, start dating someone—you name it—and I am aware it's frustrating for them when I tell them the key is knowing Jesus more. But as much as I don't enjoy seeming simplistic, I can only answer with what I know to be true, and that truth comes both from God's Word and the testimony of my own life and those closest to me. Knowing Jesus is truly the key. It's the key to every season of our followership journey, and it is especially the key as He brings us through seasons of transition.

UNCERTAINTY IN THE WAY

No one enjoys absolute uncertainty all the time. Not even the most adventurous among us would relish going without any safety gear across a dilapidated, frayed-rope bridge hanging a hundred meters high. Some of us may get a thrill from taking risks, but when it comes to our journey through life, it's hard to expect exhilaration when you can never get sure footing.

If you are familiar with any of the three seasons we just examined, you know firsthand that living through them can feel like trying to walk across a shaky rope bridge with no planks. Each season involves uncertainty, so it's understandable if you wince slightly at the thought of Jesus taking you through another one. For example, it's normal if you aren't excited by the thought of having to endure suffering or having to trust only the faintest directions that you think *might be* God's voice. I understand your hesitance, and sometimes I have that too. I'm not exactly looking forward to having to stand strong amid the increasing persecution that followers of Jesus will soon face in the Western world.

What does excite me, however—and I hope it excites you too—is thinking of Jesus' brilliance. No human leader could create a plan so genius as to take his or her people through the most unexpected lows of life to reach the highest way possible. Jesus is leading us to paradise, and that perfection is more than just His kingdom fully come on earth as it is in heaven; it's *Him*! Whatever season He has you in—and there are many others besides the ones I have mentioned—He has you there for the higher, supreme purpose of knowing Him. He knows the beginning from the end, and He never loses sight of the way because He *is* the way. Our ongoing goal is always found in Him, and our ongoing purpose is to remain in Him.

I may not always like traveling this way, where the details of my journey are ever-unfolding only as I go and the final destination is a person. Though I still struggle at times, I'm getting better at letting go so I can enjoy Him in this journey of followship. I hope you're getting better at it too. Maybe recognizing that some of these seasons are part of His plan has even lifted the burden from your shoulders. We really are best off when we let Him lead and simply trust that He knows the way. Again, this higher way of journeying through life can be simultaneously frustrating and exhilarating. But it is the way of followship, of enjoying Jesus even in and through points of uncertainty, simplicity, pain, and perseverance—the last things we ever imagined we'd be facing on our journey.

CHAPTER 14

LET HIM LEAD

JESUS IS NOT afraid of the dark.

I don't just mean the kind of dark we face when awakened in the middle of the night by a strange noise. I'm talking about the darkness that grips us with fear in life because of its unknowns—the darkness of impending bankruptcy, a cancer diagnosis, a broken engagement, or even a global pandemic that changes everything.

Jesus is not afraid of any of those things. He is not the least bit scared of heading into the dense fog of uncertainty. He's not even worried. The reason? Well, to begin with, He is all-knowing. And all-powerful and all-seeing. And He transcends all space, time, and matter. Those are some biggies, obviously.

As we end our look at followship, however, I want to highlight one reason behind Jesus' fearlessness. It's an aspect of His character that should not only motivate our trust in Him but also help us enjoy Him more as the ultimate leader of our lives.

Jesus is not afraid of the darkness because He is supreme. As God, He is completely over the darkness and all it contains. It's difficult to comprehend God's supremacy, given the limitations of our minds, but maybe this helps: Whatever is the highest, greatest, most ultimate thing you can think of in terms of power, size, rank, authority, importance—you name it—God is even higher, greater, and more ultimate. Because of this, He and He alone is supreme. You cannot have two supreme beings—that's contradictory. To be supreme, one must be over *all* others.

Colossians 1:15–17 says Jesus "is supreme over all creation. … Everything was created through him and for him. He existed before anything else, and he holds all creation together" (NLT). Jesus' supremacy over *all* creation includes every form and shade of darkness that ever existed. In the creation account, He brought light out of the chaotic nothingness we call darkness. In Isaiah 45:7, the Lord says, "I form the light and create darkness." Psalm 139:12 says of God, "Even the darkness will not be dark to you; the night will shine like the day, for darkness is as light to you." And when Jesus entered the earth, John says "his life brought light to everyone. The light shines in the darkness, and the darkness can never extinguish it" (John 1:4–5, NLT).

Why does this matter for those of us wanting to follow Jesus? Because it means He cannot be overtaken, no matter where He leads us. Throughout the journey of following Jesus, we follow the only person who can't be defeated, overpowered, or outdone. Whatever darkness we face, it can *never* extinguish Jesus. He has not only called us to be just like Him as disciples, but He's also made a way for us to live *in* Him, walking with the same power and authority He has. If His supremacy is mind-blowing for us, how much more is His invitation to us!

Jesus explained it clearly during His ministry: "I am the light of the world. Whoever follows me will never walk in darkness, but will have the light of life" (John 8:12).

As wonderful as Jesus' words sound, there is a problem: How could He say His followers would "never walk in darkness"? Didn't we just go through a chapter discussing the different dark seasons He leads us through? We have all walked through dark experiences. Whether the Lord caused, allowed, or led us through those experiences is irrelevant; they're still dark and difficult. So if following Jesus isn't all sunshine and rainbows, then what gives? Was Jesus lying?

A few years ago I knew of a Jesus-following couple whose two-year-old son drowned in the family's backyard pool. Another couple, also followers of the Lord, had to bury their teenage son when he was killed in an automobile accident. Yet both couples, only days after the tragedies, stood on the front row of their churches' gatherings, hands raised, tears flowing, and worshipping Jesus with everything they had. They didn't have many words at that point, but both later shared that they felt a divine peace and a light sustaining them through those days. In moments when the darkness grew suffocating and the despair overwhelming, they still found Jesus holding them, carrying them, being *with* them as the light in the darkness.

The light—Jesus—shines in the darkness, and the darkness can *never* extinguish Him.

Because Jesus has that kind of power, we can trust that His words are true: Whoever follows Him will *never* walk in darkness but will have the light of life.

If even the darkness is as light to Him, as the psalmist said, then so can it be for us who follow our supreme leader. Whatever seems like darkness to us can actually be light because of the one we follow and the life He gives.

FACING JERUSALEM

None of us knows the full extent of what Jesus faced in the darkness of the cross. I can't imagine going through life—or at least the last few seasons of your life—knowing that at some point you will suffer one of the most excruciating deaths contrived by humans. Yet Mark's Gospel teaches us an incredible lesson about how Jesus looked at this imminent darkness, walked right into it and, eventually, called His disciples to follow in the same way.

In Mark 10 we find a key transition point in Jesus' ministry. Prior to this He spent much of His time outside Jerusalem, though He visited the city for various Jewish feasts and undoubtedly visited the temple during each trip. After three years of teaching and displaying Messiah-like power, Jesus had risen enough in popularity to pose a threat to Israel's religious leaders, who "were looking for a way to kill him" (John 7:1). He had eluded them in Jerusalem and throughout Judea, as the sequence of events leading to His death would only be initiated when He was willing. But He now knew another trip to Jerusalem would undoubtedly light the fuse. So as Jesus made His way toward the centerpiece of Judaism in Mark 10:32–34, He knew exactly what He was heading into.

> They were on their way up to Jerusalem, with Jesus leading the way, and the disciples were astonished, while those who followed were afraid. Again he took the Twelve aside and told them what was going to happen to him. "We are going up to Jerusalem," he said, "and the Son of Man will be delivered over to the chief priests and the teachers of the law. They will condemn him to death and will hand him over to the Gentiles, who will mock him and spit on him, flog him and kill him. Three days later he will rise."

Notice how verse 32 highlights Jesus "leading the way" for those who followed. There wasn't a hint of uncertainty in Jesus. He was resolute in heading toward Jerusalem. In fact, He knew exactly what would happen there in a matter of days, and for the third time, He gave His disciples a detailed heads-up (albeit in a slightly awkward third-person way). Mark indicates that the disciples were astonished—other translations use the words "amazed" or "filled with awe" (NKJV, NLT). More than likely, they were surprised by Jesus' boldness in heading toward such danger rather than away from it. They had seen how the religious leaders looked at their rabbi. They were surely aware of the constant traps the Pharisees and scribes set for Him. Maybe they'd even heard rumors of the plots to kill Jesus. His disciples were in awe, as none of this seemed to faze Jesus in the slightest. There He was, leading the way straight into the darkness that awaited Him.

Things have not changed since then. Jesus is still unafraid of the darkness of this world, and He still leads His disciples right into it. Despite the threats of being misunderstood, wrongly accused, and persecuted, He calls His disciples to walk, suffer, and shine in the darkness, just as He did. "You are the light of the world," He told us, turning the analogy around. "A town built on a hill cannot be hidden. Neither do people light a lamp and put it under a bowl. Instead they put it on its stand, and it gives light to everyone in the house. In the same way, let your light shine before others, that they may see your good deeds and glorify your Father in heaven" (Matt. 5:14–16).

Go into the danger and darkness of this world and *shine*, Jesus said. Radiate with His life and light living inside you, and do it to such a degree that others respond by turning their faces to heaven in worship.

That's the kind of pep talk followers of Jesus need, because some of us are too often in the second group Mark notes on the way to Jerusalem: "the disciples were astonished, while *those who followed were afraid*" (10:32, emphasis added). Following Jesus can definitely seem scary at times. We are prone to fear when facing our own Jerusalems. We may be afraid of being rejected or standing out or getting hurt again. But we are never alone in facing those fears; Jesus calls us to walk *with* Him through them.

Notice that amid the fear, Jesus took His closest friends aside and offered vision, clarity, and perspective as they walked together. "This is what will happen," He essentially said, "but three days later ..." With Jesus there is always a glorious counterpoint to the darkness, a way that ultimately leads to life, even if it must take us through death to get there. Indeed, we have seen many times in the last few chapters that Jesus' leading often calls us to die so we can truly live. It's the way our Master went, so why would it be any different for us as followers?

When you think of it, we have absolutely no reason to fear. Whatever we're facing—disappointment, ridicule, disaster—Jesus is above it. He is the supreme leader, and therefore the darkness should make us cling all the closer to Him.

I once spoke with the pastor of an Asian underground church whose congregation had almost all been beaten, tortured, or imprisoned for their faith. He had the scars on his arms and back to prove his own suffering. "I do not fear beatings or even dying," he said. "I only fear that in my moment of suffering I will fall away and renounce Jesus as some have done."

We may never face such physical persecution, but we all face the threat of turning away from Jesus in the face of darkness. Maybe the Jerusalem we face is past sins coming back to haunt us. Or a familiar depression that wants to sweep over us again. Or a future taunting us with the possibility of loneliness. As one who has walked through all those shades of dark—and others—I know the only hope of overcoming such darkness is Jesus our overcomer. When we face a growing fear, we must choose to draw near to Him as if He is our next breath. He *will* lead us through. Even when we are afraid, He isn't. He knows the way, and He is leading us in light. Remember, there is no darkness that can overcome Him.

DISCIPLES, NOT STUDENTS

Whenever we lead ourselves instead of surrendering to Jesus' leadership, we will end up on a pathway in life that is frightening and overwhelming. It's not a matter of if but when. What else would we expect when facing the darkness in our own limited strength? But with the one who has overcome everything—Jesus—leading, we can rely on Him for all we need. He calls us to Himself, to walk through any darkness in His strength, His peace, and His power.

Throughout this book I have reiterated how God desires this kind of partnership, not servitude. "I no longer call you servants," Jesus said to His closest disciples. "Instead, I have called you friends" (John 15:15). Jesus has invited us into the greatest friendship ever through discipleship with Him, yet even in that call, He wants us to follow Him out of a desire for ongoing fellowship, not out of demand. This call to followship is what marks the journey of someone who is a true disciple and not just a student. A student learns primarily from books. Even when a teacher is involved, the student absorbs concepts, ideas, and information, then spits out what he has learned to pass an exam. The end goal is a passing grade and, ultimately, graduation.

For a disciple, however, the objective isn't getting good marks on a test or earning a diploma; it's to become just like the rabbi. To reach this goal requires real relationship between the disciple and master. A disciple surrenders his own way of life as he follows his rabbi; he submits to the long-term process of becoming like the one he is following. And over time, he trusts that his rabbi knows best about how to become like him. But ultimately, if the disciple never enjoys following the rabbi out of true relationship, then he will never fully become like him; he'll have only learned things like a student would.

In followship, Jesus calls us to partnership as He leads and we follow. It's a unique partnership: We are His creation, yet He invites us into friendship with Him. We were *created* for partnership; that's how much He originally formed us for friendship with Him. Yet we are *called* to followship; friendship with Him is an open invitation. He does not force us into fellowship with Him, even though we were made for such a glorious connection.

I believe the difference in rejecting or accepting this invitation to followship is the difference between enduring life and enjoying life. It's the difference between white-knuckling our way through life versus raising our hands and screaming with joy on the roller-coaster ride of our lifetime. A student endures his education to pass a test. A disciple enjoys his rabbi to become like him. Ultimately, then, the deciding factor for us as disciples is our relationship with Jesus—how much we enjoy Him. The more we enjoy Him, the more we will continue following Him regardless of where, when, or how He leads us because our ultimate joy will be in Him. He leads, we follow—and in the partnership we find the joy for which we were made.

DANCING WITH THE DIVINE

Before we had children, Amber and I were members of the oldest waltz club in America. Every Wednesday night we practiced dancing for an hour with about twenty other couples in a church gymnasium. And every week we went over the same twelve songs with the same handful of waltz patterns. I don't remember why we joined the club since neither of us are natural dancers, but we had a blast challenging ourselves with something new while enjoying some quality "couple time." The waltz club ended every year with an elegant ball in the ballroom of a famous prestigious hotel, where everyone dressed in their best and danced the night away to a live band.

I love dancing with Amber, and I love our memories from that time. But we both agree that, amid all my wife's wonderful giftings, dancing may not be one of those. There's a simple explanation: My wife has no rhythm. Whenever we waltzed, I needed to continually count in her ear so she would stay on track: "One two three, one two three, one two three …" If I ever stopped, she was immediately thrown off and lost her footing. (This is the same woman who during childbirth needed me to keep rhythm with her Lamaze breathing or else she said she couldn't push!)

To enjoy dancing, Amber had to follow my lead. She trusted not only that I would keep rhythm for her but also that I would direct her steps according to how I moved. If I moved left, she moved left, and if I pivoted, she pivoted. Her steps and movements were based on mine. And as long as I continued to lead and she continued to follow, we both could enjoy each waltz and keep dancing as long as we wanted.

But our waltzing would not have been fun for either of us had Amber not been willing to follow me. Can you imagine if both of us insisted on leading the other? Not only would we have looked ridiculous trying to pull each other in opposite ways, but we likely would have ended up in a pile on the floor. Simply put, to enjoy waltzing—or any kind of ballroom dancing—one person must lead and the other must follow. It's not an option. Anything else ends in disaster.

Not long ago I ran across an article online called "How to Dance With a Partner," which was shared among professional dance websites. The piece was not written for a Christian audience, nor was it intended to have anything to do with God. An experienced, professional dance instructor wrote this to simply relay the basics of partner dancing. But as you read a passage from what she wrote, I want you to catch the uncanny parallels between physical dancing and our followship "dance" in life with God.

> The joy of partner dancing comes from moving together in unity. ... It's simply impossible for two people, dancing in close contact, to move seamlessly if each person is making their own decisions, choosing their own timing and doing their steps independently. They must coordinate their moves perfectly—and the only way to achieve that is for one person to direct the moves and the other person to follow. ...
>
> Who leads? In a partner dance, one partner is facing forward while the other has their back to the direction of travel. Obviously, the person who should lead is the person who can see where they're going—and that is, in fact, the rule. ...
>
> It's important to get used to following right from the start ... because learning to allow your partner to lead isn't easy. ... If you're following correctly, you won't take a step until your partner tells you to. He may do that by pressure with his hand

... but whatever the signal is, you must follow it instantly. ... It's hard, especially in this day and age, to surrender so much power to a guy.[1]

I am still deeply moved every time I read this passage. What a picture of followship! It's impossible for us to "move seamlessly" with God in life when we are bent on making our own decisions, choosing our own timing, and taking steps independently. It just doesn't work! The only way to dance with a partner is by allowing one person to lead. And if by this point in the book we haven't figured out who the better leader is between Jesus and us, then we need to start all over again! As the ultimate leader, the Lord knows what He's doing. He created us to dance with Him, but for that dance to work, He must lead and we must follow. In His extreme mercy and grace, He will not force His leadership on us but instead has left the choice to follow entirely up to us.

But did you notice what qualifies the leader in ballroom dancing? It's all about vision and direction. The leader is the one "who can see where they're going." We may think we have a solid grasp on what life will look like tomorrow, next week, next month, or even next year. But honestly, do any of us have control over our lives? One heart attack changed everything for my family. One child drowning changed everything for the family I mentioned before. One job loss or divorce or accident is all it takes for any of our lives to be completely redirected. It's the same for the more positive things we may experience: one childbirth or friendship or opportunity can also alter the course of our lives. But who is not surprised by any of these events, good or bad? Who is infinitely "facing forward" and always sees where we are headed? There is only one with such supreme sight, and He is the same Lord who invited us to the dance in the first place.

He is the one with vision, and we are the ones with our "back[s] to the direction of travel." I don't know many people who like traveling backward with no visibility, and this is exactly why we must trust Jesus as the only one who can safely lead us. As the article excerpt pointed out, "learning to allow your partner to lead isn't easy." We have seen again and again how our human nature to lead and not follow gets in the way. We like control. We like to know where we're going, and when we don't, we can often end up moving out of sync with our partner. Although God created us for partnership, the fall exposed our innate desire to act in opposition to God's movements.

Yet when we are born again and receive a new life in Jesus Christ, we are given the opportunity to live out a new kind of dance. Whereas before we didn't have a chance to be close to God, now, by remaining "in Christ," we can get as close to Him as we want. (See Romans 8:1 and James 4:8.) As we know Him more in this deep way, we love Him more, and in that love we then obey Him. Can you see how this kind of obedience isn't the worldly, authoritative kind? Instead, it is a love-based obedience that comes from true fellowship.

While on earth, Jesus walked out the human experience to perfection by enjoying fellowship with the Father in perfect obedience. Therefore, Jesus leads by example because has He been in our shoes before and not only knows the way, but He *is* the way. In terms of our ongoing dance analogy, Jesus is not only the greatest dancer—and therefore the greatest lead partner—He invented dancing. So if there's anyone we would want to dance with, it's Him!

The more we follow Jesus in fellowship and dance through life in sync with Him, the more we get used to His way of leading. He may lead us by His voice, or He may just signal us "by pressure with his hand." Either way, as we enjoy His leading, less will be required for us to follow Him. We will increasingly, instinctively go the way our Master goes. And as the article says, if we're following correctly, we won't take a step until Jesus tells us to.

Followship is indeed a beautiful dance. There is nothing like enjoying Jesus and His leadership. Even when He takes us into the unknown, we can trust He has higher reasons than what we see or feel. He is the ultimate leader, leading with supreme wisdom, authority, and power. There is no one worth following more than Him, and there is no one safer to lead you through the darkness of the unknown. Sometimes He may initiate traversing through the dark, and other times He will simply allow the difficult times. Either way, He invites you to not just barely get through the journey with Him but to find joy in being with Him through the hardship of uncertainty.

So will you follow Him? Furthermore, will you *enjoy* following Him? The invitation awaits your response.

AFTERWORD

THIS BOOK IS long overdue. Although the English version of it was virtually print-ready more than two years ago, I waited to hear back from some Norwegian publishers who were interested in translating the book yet requesting that I wait to release it simultaneously in both languages. As I grew frustrated during that process, another one suddenly emerged that not only forced me to put the book aside but also has added another chapter—figuratively and literally—to my followship journey.

This most recent addition to the story began in a drab hospital office, where I sat under florescent lights awaiting results from a CT scan. I had originally come for an appointment because of nerve problems—for weeks my hands and feet had tingled to the point of numbness, and I was dealing with sharp pain down my legs and backside. When the neurologists' tests failed to reveal what was causing these symptoms, they ordered more tests and scans like the one I was about to get the results from. You couldn't have picked a more movie-like environment for my doctor to enter the room and, after the usual conversation about how I was feeling, deliver the news: "We've found a two-centimeter lesion on your right lung that looks like a tumor."

Um, what? I thought we were supposed to be talking about my nervous system.

The medical specialist continued to explain that they had also seen some changes in my liver tissue and wanted to find out if these had anything to do with a cancerous mole I'd had removed three years before. By the end of my two-week hospital stay, we had an answer more concerning than my neuropathy: I had stage-four cancer in my right lung, liver, and left thigh bone. Unfortunately, the melanoma from before had reemerged and was now spreading aggressively throughout my body.

Talk about facing the unknown. Talk about a serious test of this whole followship idea. Everything in life seemed to go on hold the moment I received news of my cancer. And yet the waves of thoughts and emotions in the following days began what would become the true test. Would I still trust—yes, even enjoy—Jesus' leadership in such a life-or-death situation?

Now, cancer is so common today that I'm guessing you have your own connection to this part of my story, whether you've personally battled cancer or have a family member, friend, or acquaintance who has. My situation is not unique, which is why I want to focus more on the followship elements of this latest season than my medical details. Because once again, Jesus and how He leads are more noteworthy than how I have followed Him.

GOD IS GOOD ALL THE TIME

Jesus is not surprised by sickness, trials, or tragedy; He reigns over them. As highlighted in the last chapter, He is the exalted King over everything "in heaven and on earth and under the earth" (Phil. 2:10); therefore, nothing happens beyond His authority and power. But that does not mean Jesus wills everything, nor does it mean He doesn't grieve or feel compassion when calamities hit us. I believe God hates cancer, just as He hates every disease or catastrophe. After all, what kind of father would enjoy seeing his children suffer under such things? We know the Lord is infinitely greater in His goodness than any earthly dad. (See Luke 11:11–13.) At the same time, He has allowed Satan, as the temporary "ruler of this world," to act within the realm of its fallenness (John 12:31; 14:30, NLT).

That tension between God's sovereignty, His divine will, and the world's sin-stained condition naturally raises some questions. More importantly, it forces us into a choice: What—or who—will we choose to believe? Will we believe God is who He says He is, and therefore He is good despite what our situation indicates? Or will we form our own definition of God—and truth—according to what we see, what we think or experience, or even what a CT scan tells us?

I faced this choice the moment a doctor told me I had cancer. On one hand, a quick online search gave me the medical outlook for those with stage-four melanoma, and let's just say the odds aren't in my favor, even with the most advanced treatment. It is very possible that I could die from this. On the other hand, the Lord is the only one who offers supreme hope and permanent healing. In fact, He doesn't just offer those elements as if they are distant "things"; He *is* them. The Lord *is* hope—the more I know Him, love Him, and enjoy Him, the more my confident expectation becomes rooted in who He is and what He says. Likewise, the Lord *is* complete healing—where else can I find such life that surpasses my physical condition? In Him I find "the fountain of life" (Ps. 36:9), which Jesus described as "eternal life" (John 10:28).

When we think of it this way, is there really any choice in what to believe? If we choose to trust that God is good, that He is our hope and our healer, and that He is for us amid a fallen world ruled by the evil one who threatens us with things like cancer and death, then we can face hardship in a different way. Then we can experience that Immanuel is truly with us. Once again, the key is in real relationship with Him. When we follow Jesus through tough seasons, mere mental assent of His goodness isn't enough; we must ultimately trust with our hearts because of authentic relationship with Him. Then, with our lives rooted in Him, we will "not be surprised at the fiery ordeal that has come on [us] to test [us], as though something strange were happening to [us]" (1 Pet. 4:12). Whenever we trust God's goodness amid trials, our "testing" can be the very means to purify us from seeking the Lord for what He can do for us rather than purely for who He is. Ultimately, we want our end goal to be God Himself, not just how He can make things better.

This reality of the Lord's unchanging goodness continues to be an anchor for me in not just enduring but enjoying His leadership through this strange season of my life. How is it possible for me to *enjoy* facing an uncertain future that could include dying too soon? Simply put, because He's the one leading, and He cannot be wrong. Ever.

The more I trust Him to lead me through this journey, the more I experience various facets of who He is—including a peace that, as cliché as it sounds, truly passes understanding. I cannot explain it, so let me at least give you an example of what this peace looks like when you're facing the unknown.

A STRANGE STRENGTH

Since my diagnosis, I have had two moments that you would expect to happen. The first was when I sat alone in my hospital room and wept while writing letters to my wife and two sons. Not yet knowing the degree of my cancer, I wanted to ensure each of them would have something from me in writing expressing how much I loved them. The second moment was when Amber was finally able to visit me at the hospital after days of us being apart since my diagnosis. Our forty-five-minute, tear-stained embrace when we met was a roller-coaster ride of emotions, most of which revolved around the uncertainty of our future together.

In both moments I didn't feel fear but only a deep sadness over the possibility of Amber being alone and my boys losing their father at such a young age. I am not exaggerating when I say that other than these two moments, which amount to about an hour and a half, my family and I almost entirely have experienced the Lord's supernatural peace, provision, and yes, even joy—and this has not ended. While we have remained open and honest with each other about how we feel (we don't want to repress or ignore things), all four of us have walked together with genuine trust in Jesus. I don't share this to boast in our ability to persevere through this season but in His unfathomable faithfulness to be our strength when we look to Him.

Almost immediately after those hospital moments, it felt like the Lord bolstered my faith with a strange assurance that I will be healed. I can't explain why, but I don't have a single doubt about being healed, which is not always the norm for me. Obviously, I could be dead wrong (sorry for the poor word choice, but it's my twisted sense of humor). Time will tell whether I am yet another believer who went to their grave contending for a physical healing that never came. But honestly, what does it matter if I am wrong? I get to be with Jesus!

At the same time, I believe the Lord has more for me to do. He has planted kingdom dreams in me that remain unfulfilled. I will admit that thinking of those dreams now is a bit strange since I have never in my life felt so weak. In the months following my first treatments, I developed an infection in my digestive system that made it extremely difficult to eat and retain food. Naturally, I lost plenty of weight; but even more, I struggled with fatigue, migraines, and a wonderful assortment of other cancer goodies. Today I still can't stand or walk without pain in my feet, I feel tired most of the time, and my limbs occasionally go numb if I have done too much. But can I tell you something? My spirit continues to soar with the Lord. If anything, I have discovered new meaning to Paul's words when he wrote, "For when I am weak, then I am strong" (2 Cor. 12:10). I wouldn't trade this kind of strength for anything if it means greater dependency on the Lord.

From the depths of my spirit, I want Him to be glorified through this journey—that people would see more of who He is whether I am healed or not. Already, my family and I have seen glimpses of this. Amid my hospital stay, doctors allowed me to leave to fulfill a teaching commitment, and thereafter I became known on that floor as "the Bible teacher." Something shifted after that, because for the rest of my time there the staff frequently commented on how unique our family was—"so full of life," they said, compared to the sadness and hopelessness they usually faced. I praise God we were able to testify about "the reason for the hope that [we] have" (1 Pet. 3:15). They saw God in action!

Likewise, believers throughout Norway have been moved as we've shared how the Lord continues to lead us through this storm. He is getting the glory and the attention, not our faith or my healing—hallelujah! After all, since He's the one leading, He's the one worth talking about! May we all follow Him in such a way that people see our great Rabbi—Jesus, the one who is worth following in every season of life.

NOTES

Chapter 1: A Call for All

1. Wikipedia, s.v. "Simon Says," modified November 29, 2022, 21:43, https://en.wikipedia.org/wiki/Simon_Says.
2. David Platt, *Radical* (Colorado Springs, CO: Multnomah Books, 2010), 167.
3. Dr. and Mrs. Howard Taylor, *Hudson Taylor's Spiritual Secret* (Chicago, IL: Moody Publishers, 2009), 208.
4. Charles Spurgeon, "Christ Is All," sermon, Metropolitan Tabernacle, August 20, 1871, The Spurgeon Archive, https://archive.spurgeon.org/sermons/1006.php.

Chapter 2: Following on Jesus' Terms

1. John Maxwell, *The 21 Indispensable Qualities of a Leader* (Nashville, TN: Thomas Nelson, 1999), xi.
2. Shmuel Safrai and M. Stern, "Education and the Study of Torah," *The Jewish People in the First Century* 2 (1976): 953–955.
3. Lois Tverberg with Bruce Okkema, *Listening to the Language of the Bible* (Holland, MI: En-Gedi Resource Center, 2004), 126.
4. Martina Gracin and Ervin Budiselić, "Discipleship in the Context of Judaism in Jesus' Time, Part I," *KAIROS: Evangelical Journal of Theology* 13, no. 2 (2019): 205–222, https://doi.org/10.32862/k.13.2.3.

Chapter 3: The Ultimate Fellowship

1. John Piper, "What Is It Like to Enjoy God?" Desiring God, January 2, 2018, https://www.desiringgod.org/messages/what-is-it-like-to-enjoy-god.
2. *Dictionary.com*, s.v. "phase," accessed December 17, 2022, https://www.dictionary.com/browse/phase.
3. "The Westminster Shorter Catechism," The Presbytery of the United States, accessed December 17, 2022, https://www.westminsterconfession.org/resources/confessional-standards/the-westminster-shorter-catechism/.

Chapter 4: Jesus, the Perfect Leader

1. "Leadership," BI Norwegian Business School, accessed December 17, 2022, https://www.bi.edu/campaign/full-time/fresh-perspectives/norway/leadership/.
2. Lao Tzu, *Tao Te Ching* (Boston, MA: Hackett Publishing: 1993), 17.
3. Laurence Leamer, *Fantastic: The Life of Arnold Schwarzenegger* (New York, NY: St. Martin's Press: 2005), 106.
4. Timothy Keller, *The Reason for God* (New York, NY: Penguin Books, 2008), 224.
5. Jeff A. Benner, "Messiah," Ancient Hebrew Research Center, accessed December 17, 2022, https://www.ancient-hebrew.org/definition/messiah.htm.

6. Todd M. Johnson and Gina A. Zurlo, "Christian Martyrdom as a Pervasive Phenomenon," *Society* 51, no. 6 (December 2014): 679–685.

Chapter 5: The Original Plan

1. K.J. Went, "Hebrew Thoughts: *Tselem*," accessed January 21, 2023, https://www.studylight.org/language-studies/hebrew-thoughts.html?article=592.
2. Sam Storms, "A Christian Theory of Everything," Enjoying God, accessed January 22, 2023, https://www.samstorms.org/all-articles/post/a-christian-theory-of-everything.
3. " Spiritual Beings Study Notes," The Bible Project, accessed June 27, 2023, https://d1bsmz3sdihplr.cloudfront.net/media/Study%20Notes/Spiritual-Beings-Study-Notes-Collection.pdf.
4. "Spiritual Beings Study Notes," The Bible Project.
5. C.S. Lewis, *Mere Christianity* (New York, NY: Simon & Schuster Touchstone edition, 1996), 112.
6. Ken Ham, ed., *The New Answers Book 1* (Green Forest, AR: Master Books, 2006), 125.

Chapter 6: After the Reboot

1. Steph Koyfman, "What Language Is Spoken in the Philippines?" Babbel Magazine, February 6, 2023, https://www.babbel.com/en/magazine/what-language-is-spoken-in-the-philippines.
2. A.V., "Papua New Guinea's Incredible Linguistic Diversity," *The Economist*, July 20, 2017, https://www.economist.com/the-economist-explains/2017/07/20/papua-new-guineas-incredible-linguistic-diversity.
3. Flavius Josephus, *The Antiquities of the Jews*, accessed February 7, 2023, https://www.gutenberg.org/files/2848/2848-h/2848-h.htm#link2HCH0004.
4. Myra J. Siff, "Tower of Babel," Jewish Virtual Library, accessed July 12, 2020, https://www.jewishvirtuallibrary.org/tower-of-babel.

Chapter 7: The Forgotten King

1. Ernst Sellin and Carl Watzinger, *Jericho: die Ergebnisse der Ausgrabungen*, (Osnabrück: Otto Zeller Verlag, 1973), 58.
2. Mark Rutland, *David the Great* (Lake Mary, FL: Charisma House, 2018), 3–4.
3. John S. Knox, "King David," World History Encyclopedia, October 18, 2017, https://www.worldhistory.org/King_David/.
4. John Barnett, "How David Systematically Invested His Hard-earned Treasures With God," Discover the Book Ministries, accessed February 6, 2023, https://dtbm.org/lod-41-how-david-systematically-invested-his-hard-earned-treasures-with-god/.
5. Wikipedia.org, s.v. "Mesha Stele," modified January 18, 2023, 15:52, https://en.wikipedia.org/wiki/Mesha_Stele#Parallel_to_2_Kings_3.

Chapter 8: The Complex Messiah

1. Anne Frank, *The Diary of a Young Girl: The Definitive Edition* (n.p.: Grapevine India, 2022), 272.

2. Ake Viberg, "The Concept of Anointing in the Old Testament," *Journal of the European Pentecostal Theological Association* 16, no. 1 (1996): 19–29.

3. David Brickner, "Jesus as Messiah in the Gospels," Jews for Jesus, July 1, 1999, https://jewsforjesus.org/publications/issues/issues-v12-n06/jesus-as-messiah-in-the-gospels/.

4. Joseph Klausner, *The Messianic Idea in Israel* (New York, NY: Macmillan, 1955), 128.

5. "Mashiach: The Messiah," Judaism 101, accessed February 17, 2023, https://www.jewfaq.org/mashiach.htm.

6. Rabbi Dr. Ezekiel Isadore Epstein, *The Babylonian Talmud*, vol. 20 (London: Soncino Press, 1935), 658.

7. See Deuteronomy 18:15.

8. Matthew 1:23.

9. Wikipedia, s.v. "Semikhah," modified February 5, 2023, 08:39, https://en.wikipedia.org/wiki/Semikhah.

10. Michael L. Brown, *Answering Jewish Objections to Jesus, Vol. 3: Messianic Prophecy Objections* (Grand Rapids, MI: Baker Books, 2003), 49–50.

11. David Mishkin, "The Emerging Jewish Views of the Messiahship of Jesus and Their Bearing on the Question of His Resurrection," *HTS Theological Studies* 71, no. 1 (2015): 01–07. https://doi.org/10.4102/hts.v71i1.2881.

12. C.G. Montefiore and H. Loewe, eds., *A Rabbinic Anthology* (New York: Schocken Books, 1974), 544.

13. Ludwig Schneider, "Messianic Jews and Their History," Israel Today, March 29, 2022, https://www.israeltoday.co.il/read/messianic-jews-and-their-history-2/.

14. "Findings of New Research on the Messianic Movement in Israel," One for Israel, April 11, 2018, https://www.oneforisrael.org/bible-based-teaching-from-israel/findings-of-new-research-on-the-messianic-movement-in-israel/; Sarah Posner, "Kosher Jesus: Messianic Jews in the Holy Land," *The Atlantic*, November 29, 2012, https://www.theatlantic.com/international/archive/2012/11/kosher-jesus-messianic-jews-in-the-holy-land/265670/.

Chapter 9: A Different Kind of King

1. "King Abdullah Goes Undercover," BBC News, July 29, 1999, http://news.bbc.co.uk/2/hi/middle_east/407193.stm.

2. Jamal Halaby, "King of Jordan Visits Tax Office Disguised as Bearded Old Man," *The Independent*, July 31, 2001, https://www.independent.co.uk/news/world/middle-east/king-jordan-visits-tax-office-disguised-bearded-old-man-9273961.html; Associated Press, "Jordan King Goes Undercover," *Deseret News*, July 30, 2001, https://www.deseret.com/2001/7/30/19598858/jordan-king-goes-undercover.

3.   Alexa MacDermot, "10 Unbelievable Times Royalty Went Undercover," Listverse, August 11, 2018, https://listverse.com/2018/08/11/10-unbelievable-times-royalty-went-undercover/.

4.   "American Worldview Inventory 2020 Results—Full Release #8: Views of Sin and Salvation," Arizona Christian University Cultural Research Center, August 4, 2020, https://www.arizonachristian.edu/wp-content/uploads/2020/08/AWVI-2020-Release-08-Perceptions-of-Sin-and-Salvation.pdf; YouGov.co.uk, "YouGov Survey Results," YouGov, August 16–17, 2015, https://d25d2506sfb94s.cloudfront.net/cumulus_uploads/document/zcui1w66ie/Copy%20of%20Opi_InternalResults_150817_Death_R_W_2.pdf; "Views on the Afterlife," Pew Research Center, November 23, 2021, https://www.pewresearch.org/religion/2021/11/23/views-on-the-afterlife/.

5.   Grant Castleberry, "Repentance: The Lost Doctrine of the Twenty-First Century," Reformanda, May 14, 2019, https://www.reformandamin.org/articles1/repentance .

6.   David Wilkerson, "Whatever Happened to Repentance?" World Challenge, accessed February 19, 2023, https://worldchallenge.org/newsletter/1999/whatever-happened-to-repentance.

7.   Sinclair Ferguson, "Faith and Repentance," Ligonier, May 25, 2013, https://www.ligonier.org/learn/articles/faith-and-repentance/.

8.   Joseph Shulam, "Rabbis and Their Disciples Between the 1st Century B.C. and the 2nd Century A.D." Renew.org, accessed February 19, 2023, https://renew.org/rabbis-and-their-disciples-between-the-1st-century-b-c-and-the-2nd-century-a-d/.

Chapter 10: A Kingdom Fit for Its King

1.   Bob Sorge, "Jesus' Most Common Teaching," BobSorge.com, November 3, 2014, http://bobsorge.com/2014/11/jesus-most-common-teaching/.

2.   Mark Cartwright, "Roman Triumph," World History Encyclopedia, May 5, 2016, https://www.worldhistory.org/Roman_Triumph/; T.E. Schmidt, "Mark 15.16–32: The Crucifixion Narrative and the Roman Triumphal Procession," *New Testament Studies* 41 (1995): 1–18, https://doi.org/10.1017/S0028688500022918.

3.   Thomas Schmidt, "Jesus' Triumphal March to Crucifixion," *Bible Review* 13, no. 1 (February 1997): 30–37, https://www.baslibrary.org/bible-review/13/1/11.

4.   Schmidt, "Mark 15.16–32: The Crucifixion Narrative and the Roman Triumphal Procession," 1 18; Schmidt, "Jesus' Triumphal March to Crucifixion," 30–37.

5.   Adriano La Regina, *Archaeological Guide to Rome* (Segrate, Italy: Mondadori Electa, 2004, 2007), 105.

6.   Schmidt, *New Testament Studies*, 1–18.

Chapter 11: The Return of the King

1. "Jesus: Man, Myth or God?" Barna Group, April 13, 2017, https://www.barna.com/research/jesus-man-myth-god/.
2. "Dalai Lama XIV Quotes," Goodreads, accessed February 21, 2023, https://www.goodreads.com/author/quotes/570218.Dalai_Lama_XIV.

Chapter 12: From Fellowship to Followship

1. Oswald Chambers, "After Surrender—Then What?" My Utmost for His Highest, accessed February 24, 2023, https://utmost.org/after-surrender%E2%80%94-then-what/.
2. David Nixon, "Top 15 Most Expensive Countries in the World – 2014," Insider Monkey, May 5, 2014, https://www.insidermonkey.com/blog/top-15-most-expensive-countries-in-the-world-2014-321059/?singlepage=1.
3. Janet and Geoff Benge, *George Müller* (Seattle, WA: YWAM Publishing, 1999), 196; George Müller, *Autobiography of George Müller* (Vestavia Hills, AL: Solid Ground Christian Books, 2004), 693.

Chapter 13: Walking the Way of Uncertainty

1. J. Warren Smith, "See How These Christians Love One Another," Christian History Institute, accessed February 25, 2023, https://christianhistoryinstitute.org/magazine/article/see-how-these-christians-love.
2. Oswald Chambers, "God's Silence—Then What?," My Utmost for His Highest, accessed February 24, 2023, https://utmost.org/god%E2%80%99s-silence%E2%80%94-then-what/.
3. C. S. Lewis, *The Problem of Pain* (New York, NY: HarperOne, 1940, 1996).
4. Dietrich Bonhoeffer, *The Cost of Discipleship* (New York, NY: MacMillan, 1963), 73–74.

Chapter 14: Let Him Lead

1. Kate Swanson, "How to Lead and Follow (The Secret to Dancing With a Partner)," HobbyLark, November 23, 2020, https://hobbylark.com/performing-arts/Ballroom-how-to-lead.

ABOUT THE AUTHOR

MARCUS YOARS lives to know God, love Him, and walk as closely with Him as possible. In the process, he enjoys helping others to do the same through, among other things, his teaching, writing, and music. Marcus worked as a journalist in the US for more than twenty years, including being the editor of *Charisma* and *Ministry Today* magazines. As a ghostwriter, he has written books for several *New York Times* bestselling authors, and some of those projects have also been bestsellers.

Marcus currently serves as the director of the Mountain Bible School (Fjellbibelskolen) in Hemsedal, Norway, where he and his wife, Amber, have lived as missionaries for more than a decade. They spend most of their time training and equipping young adults through Fjellbibelskolen's various courses, which range from weekend Bible-teaching events to a three-month discipleship course blending outdoor adventures with classroom education. Their passion for discipling and helping others experience more of God is the core of their ministry. Having been married for almost twenty-five years, Marcus and Amber are also seasoned counselors who love helping couples thrive in marriage.

Marcus' parents were missionaries for almost thirty-five years in Hong Kong, where he was born and raised. That international upbringing shaped his worldview and has been invaluable in equipping him for living in different cultures. He and Amber have two sons, Brayden and Xander, and they couldn't be prouder of them.

www.ingramcontent.com/pod-product-compliance
Lightning Source LLC
Chambersburg PA
CBHW030825090426
42737CB00009B/879